THIN ICE

By Larry Sloman

Thin Ice

Reefer Madness

On the Road with Bob Dylan

THIN ICE

A Season in Hell with the New York Rangers

LARRY SLOMAN

WILLIAM MORROW AND COMPANY, INC.
New York   *1982*

This book is dedicated to

Michael Bloomfield (1944–1981)
and
Judy and Zoë, the future

Copyright © 1982 by Larry Sloman

The Ron Duguay interview reprinted with permission of Scott Cohen and *Interview* magazine from *Interview*, March 1980.

Lyrics to "Skating on Thin Ice" by Kinky Friedman, copyright 1980 by Kinky Music Inc., BMI. Reprinted with permission.

Lyrics to "Ol' Ben Lucas" by Kinky Friedman, copyright 1976 by Kinky Music Inc., BMI. Reprinted with permission.

Portions of this book have previously appeared in *Playboy, Inside Sports,* and *Oui.*

Library of Congress Cataloging in Publication Data

Sloman, Larry.
  Thin ice.

  1. New York Rangers (Hockey Club)
2. Hockey players—Biography. I. Title.
GV848.N43S58   796.96'2'097471   81-16937
ISBN 0-688-00628-0   AACR2

Printed in the United States of America

First Edition
1 2 3 4 5 6 7 8 9 10

BOOK DESIGN BY MICHAEL MAUCERI

THANKS TO:

My parents who nurtured my interest in hockey by driving me to my games at extremely odd hours of the night; Rosemary Lewandowski-Lois who picked up on the sensuality of hockey and encouraged me to do this book; her husband, George Lois, who once again was too creative for comfort; Robert Marcus, who despite being a character in the book did some outstanding legwork and provided me with some fascinating interview material; George Barkin, Lou Gorfain, Charlie McDade, and Michael Bloomfield, who read the manuscript and made valuable suggestions; Jim Cusimano, who not only read the manuscript but sat with me one weekend and helped pare the year into acceptable word-length; his wife, Beverly, who snapped great pictures on ten-minute call; Marsha Stevens, who organized me in ways way beyond the call of duty on the secretarial front; Benny and Mary, who held the papers for me every day at their general store on Spring Street; everyone at *High Times* magazine, who put up with me while I was writing the book; Steve Oren and Kenny Aretsky, who made their bar feel like home; Mike Cosby of Gerry Cosby Sporting Goods, who provided me with the Ratso Ranger jersey; David Cooperman, who persuaded his father, Mort, to let us run rampant at the Lone Star Café; John and Janet Halligan and the Ranger organization, who got me seats at the games and access; Bobby "Tileman" Caserta, who gave me better seats; John Brockman, who sold the book; Jim Landis, who bought it and was a pleasure to work with; Dick Sugarman, who gave the green light; and Laurie Rockett, my favorite legal beagle, who knew the law.

A SPECIAL THANKS TO:

The New York Rangers of 1979, 1980, 1981, who opened up their lives to a journalist with a lousy slap shot.

THE LINEUP

THE PLAYERS

Mike "Red" Allison
Steve "Bakes" Baker
Frank "Beater" Beaton
Barry "Bubba" Beck
Tim Bothwell
Pat "Charlie" Conacher
Cam "Bam Bam" Connor
John "JD" Davidson
Lucien "Louie" DeBlois
André Dore
Ron "Doogie" Duguay
Phil "Flipper" Esposito
Dave "Omar" Farrish
Nick "Pieface" Fotiu
Ron "Honker" Greschner
Josh Guevremont
Anders "Andy" Hedberg
Pat "Hitch" Hickey
Ed "Boxcar" Hospodar
Ed "Ciggy" Johnstone
Chris "The Big Greek"
  Kotsopoulos
Tom "Ledge" Laidlaw
Claude "Rosie" LaRose
Dave Maloney
Don "Slip" Maloney
Ray "Too-Tall" Markham
Mario "Frenchie" Marois

Jim Mayer
Mike "Q" McEwen
Warren "Barney" Miller
Don "Mud, Murder" Murdoch
Lance "Lanceford" Nethery
Ulf "Lil' Person" Nilsson
Jim "Seaweed" Pettie
Pierre "Pepe" Plante
Bobby "Sheecat" Sheehan
Dave "Silky" Silk
Dave "Snowy" Snopek
Doug "Soapy" Soetaert
Doug "Sully" Sulliman
Dean "Deano" Talafous
Wayne "Twinky" Thomas
Walter Tkaczuk
Jim Troy
Carol "Vad" Vadnais
Steve "Sarge" Vickers

THE COACHES

Fred "The Fog" Shero
Mike Nykoluk
Mickey Keating
André Beaulieu
Ed Giacomin
Herb Brooks
Craig Patrick

THE TRAINERS

Joe "Bukka" Bucchino
Joe Murphy
Jimmy Young
Danny Moscowitz
Nick Garen

THE BRASS

Jim Judelson
Sonny Werblin
Jack Krumpe
Rod "Rocky" Gilbert
John Gfeller
John Halligan
Janet "The Jewel" Halligan
Mike Burke

THE PRESS

Marv Alpert
Larry Brooks
Frank Brown
Bill Chadwick
Scott Cohen
Hugh Delano
Stan Fischler
Jim Gordon
Norm McLean
Walt McPeek
Sal Messina
Lawrie Mifflin
Malcolm Moran
Tim Moriarity
Tom Murray
Jim Naughton
Betty Rollins
Larry "Ratso" Sloman

THE WIVES

Diana "Beaver" Davidson
Donna Esposito
Gun-Marie Hedberg
Sue Johnstone
Vicki Frost Maloney
Barbro Nilsson
Valerie Tkaczuk
Joanne Vickers

THE FRIENDS

Ken Aretsky
Peter Beard
Marc Beneke
Kinky Friedman
Catherine Guinness
Steve Herlihy
Reggie Jackson
John McEnroe
Audrey & Irene Nicen
Steve Oren
Cheryl Tiegs
Andy Warhol
Richard Weisman

THE FANS

Robert Marcus
Bob "The Chief" Comas
Head Esposito
Dom
Susan R.
Sid the Lawyer

THE AGENTS

Larry Rauch
Mark Stewart

Introduction ═══════

I could have sworn I saw a UFO. It was made of shiny metal, about four feet long. Cylindrical for the most part, but tapering off on top into an odd bowl shape. There was light reflecting off it, giving it an unearthly hue. As I gazed at it, I felt almost hypnotized, and a nice Sunday-morning-secure feeling came over me. As the object bobbed about, I couldn't take my eyes off it.

Neither could Vic Hadfield. Or any of the 18,000-odd screaming Frenchmen who had sardined their way into the old Montreal Forum that night to see their beloved Habitants run roughshod over the upstart New York Rangers and clinch the 1978–1979 hockey championship. And keep possession of that shimmering legendary hardware, the Stanley Cup, hockey's holy grail, which was slowly making its way around the arena, proudly held aloft by designated Captain Serge Savard, as the rest of the Montreal skaters tagged along for a few victory laps.

By then the Rangers had retreated into their dressing room, one, Nicky Fotiu, pausing to strong-arm a young souvenir hunter who made motions toward teammate John Davidson and his big goalie stick. Only Vic Hadfield lingered. Hadfield had patrolled left wing for fourteen years in a Ranger uniform, and now he was crisscrossing the continent scouting new blood. Hadfield lingered to catch a glimpse of the Cup. This was the closest the Rangers had come to capturing it in forty years.

I lingered because I was a bit hesitant to go into the Ranger room. I was in Montreal on assignment for *Playboy*, doing a story on Ranger coach Fred Shero, whose unorthodox coaching techniques owed as much to Zen wisdom as they did to conventional hockey play books. But I had more than a journalistic relationship with the Rangers and their coach.

I was a hockey fanatic. Most fans of ice hockey cross that thin line. I started back in Russell Sage Junior High School, listening to the Rangers on the radio while I was doing my algebra homework. Then I went to a game and I was hooked. The action was inexorable, end to end, skating and bumping and fancy passwork, and new players hopping over the boards and joining the seamless flow, the tension building and building till someone managed to whisk the small dull-black rubber disk past the masked, padded goalie, popping the pristine nylon-mesh netting of the goal. The release was staggering. A huge collective roar and thousands on their feet, horns blaring, whistles trilling, backs thumped and hairdos mussed. Here, at last, was a game where scoring meant something.

But I was soon more than a spectator. I started playing hockey twenty years ago in the grimy back corridors of the old Madison Square Garden. I'd kick around a crumpled-up old soft-drink cup between periods, stickhandling with my feet just as smoothly as my hero, Andy Bathgate. From that I graduated to roller hockey on the tarred schoolyards of Queens, grinding down innumerable pairs of Chicago metal-wheeled roller skates while prodding a roll of plastic electrical tape over the cracks and crevices of the playgrounds. Then, one winter's afternoon in my seventeenth year, behind my apartment house in Bayside, Queens, I discovered ice.

It was a revelation. This was the way God meant for men

to play hockey. No buckling, salt-ravaged concrete, no runaway tape rolling on its edge, no cops breaking up the game by kicking the crumpled cup off the subway car. Just you and the ice and your two thin blades and the puck on your stick. I was hooked.

It didn't take long before I was rising at four in the morning Sundays to get to a rink by 6 A.M., and play choose up for a few luxurious hours of rental time before the dilettante general-session figure skaters came on. Oh, how I loathed leisure-time skaters. All the precious ice, begging for nets and sticks and pucks and a goalie to stand guard, instead of being despoiled by old farts and snotty-nosed brats circling around and around like mindless robots while the PA system pumped out Muzak pablum. The odd time that we'd follow a general session, I made sure I was on the ice prematurely, throwing snow on little girls in tutus and terrorizing senior citizens with my long stick. Ice was made for ice hockey. I was a deviant.

In Goodsoil, Saskatchewan, Ron Greschner was doing the exact same thing at that time, only he was eleven. And it was normal. Every day he'd get up and walk a mile through the blazing cold, accompanied by his dad, a nonskater, who would give him instructions and encouragement. They'd often practice together in front of the house, the young Greschner twenty feet down the driveway shooting pucks at his business-suited father, who would inevitably limp away with welts decorating his shins. In Canada people took their hockey seriously.

Our paths crossed in 1978. I met Greschner at the Lone Star Café, along with his teammates, John Davidson and Wayne Thomas, when they chanced in one night when my friend Kinky Friedman, the legendary Texas Jewboy, was playing. Being the semiofficial custodian of Kinky's guest list, I grabbed the Rangers as soon as they came in, sat with them through the set, and dragged them backstage later to meet the Kinky man. Soon the whole team was coming down.

They loved music and, after a few games' training, Kinky loved hockey and a curious friendship grew between us all. We became their cultural ambassadors to New York City, a frightful place for young men fresh out of Canada. We took them to Chinatown for *dim sum* and to Little Italy to Luna's and Umberto's, where they marveled at the bullet hole mementos of the massacre of Joey Gallo. We went to rock clubs and SoHo bars.

In return Kinky and I got yellow seats, the players' tickets, three levels above the Garden ice—and the rub-off status that flowed to anyone who hung out with the Rangers at any of their Upper East Side haunts where the groupies elbowed each other, jockeying for position on the jocks. Many was the night that I'd be sprawled in the back seat of a cab, hurtling down Second Avenue at bartime, 4 A.M., after a beery night with the young men who wear Ranger jerseys.

They were celebrities. They were young and attractive and playing in a fishbowl. And, for a change, they were playing well. Under Shero's tutelage the team had improved by eighteen points during this, his first year, and then in the play-offs, when Ranger teams traditionally fade to Blue, they came on strong. They trampled LA in the first round and they soundly defeated the Philadelphia Flyers, Shero's old team.

Then came the Islanders. It was a battle for New York supremacy, and amazingly enough the underdog Rangers sent the Islanders packing in six games. In the process they won the hearts of millions. The night they eliminated the Islanders, New York went crazy. As soon as the buzzer sounded and the Rangers mobbed John Davidson, the carnival was on. Thousands of fans spilled into the streets surrounding the Garden, dancing and cavorting and taunting the Islander bus as it inched its way back to Long Island with a hearty chorus of "ISLANDERS SUCK." In Charlie

O's, where the Rangers routinely stopped for postgame beers, they had to pull down the metal gates to protect the windows from the mob, who were peering in through the glass at their heroes like extras from *Dawn of the Dead.* Even in the boroughs they took to the streets, stopping traffic.

So the Rangers went to the finals and they won the first game in Montreal and then their past caught up with them. There were whispers that some of the guys had been leaving their game in the Vieux Montreal bars. And Bobby Sheehan, a fleet journeyman center who was brought up in the middle of the Flyers series and gave the Rangers the break-out speed they needed to counter Philly's forechecking, also was said to be suffering from his old nemesis: too much booze.

The Canadiens countered with tradition. Four straight wins, and suddenly it was white uniforms lugging that Cup around in the Forum. And I was watching because I didn't relish seeing the Rangers at their lowest. But the journalist in me outvoted the comrade, and even then, before I would inform management, I knew that I wanted to follow these guys around the next season and chronicle the lives of young Canadian hockey players who happened to be playing in the center of the universe. Duty drew me into the losers' locker room.

It was quiet but it was no wake. After all, it was mid-May and nobody in their right mind at the beginning of that season would have thought that the ragged Rangers, the per-ennial NHL whipping boys, would be peeling tape and pull-ing off cups and popping beer cans at that juncture. May had always meant Moose Jaw or Goodsoil or Cranbrook, fishing or golfing or just watching the Canadian grass grow. To be in Montreal on ice in May was valiant, so there was no need to hang one's head.

Someone forgot to tell Donnie Murdoch, though. He was twenty-two and cherubic and forever living down a cocaine bust, and he'd thrown a towel over his head to shut out the room that was beginning to fill with deadline-crazed bilingual reporters. To his right, Don Maloney, a twenty-year-old who had joined the team in midseason and burned up the ice from that point on, in the process breaking the record for most play-off points by a rookie, sighed a bit, clenched his teeth, and bit down hard on his lower lip. Then he cried like a baby.

Which was quite a contrast to Fred Shero. Shero was at that moment around the bend, meeting with the press. To call him stoic was a little like calling Trotsky a reformer. His enigmatic, passionless demeanor continually confounded reporters who were programmed for Knute Rockne types who filled their pads with give-'em-hell copy. But a session with Shero was more like meeting with a Zen master; if you got away without getting your nose tweaked, you were ahead of the game.

First of all, it was hard to get words out of Freddie's mouth. Just ask his players, most of whom spent the entire year wondering if their coach even knew their names. In fact, the few odd times when Shero would talk, usually behind the bench during a game, directed at no one in particular, the Rangers would all lean in, looking like stand-ins for an E. F. Hutton commercial.

But Shero was expected to talk to the press. That didn't mean they'd get straight answers. Non sequiturs, if they were lucky, a grunt or a grimace if they weren't. But for all his evasiveness, Shero had a backwoods bullshit country Zen wisdom that made his frequent forays with the press memorable. Of course, often Fred's *koan*-like responses would evade the eager scribes' cognitive grasps. After all, most hockey writers, like hockey players, aren't brain surgeons. So the writers would leave the encounter feeling unsatisfied, joking about the man they dubbed "The Fog," rolling their eyes at each other, whispering about his rumored proclivity toward suds. What is the sound of one head shaking?

But Fred was surprisingly straight that night in Montreal, the only concession to quaint human traits like emotion and tension and release being the Lucky Strike that he pulled on throughout the interrogation. He praised the Canadiens and admitted to being thankful for getting to the finals. Then he leaped to the defense of his defense, after someone noted the Rangers couldn't get going against the Canadiens' fore-checking.

The questions turned toward the impending expansion draft, since the next year would see the entrance of four new teams into the NHL and, consequently, general managers were scrambling around making last-minute deals. Except no one had been dialing Fred.

"Since the play-offs started, no one's called. That's unusual." He shrugged. "No one wanted anybody, except Davidson."

But Davidson seemed untouchable. The big goalie had carried the team through the first rounds of the play-offs, virtually unbeatable, doing it on a left knee which when opened would resemble the inside of a Ronzoni spaghetti can. News of his injury had only leaked out before this, the last game, and in retrospect his achievement was all the more remarkable.

Right now he was sitting at his stall, rubbing his mangled left knee, chatting with Jim Judelson, who had interrupted the press to greet John Davidson. Judelson can do that. He runs Gulf and Western, which owns Madison Square Garden. Along with every last player, jersey, stick, and water bottle in the room.

"You played great, super." Judelson squeezed Davidson's good knee. "This was your first year in the finals. You guys can do it. You saw all those flags up there." Judelson was referring to the Canadiens, who owned twenty-one previous championships.

"We'll get them again." Davidson managed a smile. "This time we learned, it was a . . . rehearsal." Judelson would understand. After all, Gulf and Western also owned Paramount.

"Look" the owner squeezed the good knee again—"after three times you don't win, I'd be upset, but not the first time."

At the other end of the room, Esposito was thinking it might be the last time. Phil Esposito, the living hockey legend, seventeen seasons under his belt, myriad scoring records, forty-two goal season this year, was thinking the unthinkable. Out loud, for a bevy of reporters.

"Next? We go to training camp in September and work our asses off and we'll be a stronger team next year. I'm sure that some of us will be here but those that aren't here, if it's me or anyone else, can always remember this because this is the year that the Rangers put New York back on the map as far as hockey is concerned. Not the Islanders. These guys are fantastic. I'm proud of every one of these kids. They're gonna be back for a long, long time. I may not be around, but they're gonna be."

With that Esposito slowly got up, carefully nestled his feet into his rubber shower thongs, and grabbed his towel and his toiletries bag. Halfway to the shower he paused. "Hey, John," he yelled over to Davidson, interrupting Judelson, "come in the shower with me 'cause I'm lonely in there. I don't want to go myself." The goalie managed a grin.

Something few others could do. Murdoch and Maloney were still bawling softly, and Dave Maloney, Don's older brother and the captain, was brooding by himself. All around the room the players were saying their good-byes to the press, accepting congratulations for having gotten this far. True, they beat the Islanders and Philadelphia to get to the finals, but, ultimately, they won nothing. That realization gnawed at them as they picked up their hand luggage and slowly filed out of the Forum and onto the bus that would take them to their charter for the flight home.

I stayed. I didn't fly the charter or, for that matter, the Gulf and Western jet that was whisking Judelson and Sonny Werblin and a few other Garden execs home to New York. I wandered back into the Forum, eerily empty now, silent except for the strange sound of typewriters clacking away from the overhead gondola press box where the deadline crew were churning out their copy. I stayed to see Larry Robinson, the Canadiens' 6-foot 3-inch, 210-pound defense-man, scheming to avoid walking out the players' entrance into a mob of thousands of shit-faced Frenchmen screaming and squirming and blowing horns and kissing each other, threatening to shatter the thin plate-glass Forum doors in the process.

I also stayed to see Mark Napier exit that way. Napier was a young right wing who had actually sacrificed salary and spurned an offer from the World Hockey Association to play for the Canadiens, muttering something about pride and tra-dition. The sweet innocence of youth. We walked past the old guard and out the door together, and the last I saw of Napier he was halfway down Atwater Street, propelled on the hands of his public, as helpless as Gulliver in the land of the Lilliputians.

He survived to parade down St. Laurent again the next day for the traditional massive Stanley Cup parade. Well, not actually parade. You see, the Canadiens were whisked past their admiring fans in a few chicken-wire-reinforced police vans and flatbed trucks, one of which contained the cherished Cup. So much for adulation.

The Rangers had no such problem. Sure they lost, but it was the closest thing to success in years for the Broadway Blues and damned if New York's rah-rah mayor, Ed Koch,

was about to let the near victory slip away without cere-
monial acknowledgment. So a few days after the Canadiens
barreled down St. Laurent, the Rangers were honored at
City Hall in Lower Manhattan.

It was an overcast humid day, and about fifty curious
lunch-hour secretaries and a few scattered diehard fans were
lured to the City Hall steps by the sounds of a Salvation
Army-like band playing, inappropriately enough, "Take Me
Out to the Ball Game." Periodically, one of the Mayor's men
would make a short announcement, desperately trying to
drum up a crowd. Back at the Garden the Rangers were
trying to drum up a team.

It seemed that since that charter had kissed the friendly
runway of LaGuardia, the Rangers had been celebrating the
end of the season with their annual blotto bash. Most of
them had gone that same night to Herlihy's, a favorite watering hole of the icemen, and after Herlihy's squeezed the last
few out before the crack of dawn, an obliging acquaintance
of the guys had opened his posh duplex to keep the party
going nonstop. And it did. Which was why John Halligan,
the PR man, was having such trouble rounding up the troops
three days later.

But he herded the survivors into a bus and sneaked them
through the back door of Koch's workplace, and slowly,
somewhat unsteadily, they filed down the City Hall steps
and sat on the makeshift stage. By now the crowd had
swelled to a few hundred.

Koch, a rather large, balding, dynamic man, seized the
mike. After saving the city from the jaws of bankruptcy, this
was a piece of cake. His booming, slightly squeaky voice
made several Rangers wince. Of course, in their condition
the sounds of silence would probably have driven them
crazy.

"I want them to know," Koch crooned in his unique sing-
song way, "they represent New York, because they came

from the very bottom and they are reaching the top just as the City of New York is not yet out of the woods but we will be, so they have demonstrated that they too will be number one next year." The applause threatened to wake a few of the players.

Koch then pulled out some replica keys to the city and presented one to Sonny Werblin, the Garden's president, a crusty old entrepreneur who had made Joe Namath a household word and was intent on doing the same for his Rangers. Werblin rasped for a bit, then he brought up Shero.

Shero grasped the podium delicately. "I only have two regrets today." He paused dramatically. "One, that I couldn't bring the Cup today . . ."

"We beat the fucking Islanders," someone screamed encouragement. Everybody cheered.

". . . and secondly, I picked up a newspaper today and I couldn't believe what I read." He was referring to a *New York Post* article that claimed that several of the Rangers were on the trading block.

"Don't trade Espo." Another voice shattered Shero's silence.

"Someone said in that story that I didn't like some of my players." Shero seemed hurt. "I *love* my players."

The last admission just sort of squirted out and the crowd cheered Shero's vulnerability. "Even though I couldn't bring you the Cup today, I got the key to the greatest city in the world. I know it and my players know it. Thank you."

Even Koch was impressed by the performance. He patted Shero on the back and then introduced the players, one by one. McEwen, the fleet, impressive defenseman, Pierre Plante, a digger of the first class, Murdoch, Greschner, Tkaczuk, Espo, John Davidson, backup goalie Wayne Thomas, the oh-so-blond Pat Hickey, the Super Swedes, Anders Hedberg and Ulf Nilsson. And Captain Dave Maloney, who bears a striking resemblance to Warren Beatty.

Maloney accepted a key on behalf of his teammates, made a short speech alluding to losing a good portion of the team the last few days, then that was that. The band started up and the photographers swamped the stage, and the cassette crew stuck out their mikes. The old vets like Tkaczuk were gone like a shot. Davidson, perhaps favoring his knee, got snared. After a few dozen autographs he disentangled himself and limped toward the bus. "I can't believe I'm alive," he whispered to me. "These last few days . . ."

Meanwhile on the steps of City Hall, Murdoch was fighting back the bitterness. "Now I read in the papers they want to get rid of me, so I'll have to wait for the summer to see what's going on," he told a microphone from a local radio station.

He finished and I walked him toward the bus, reminding him about my *Playboy* piece. "I need to sit down with you, what's your script for the next few days?"

"I don't know," he mumbled. "I gotta see if I can get a house in Colorado."

They were runner-ups. In a city that doesn't exactly reward second-place finishes. Just ask the guy that lost to Ed Koch, what was his name? Next year would be an interesting season.

The Swedes, Ulfie and Anders, who had come to New York the same season as Freddie, lured by the big bucks of Gulf and Western, were the last to get away from the crowd. They were patiently signing autographs out in back of City Hall. Anders, the blond one, Ingmar Bergman earnest, shook his head in awe. "Nice spot, nice spot here. And that Koch, what a politician, what a politician."

He grabbed another ragged piece of paper. "Write something Swedish to my mother," the young girl ordered. Just then the buses started pulling away, and $600,000 worth of wrist shot and stickhandling had to run like hell to scamper aboard. His dryland training had begun.

- JUNE 13, 1979

The Cinderella Rangers lasted intact for about a month. But today they had the expansion draft for the four new teams, and the reason no other teams had called Freddie the last few months was because they were too busy calling all the other teams, making deals to protect their own players.

That's what they had been doing the last week in the Bahamas prior to today. The Rangers neglected to send someone down early, so as a result they lost Dave Farrish, Greschner's defensive partner, Nicky Fotiu, one of the best fighters in the league, and Pierre Plante, a hardworking defensive forward. And nobody else seemed to lose anyone of note.

- SEPTEMBER 3, 1979

Pat Hickey

One of the fastest skaters on the Rangers . . . last season his best yet . . . was national hero in Canada in Spring of 1978, after his dramatic goal gave Canada third place medal in world championship play . . . Picture was page one material across Canada . . . A real favorite with the fans and a recognizable face around Manhattan . . . Loves the City life . . . Brother Greg also a hockey player . . .

—New York Rangers Yearbook, *1979–1980*

I was standing in the back of the boat, trying to look incredulous. At my feet Glenn was hunched out of view, pointing a shotgun mike at me to pick up my reactions. Halfway up the shoreline hill, Martin was focusing his big camera. "Okay, action," Bill, the director, yelled. Forty feet above us Pat Hickey took a few running steps and jumped off the cliff.

The splash was enormous. I muttered something suitably dramatic and then began to worry. A couple of seconds later Hickey surfaced and pulled himself onto the motorboat. "How was that?" He shook the water off his body. "Was it a take?"

We were in Pat's boat, floating somewhere in the Lake of Bays, a picturesque retreat about two hours north of Toronto. We meaning me, Pat, his brother, Greg, and a four-man film crew who had contacted me in New York and hired me as a consultant to a hockey movie about the Rangers. They wanted to focus in on one player, so I suggested Hickey or McEwen or Duguay. They chose Hitch.

The first thing about hockey players is that they all have strange nicknames. Pat was called Hitch because one summer a few years back, he had hitchhiked across America. Greg was called Little Hitch because he was Pat's smaller brother. I was called Ratso, but that was another story.

We had been holed up in Pat's guest bungalow for three days now, filming Hickey and his family, who had amassed at his summer home for their annual Labor Day reunion. There were scenes on the boat, cruising through the spectacular waterways of the Lakes Bay, a setting that rivaled *Apocalypse Now*. Scenes in a little rundown hockey rink in South River, where Hitch was practicing with the old-timers to keep his legs in shape. We rose with the birds to shoot Hickey as he went through his morning ritual—push-ups, sit-ups, jogging. We shot him in the sauna ("that's what I love about my job, the s's—shit, shower, shave, sweat") and followed him from there to the pier, where he jumped into the bay and did pull-ups off the diving board. Hickey was getting ready for his job—left wing on the Rangers' first line.

A job that paid nice dividends. Like this marvelous summer retreat, a nice four-bedroom job complete with small guesthouse overlooking the water. It seems that Pat had taken advantage of the megabucks Gulf and Western had pumped into the Rangers after the giant corporation purchased the Garden a few years back. Hickey was fortuitously a free agent without compensation through a careless clause in his old contract. And the Garden had just splurged to the tune of $2.4 million to sign the Swedes for two years. As their designated left wing, Hickey walked off with a bundle.

But he didn't blow it. After all, he was twenty-six now and smart enough to have professionals to consult in legal and business affairs. No, the home was a solid investment, a part of something called Double Hitch Enterprises. "We pool our resources," Pat told me. "You know, love your brother as yourself. It's a close-knit family."

Remarkably close, considering the natural bitterness and rivalry that might have grown between the two Hitches.

Greg, who was two years younger, was also about four inches smaller and thirty pounds lighter than Pat. Which was why he had been laboring in New Haven, the Rangers' farm team, for the last few years. And this summer things had come to a boil. Greg had gone through three different sets of management in his four years in the Rangers' organization, and the latest crew, Shero's regime, had no designs on the small winger. After all, Shero's right-hand man, Mickey Keating, had flat-out told Little Hitch that they could use him. If he was only two inches taller.

But his height was no handicap in building a shed. That's what Pat and Greg and their dad were doing today in the backyard, under the scrutiny of the camera. I was sitting in the dining room, talking with Emma, Momma Hitch. She was wearing a Pat Hickey Fan Club T-shirt.

"How did you ever get close to Shero for that *Playboy* article?" Emma wondered. "Pat says he doesn't even know his name. It's incredible. You know, there are a lot of people that feel that Greggie has the talent and he's colorful. New York is crazy to let Fotiu go but let this kid out. They would have something to cheer about. They really blew it, I think, not because he's my son, but he's thrilled many Canadians and hockey players. He might just be phased right out of hockey, for heaven's sakes." Emma looked perturbed.

After the shed was built and Pat's father reminisced on camera about his son's bantam hockey days, the crew moved in and set up a scene where Emma sketched me. Pat was the back-seat artist. The cameras started rolling.

"I'm lucky if I get a likeness," Emma sighed.

"We used to sit down and she'd play a game with us," Pat remembered. "We'd put a squiggle on a piece of paper and hand it to her and she'd turn it into something like a cow or a chicken. I remember when I was about twelve or thirteen, I'd sneak into her anatomy books to find out what a woman's breast looked like, you know, see all the parts of the body they didn't want you to see. She caught me one day sort of sniffing at it and she casually explained to me some of the birds and the bees, how beautiful the body was and how it worked, how it flexed and relaxed.

"She came to a couple of my hockey games and did stick figures of me and she'd show me the sketches she did and it gave me a different outlook on the game. It wasn't all strictly hockey, it was maybe even how you looked or did you make yourself happy?"

"Hockey's poetry in motion," Emma interrupted. "And it's a challenge for an artist too to see under all that heavy equipment."

"I like to say that hockey is the ballet of sports," Hitch continued, "because under our clothing we're just dancing. I went to the ballet recently and I was getting off on the whole thing. I think people at a hockey game do the same thing. Whatever my sexual drives, it ticks off my sensuality. Like I saw a male dancer in tights, his ass, the muscles, and I said, 'Hey, I wouldn't mind building up my legs to look like that to play hockey,' and that gave me a rush." Hitch got up to turn over the Neil Young album that was playing.

"Hockey's the same type of movement. We're covered by pads, so you can't get right down to the physical but you can see the pain in our faces and the recovery from that physical exertion. And the desire in the eyes.

"What we do and how we affect people is very sensual, very sexual." Pat peeked at his mother's progress. "We get girls in the crowd going the same way that rock stars do. Like I'm very spastic and spontaneous on the ice. I enjoy being flipped. When the defenseman goes down and I go up. It's jarring for someone to watch, but for me it's like art because I go over the man's body and way up in the air and everybody thinks, 'Oh, man, he's already half-dead because he got hit so hard and now he's going to come down and he's going to hit on his head and be out of it.' And you just roll with it and you bounce back up and keep going and there's that exultation that I have when I finally get back on my feet all very smoothly and poetically, and I skate away and I hear that 'Ahhh,' almost like laughter."

"So you really view hockey as an art form?" I interjected.

"Is he way out thinking that way?" Emma wondered. "He's definitely in the minority. Lots of people are going to games to see a little violence."

Emma squinted at me and resumed sketching. "Did Pat tell you about the alpha waves?"

I shook my head.

"I subscribe to *Psychology Today*," she continued. "And those alpha waves really sent me. So I told Pat."

"I used to do it on the bench." Hickey smiled sheepishly. "When things were going bad, I'd look at the crowd and go into it. Nobody knew. They might have seen me on the bench, probably thought I was picking my nose or something."

"It works," Emma said. "This guy wasn't doing anything and he got three goals. I didn't talk to him about it, but I was in New York at the game and I went into an alpha state and he got three. So I tried it again and he got three again. Then I told him to buy the book. I told Pat I was sick of praying and he phoned me once and said, 'Hey, Mom, better get those waves going.' But I said, 'No, it's too spooky.' I felt witchy about it."

"Sometimes you just use the energy around you," Hitch continued. "Like even winking at the girls in the stands. I did that a lot of times. Waiting for the face-off and you catch someone's eye in the crowd. It's a little like Babe Ruth pointing to the fence. I always play little games with my head. Like I see a girl and wink at her and then I look at the net and I point and say, this is for you. Then the puck is dropped and it's all forgotten in my head, but I needed something to get me up. It's worked a couple of times. And then I go back and say, 'Thank you very much for being there.'"

My neck was getting stiff from posing. I looked out the window, out at the magnificent lake and the islands in the distance, and thought about what Hickey had said. It was definitely a minority view. All that talk about aesthetics and art and alpha waves and Danskins. What about violence? Wasn't it a brutal, bloody, violent game?

Hickey scoffed. "Not at all. Not at all. The only violence in it is premeditated and that goes along with the social world. You want to go to the store and get some milk and you don't have any money, so you steal it, and if you get caught and someone hails you down, you're gonna punch him in the head and run away with the milk."

"Isn't there spontaneous violence?" I asked.

"Is that violence? I don't know." Hickey shrugged. "Fighting in hockey is pure. That's human, a challenge, one-on-one combat. Man against man. That's honor. I've been in fights. Most of them start, you bang together, you look each other right in the eyes, you say, 'Let's fight.' And the feeling is equal on both sides and you fight for your thirty seconds and you're completely exhausted and you say, 'Hey, that was a good one,' and you pat each other on the back and away you go."

Pat laughed and his blue eyes sparkled. " 'I gave you a bloody nose, I guess I won. Ha ha ha. See you later.' Most fights are pure and they're fair and nobody really gets hurt."

Hickey jumped up and began to demonstrate. "The guys that swing sticks. I can wield that stick around your ears for twenty-four hours and never touch you. Right in front of your face and everybody's going 'Ooooh and ahhhh,' but I know that I'm not gonna hit you because that's one of my tools. I also know where your equipment is. I can whack you in the shoulders or on the shins and it's gonna hit you right on the pads and it's gonna look great and sound great, but it's not gonna hurt you at all."

Hitch sat down. "Look, I'm not gonna let you score or get the pass, but you're not gonna get hurt getting whacked on the shins and the thigh. But if I don't want you to get the pass and I say for sure he's not getting the pass, then I'd pull you down right in the crotch or I'd stick it in your stomach where you can possibly get hurt and that's premeditated, that's violence. You look for it. Look at some of the brave guys around the league wielding their sticks. Bobby Clarke. He's mastered that game. Clarke never hurts anybody. You look at a guy like that you want to say, if you want to look like you're gonna spear me, spear me in the gut where I'm gonna get hurt and I'll get mad at you and beat your brains out. Don't spear me right in the *pad*"—Hitch spat the word out derisively—"where it looks good for you and it doesn't even hurt."

• SEPTEMBER 4

The next day we waterskied and jumped off the cliff again. That evening we were filming at the local rink, just Hitch and Little Hitch going through pretraining camp practice. Joined by Mike McEwen, who had driven up from Toronto to spend the day with Pat.

McEwen was a young defenseman whose tremendous acceleration and smooth stickhandling made him an offensive threat whenever he would rush the puck. Which was often, making his greatest asset a liability. Many was the time that Q, as he was called, would prance up the ice, stickhandle around the opposing wings, only to lose the puck and get burned on a two on one coming back. But he was still young, barely twenty-three, and coming off a twenty-goal season, practically unheard of for a defenseman. He was looking forward to training camp.

Q finally arrived, sporting longish hair and about five more pounds of upper body weight, thanks to a Nautilus machine. The camera crew left ahead of us, armed with directions to the nearby town where the rink was located. We took Little Hitch's jeep.

Most of the ride was spent speculating on the success of teammate Ron Greschner's PR-arranged date with a Penthouse Pet of the Month, one of the more pleasant dividends of the Rangers' success last year. For the first time since Rod Gilbert was palling around with Joe Namath and former Yankee Phil Linz, the New York Rangers were becoming items around Manhattan.

A fact Q never failed to mention whenever cameraman

Duckworth aimed the lens at him that evening. On the bench resting, on the ice skating lazily, every time the boom mike picked him out, McEwen smiled and said, "I hope Gresch gets laid tonight. Fuck, a Penthouse Pet!"

After shooting parts of the old-timers' game, where McEwen's summer of skating was a marked contrast to Hickey's plodding out-of-shape forays up and down, Pat and his brother and McEwen remained on the ice, taking shots on the open net. I skated over to Greg, who was practicing his wrist shot.

"See Rats,"—he blasted the puck, hitting the top corner of the net—"it's all in the wrists."

I marveled at his incredibly strong shot.

"Ah, all Canadian boys have strong wrists," Greg said. "From pulling their wires. We don't get much pussy, you know."

Martin shot some more practice footage, including a hilarious mock fight that ended with Greg sprawled on top of Pat and Q, chewing on a puck. Then we headed back to Pat's. The next day we were flying back to New York, with training camp only a week away. For Hitch it was time to close up the house and get mentally prepared for the season. For Little Hitch it was the uncertainty of trying out for a new team. The Rangers had not invited him to camp.

"Shero told me last year that he thought I was gonna be a center. Be like Bobby Clarke." Greg laughed ironically. "Then I knew I'd be down there forever. I never played center in four years there."

We traveled on in silence. Until a horrible stench filled the jeep. Pat looked back and smiled.

"Shit, horrible fart." McEwen lunged for the window.

"That's country living, boys." Pat grinned. "There's vegetables in that one."

McEwen shuddered. "New York." He shook his head in trepidation.

"It's like a human filing cabinet," Little Hitch lectured. "They take you out and use you. I hate it. I like it for three days."

"That air hits you. And the tap water, I won't drink it," Q said. "It's eerie. All the cement and people. No fucking grass. No fresh air. You never go . . ." He slammed his fist against his chest, a Tarzan move. "You gotta walk on one side of the street to get sun."

"The heat coming off people melts all the snow," Pat said with some awe. "It's a whole new world."

And as the jeep hurtled through the clear, crisp Canadian night, I thought about that other world. And I hoped that Gresch got laid that night.

• SEPTEMBER 6

He didn't. Oh, Gresch tried. They ate at Oren and Aretsky, a hot celebrity hangout on the Upper East Side of Manhattan, then they went to Studio 54. And even hung out till 6 A.M. at Rod Gilbert's house. But no Penthouse nooky.

That wasn't the only reason Gresch was grumpy as hell these days. He was also holding out, refusing to go to camp unless the Rangers came up with more cashish. At $85,000 a year Greschner was underpaid by NHL standards, since he was arguably the best defenseman on the Rangers, and one of the top five in the league. True, he was a slow, deliberate skater and he would rarely deign to throw his body in the way of opposing forwards. But with the puck caressing the blade of his stick, he was magic. He moved like a snake, the sinuous motion of his hips alone was enough to mesmerize defensemen, and with his long reach, odds were that Greschner would break in for a shot on a goal, leaving the defenseman and his pants yards apart at the blue line.

But it wasn't just the contract either. Greschner is an honorable man. Honest as the day is long. Pure as the wheat-fields of his native Saskatchewan. And he was upset because there was trouble with the Rangers.

It started as soon as the season was over, as soon as the Key to the City opened doors for the young immigrants from the North. Suddenly the Rangers were hot and in demand. Speaking engagements, appearances in shopping centers and at bar mitzvahs, overtures from big corporations looking for celebrity endorsers. Why, John Davidson had picked up $400 just to show his face for an hour at some Wall Street financial lunch. "Four hundred bones," he said. "I didn't even have to talk, just autograph photos." How about Don Maloney? He spent half the season in the Crabapple, New Haven, got called up to the big team, skated on a line with Esposito and Murdoch, and the season ain't three months dead and he's doing a TV commercial for Seven-Up. And his brother's all set to do his own, this one for designer jeans.

That was another problem. His brother, Dave Maloney. It seems that there was a growing feeling among a large cross-section of the players that their captain was a company man. The perception was that Maloney was getting too palsy-walsy with Assistant Coach Mike Nykoluk. They even came up with a new name for their captain, these fun-loving guys. They called him Davey Brown.

Behind his back. But still, the dissension was brewing. Maloney had seemed to isolate himself from the others. His closest friend on the team, some would say only, was his defensive partner, Carol Vadnais, who would not exactly win a popularity contest with the other guys. And Vadnais and Maloney were being blamed for the Rangers losing Nicky Fotiu to Hartford during the expansion draft.

Of course, it was Nicky himself who was fueling that rumor, telling nearly everyone he ran into during the off-season of his loathing for those two defensemen, who had managed to have him exiled from his native New York. Nicholas Evlampios Fotiu was New York. The PEOPLE'S CHOICE. The first city kid to hop out of the stands and proudly wear Ranger Blue. A big, beefy winger, who substituted drive for the subtleties of the game. Look, he didn't start playing hockey till he was fifteen, okay, so how could he skate like all those frogs, fancy and stuff, huh? So Nicky did the next best thing, he just built up steam like a runaway freight train, and if you happened to be in his path, look out. How did he stop? That's what boards are for, ain't they?

But Nicky in some ways was the heart and soul of this Cinderella Ranger team. He was the policeman, one of the best fighters in the league. Having Fotiu on the bench was like dressing a hydrogen bomb. Anyone for deterrence? And Nicky was also the primo practical jokester. Everyone still talks about the time that he grabbed a lobster from the tank at the dining room of some hotel the team was at and rode up the elevator with the rather large crustacean, only to dump it on his roomie Bill Goldsworthy's bare midriff as he slept.

And now Nicky was gone, in the expansion draft. And everyone knew that Captain Davey wasn't about to protect them in a scrap, he whose idea of fighting was to drop his gloves and make a beeline for his opponent's knees.

So Gresch was not in the best of moods when I phoned him after coming back from Huntsville:

ME: So when are you gonna start skating? You going out to Chadwick's rink?

GRESCH: Some of the Islanders are skating there. I could. I don't give a shit. I might be playing there. We'd beat the fucking shit out of the Rangers. I'd skate by and fucking spit right in Keating's eye.

ME: What was the latest offer he gave you?

GRESCH: A hundred seventy something.

ME: They'll keep going higher.

GRESCH: Tuesday morning, I'm telling them I'm not going to camp if they don't. I'll go play in Europe. Tuesday morning, it'll be all over one way or the other. I'll go back to Canada for a while and visit.

ME: But you gotta play.

GRESCH: I don't have to play shit. I'm not playing for fucking no money. Think I play this game for love?

ME: You don't love the game?

GRESCH: I do. But I'm not playing for nothing and everybody else is making money on it. If the money comes then the Greascher comes. As soon as I put my name on the bottom then I'll be okay. 'Cause I got enough money to live for two or three years without working.

ME: Yeah, but you wouldn't do that. You got a responsibility to yourself.

GRESCH: Yeah, I do. I'd get a job in a bar here. I'd get a job at Oren and Aretsky's.

ME: You're talking like a maniac now. You'd get a job at Oren and Aretsky's. You're one of the best hockey players in the world and you want to work at a bar.

GRESCH: I'm saying if they don't come across with the money, I'm not playing, right? So I'd work there as maître d' or something. That'd be pretty cool, I think. Wouldn't that be fun?

ME: You're crazy.

GRESCH: I think it would be. It'd make all the fucking papers.

• SEPTEMBER 8

Ron Duguay was hunched over, adjusting his socks. He stood up and straightened out his uniform top, pausing to look at himself in the mirror. He seemed to like what he saw. So did nearly every female who could see. "Bukka," he yelled, "where's my hat?" Joey Bucchino, the Rangers' young trainer, came running into the locker room, his arms full of caps. Duguay grabbed one and made his way down the stairs and into the bright daylight of Central Park West. Today the Rangers were playing the Islanders. Slow-pitch softball.

Murdoch and I caught up to Doogie, and the three of us made our way from the YMCA over into Central Park. We weren't a hundred yards into the park when the screaming started.

"There they are." Two subteens pointed at us. Duguay grimaced and broke into a trot. By the time we neared the playing field our entourage had swelled to twenty.

One girl nudged her partner. "Murdoch looks so short."

"Hey, Doogie," one kid yelled, "you got a gut."

We were sprinting now, in the homestretch. "Hey, it's Donnie Murdoch," Duguay yelled out at the top of his lungs. A cluster of young girls squealed and took off after Murdoch. "Who you?" Duguay screamed. "What you do?"

By the water fountain we got waylaid. Murdoch paused to sign one of a sea of papers. "Want my phone number?" he asked a comely young blonde. "Your phone number?" She blushed. "I have a boyfriend."

Murdoch shrugged. "If that changes, call me." He turned to me, scribbling his name on another paper. "I like the ones that want you to write a book." Murdoch finished his signature and handed it back to a cute ten-year-old. "See me in ten years, kid," he rasped and made his way to the field.

Today was a charity affair, organized by Rod Gilbert in his role as assistant to the Ranger president. And he had convinced about eight of his charges to don their special Ranger softball uniforms and place their images in jeopardy playing an American game. There was Pat Hickey at short, sporting an off-season beard. Jim Troy, a minor leaguer, was in the outfield along with Anders Hedberg and Doog. Dave Maloney was at first, Espo was pitching, Murdoch catching. Vickers was available for designated hitting.

And, thankfully, Gilbert had also convinced some of the finest leg this side of Herlihy's to wear tight shirts and very short pleated dresses and to lead the cheers. There were Playboy bunnies and shapely stewardesses and the Penthouse Pet that Gresch had dated and Rod's wife, Judy, a former model, and they were all bursting out of their official "First Annual New York Hockey Softball Classic" T's and singing, "We love New York, so let's make a bid. Don't everybody here want to help the kids." It was slightly surreal.

Murdoch stole the show. The first time up he swung at the first pitch and missed. "Nice swing, Alice," Maloney yelled. Next pitch, another swing and miss. He dropped his bat. Duguay ran up with another one. No help. Swinging strike three. The second time up was more of the same. Strike one. Strike two. He waved to the crowd. Swinging strike three. "Donnie, use a hockey stick," someone yelled.

Between strikeouts the Islanders were winning. That is, Gary Howatt and Bobby Bourne. The rest of the team were minor leaguers and ringers. At one point the Rangers threatened, but Murdoch came up as the Unknown Hitter. The bag over his head didn't help as he took a call, third strike. The Islanders won 9–7 on Duguay's throwing error.

But Murder was forgiven by the girl who pushed her way into the throng and confronted him and Doogie.

She was blond and from Queens and her name was Diane. She was standing to the side, popping out of short shorts and tank top, along with her winger, who was far less attractive. Murdoch took a shot.

"How are you?" He batted his baby blues.

"What are you guys here for?" the young blond wondered.

"I'm here to benefit my own charity." Murdoch fingered the gold initial D she had around her neck. "The two D's." He smiled. "Wanna party?"

"I like to party." She stood her ground.

"No use holding things back." Murdoch nodded at me. He obviously wanted me to cover the wing. "Whaddaya say Rats?" He smiled at me. "Should we give the girls from Queens a matinee?"

Diane was weakening. "You only live once." Murdoch was relentless. "The two D's. Let's put the two D's together and come up with sixty-nine. Let's go for a few beers." Diane huddled with her friend, who decided to take the subway home. I heaved a sign of relief and set off with the two D's toward the East Side. We walked through the winding roads, then cut through the zoo. "What is this, a road trip?" Murdoch complained. "Jeez, my hand got sore from all those autographs. I must have signed like three hundred. After a while it was like I was on Quaaludes. How'd you like that one that kissed me, eh? That was the first one I got that I didn't ask for. And she slipped me the tongue. Can you believe that? An eighty-year-old woman slipped me the tongue." Murdoch recoiled in disgust.

We made our way back to the apartment where Murdoch was staying. After serving drinks the Ranger turned on the TV and punched up the Betamax. Within seconds the screen was filled with fornicating bodies.

"What is that shit? That's disgusting." Diane frowned and escaped into the bathroom.

Murdoch turned off the video tape machine. "I got to get into her, Rats," he said. "She didn't go for the porno film, eh?"

Don Murdoch

Considered one of the most explosive players in the National Hockey League . . . Missed first half

of last season, but returned for tremendous second
half after long layoff . . . Knows where the net is
and has finesse touch up close . . . Dramatic type
of scorer . . . Older brother Bob with St. Louis
Blues . . . Nicknames "Doc" and "Murder" . . . Not
married.

—New York Ranger Yearbook, *1979–1980*

Diane went for the sweet talk, though. And Murdoch is one sweet talker. One chubby-cheeked, cherubic goal and girl scorer. The kid was a natural from his first shift with the Rangers back in 1976 when he pumped in a goal the first time he touched the puck. He scored thirty-two goals in all that rookie season, including a five-goal game that set a Ranger record. He was the toast of the town. Till he got popped at the border.

He had never had trouble before at customs. But there he was in August, 1977, flying to Toronto to meet his brother, Bob, en route to British Columbia to run a hockey school with teammate John Davidson. But it was something about his immigration status, his card was pink, not green, and this is standard, just a routine search and . . .It didn't take them long to find the 4.8 grams of cocaine stashed away in his sock. Or, for that matter, the five joints of marijuana residing in a cigarette pack in his coat pocket.

Murdoch played the whole next season with the court case still pending, and despite the frequent abuse from a minority of fans, he still managed to score twenty-seven goals in sixty-six games. On April 24, 1978, a week after the Rangers were eliminated in the first round of the play-offs, Murdoch pleaded guilty to possession of cocaine. He was fined $400 and reprimanded by the judge. In July of that year, the NHL fined him $500, reprimanded him, and suspended him for forty games, half a season.

The next day, at the NHL Players Association meetings in

Toronto, Alan Eagleson, the association's executive director (and agent for a number of NHL stars), pronounced his own judgment. "It was the unanimous decision of the representatives that although Don Murdoch's suspension seems severe, he knew the problems he was creating by pleading guilty. Therefore the Players Association does not condone—and has little sympathy for—his present plight." Obviously Eagleson didn't represent Murdoch.

Olga Murdoch, Donnie's mother, made her own pronouncement. "I wish he had never been a hockey player," she said sadly. "I wish he had become a lawyer."

Drugs were one of the prime topics when I finally went to interview Murdoch a few days after the Rangers had sleepwalked through the City Hall ceremony. He was more cheerful that day, the rumors of a trade had passed, and he never did have to go househunting in Colorado. In fact, he was ensconced in Dave Maloney's apartment in Westchester, where he had spent the last half of last season, the only half of that season that the NHL had let him play. He was stretched out on a sofa watching Marcus Welby, who was helping a distraught father track down the "supplier" of the marijuana that was ruining his teenage daughter's life.

Naturally I brought up the cocaine.

"They made it look like I was the only person around." Murdoch sneered. "There's everybody doing it—doctors, lawyers, pro athletes. It's always around and probably always will be for a long time."

"But how'd you get involved? All the accounts made it sound like the old 'too much, too soon' story," I said.

"When it first happens to you, the first time you get busted, the first thing in your mind is trying to get out of it the easiest way. If that means kissing somebody's ass, if that means blowing someone, you're gonna do it," Murdoch said.

"You're so scared, it doesn't matter what happens, you just want to get it done and over with.

"I didn't talk to the press for a good six months. I wouldn't talk to nobody and everybody wrote it up like that and it was fine with me. I knew what was going on, I'm not gonna say that I was a dummy. But I was coming out pretty good and everybody was happy so I wasn't about to step in and say, look, I'm gonna change it around."

"But still there must have been some degree of truth to that interpretation," I said.

"Well, there were a lot of doors opened up to me. If you're just your ordinary average player, not many people go out of their way to meet you, but since you were coming up like a star they all went 'Hey, the star Murdoch.' People were inviting me to parties, 'C'mon, wanna meet chicks?' and I'm twenty years old, I guess I want to meet chicks." The words were gushing out of the right winger now. "Everything was handed to me on a silver platter."

"Including the blow," I said.

Murdoch smiled. "I was getting drinks bought for me, people wanted me to come to their house for dinner. I ate it up. But maybe too much, too soon is right."

The phone interrupted us. On the other end it was Richard Weisman, a financial consultant. Weisman's connection to the Rangers is simple. He has a large, beautiful duplex. He has wonderful all-night parties. He has a lot of female friends who are all very attractive. So, he draws a lot of Rangers to his parties.

"You just got back from France, eh?" Murdoch paced the kitchen while he talked. "They need some Canadian guys to invest. Dynamic deal. Sure bet, hey, I'll listen, no problem . . . Yeah, and there's another party tonight too, this restaurant, Marco's, on forty-fifth. Invitation only."

Murdoch hung up and came back into the living room.

"That was Weisman. He's always got broads around. He likes to be around athletes. What a pad he's got. He let me use it for about three days there, I brought in this chick from Atlanta. Fuck, she thought that I was about the best thing since Scotch tape. I had a limo that night, holy fuck. We wheel in there, she says, 'How long you had this place?' I said, 'I'm only trying it out.' She was creaming in her pants just looking at the place."

Murdoch paused. "It's funny. Even when I got busted and I come back, everyone thinks I'm fucking Joe Cool. 'Hey, this guy's been busted for cocaine, he's cool.' Like when I go down to the can in a bar I hear the guys in the can, they come out and say, 'Hey, you're Murdoch, you wanna do something?' But you say, 'No, I'm just taking it easy.'"

"C'mon," I interrupted, "that bust was the best thing that happened to the NHL."

"They don't realize that they got a lot of publicity out of it. It's not like good publicity, it's never good publicity." Murdoch stretched on the sofa. "But I get recognized as much as anybody on the team, even more than other guys. But it was rough at first. That year I played after coming back was really terrible. In the back of my mind was still that court case. When I finally went to trial my lawyer said, 'Pack a toothbrush and get a five-hundred-dollar suit.' That was heavy. There were big faggots in jail there. Fuck, I would've skipped the country if I had to go to jail.

"But that year, you're playing hockey and people are calling you doper, junkie, shit like that. I was having hassles with my parents then because they didn't know what was going on. I was drinking a lot, I couldn't handle just being alone so I always had to go out. I was staying up late, not getting a good hour's sleep.

"Now, when things are going good you always try to dream that this was a bad dream. This really didn't happen. It's three summers ago this summer. It's time to flush it down the drain and let people forget about it, but every time there's no news around they always bring up old news. Instead of Don Murdoch scored two goals for the New York Rangers, it was Don Murdoch, busted for drug charges, scored two goals."

Murdoch watched as Marcus Welby sermonized on the dangers of drugs.

"I spent a whole year going around with about a thousand pounds of bricks on my shoulders." Murdoch fluffed the pillow up behind his head. "It didn't matter even if I scored five goals in five games, it meant I still had troubles.

"It's the heaviest thing to get busted and then have to go home and tell your parents, have to face your hometown people where you were once an idol. I said to myself, there's two things you can do: you can be a fucking pansy and quit hockey. Take the money that you have and run and do what every other kid does that you hang around with. I have a lot of friends that are just working. They're having a good time. But they never smelled the fucking caviar. They've never been able to jump on a plane and go anywhere you want. They've never had the broads. They don't know what it's like, so they don't know they're missing this much and I did.

"So I'm sitting there thinking, 'Well, Jesus, I've tasted it. I'd rather eat steak than hamburger.' So I said to myself, you have to turn these people's minds around. By going back out and taking all that shit. By playing hockey and coming back and doing good and having the people say, 'Well, at least he had the balls to come back.'

"Now when I go back home this summer, I'll be excited to be back. You don't have to hang your head no more. You don't have to sneak into a bar. You can walk into a fucking bar like you owned the place. That's the way I like it."

I asked him what it was like sitting out that half season.

"It was like going to jail," he huffed. "I had to stay inside. I was back home in Canada skating in my hometown. Then I went to St. Catherine with the Niagara Falls Flyers. All I was doing every night was listening to the news. Every day was so long and slow. Nothing to do. Holy Christ, I was eating four times a day. I was getting to be a fat pig. I'd want to talk to the guys, but I couldn't come down to New York. What am I gonna do, sit around New York for three months, start getting into trouble again? So I just laid low. Every night I'd hear that the team was winning, they're playing great. I haven't met Shero yet, so I don't know what to expect. Things run through your mind like 'Do they want you back?'

"But Shero was great. We went to the meeting together and talked to the president and they lifted the suspension. Then we went to a press conference and they asked him if Murdoch was gonna play right away and Shero said he missed enough games already. Afterward he takes me aside and says we're gonna get along really well 'cause he finally met someone who could bullshit as good as him. I had to kiss a little ass.

"Shero made me feel like I could fit right in. He amazes me. I watch him so much. I'm really into him because he doesn't say nothing. He always throws a phrase at you when he talks to you, he never comes straight out and says blah blah blah. He used to come in the morning and write a little phrase on the blackboard. Like everybody was counting us out in the first round of the play-offs last year 'cause we had a bad streak. So Freddie comes in and writes 'A little mouse by gnawing at a dike can flood a whole nation.' "

Murdoch laughed. "So first I say, 'What the hell's this?' Then you sit there and look at it and in other words it's easy if you work hard and keep working hard you can make it to the top. It might take that fucking mouse two or three years of working his ass off just to make a hole, but once he did he'd flood the whole nation and flush everybody out. Shero's so intelligent. He doesn't come right out, if he gives you an answer he makes a person work to get the answer too. I learned a lot off Shero just by watching and listening to him.

"I like to listen to all kinds of people. Like when I first came to New York I didn't know how to dress for the styles. I didn't know how people acted. When I came here I was wearing country-boy plaid shirts and fucking jeans. Here I gotta go and start buying three-piece suits and fourteen pairs of shoes and a hundred shirts. Shit, half the times I go to discos I go there to watch. When I first came here I didn't know how to dance more than your basic cowboy. You can sit and listen and everything, but you have to get out and try it. Once in a while I'd see the stars like in Studio and I would know that one time I'd have to get up there and try it, get pissed out of my head so I'd have enough nerve to get up there and dance."

Murdoch seemed happy to have changed the thrust of the conversation. And it was inevitable that the talk would turn to girls, one of his favorite topics.

"Hey, I come from a small town where you might get ten good-looking chicks out of the whole fucking town. And remember there's five hundred guys going for them. So I come to New York and I used to get sore necks from turning around looking at all these chicks. I used to walk around with a semiboner all the time. Anywhere I'd go, all these nice-looking chicks were coming up to me. I had nothing to do. I didn't have to work up any lines or anything. Fuck, they'd come up and ask the questions and they'd do all the answering and it was no problem taking a chick back home. It was too easy. I used to say to myself, this isn't right me taking home a beautiful chick and giving her a quick shot."

"But wasn't that boring after a while?" I was trying to convince myself. "I mean, didn't that change the way you viewed women? Wouldn't you become contemptuous of those women?"

"My first year anytime I had a chance to get laid I would

have taken the opportunity. Fat, skinny, ugly, good-looking, it didn't matter. All I was worried about was getting my rocks off." Murdoch smiled wistfully at the memory. "But now these chicks come up and Doogie and I will make fun of them, cut them right down, tell 'em they're pigs, and they'll sit around and like it. If we have them oink for us, they'll probably oink for us. Like we'll be sitting there calling them out, like 'Yeah, you like it, how hard do you want it?' shit like this to these nice broads, and fucking laughing. These chicks would eat it up. We'd abuse them and they would stick around and take it. If you were nice to them, fuck, you'd never get laid. I don't know if 'treat 'em mean, keep 'em keen' is the word, but the more you abuse them, the more they seem to like it."

"But it's sad, isn't it, how empty some of their lives seem? The groupies, the hangers-on," I said.

Murdoch nodded. "You get some of the fan letters they write to you, holy fuck. They send pictures too, that's the biggest joke. When you get a picture they'll send you, everybody in the dressing room has got to have a look at it. One girl from LA sent Christmas cards out to some of the guys with her lips on it. She sent a nude picture of herself in the swimming pool and she's like a big Amazon, fucking six feet, big tits. Oh Christ."

The phone rang again. It was Murdoch's current girl friend. She used to go out with Bobby Murdoch, Donnie's older brother, who also plays hockey. In fact, Bobby introduced them one night at Studio 54, while he was still seeing her. Later that night he was no longer seeing her.

"Oh, it's honey now, is it?" Murdoch's voice floated into the living room. He talked a while and then he came back in. "That's why she likes me, 'cause I'm such a fucking dink!" He laughed.

"I can't believe you stabbed your brother like that," I marveled. "You'd be a good litmus test for a girl's loyalty."

Murdoch cracked up. "Bring 'em over to Murdoch's place," he announced. "Leave 'em for an hour here. We'll see if they're faithful."

"I still can't believe those girls in Charlie O's," I said. "I mean, if you told them to take four laps around the dining room, they'd do it."

"If I found a chick that would tell me to fuck off, I'd probably marry her," Donnie said wistfully. "But I don't care. I'm only twenty-two. I just want to get fucked anyway. They can use me all they want as long as I get laid out of the deal. I don't spend money on them. When it comes time to get a steady girl, I'll get a girl that doesn't know what I do." Murdoch paused. "It's like this girl. That's why she likes me. Bobby's pampering her and babying her and I was getting pissed, leaving her at the bar, going to talk to everybody. She's never been treated shitty like that before. Now she fucking loves me." He smiled with some satisfaction.

"But you seem to have settled down a bit out here," I said. "Almost like you've taken on some suburban values. You seem like you're growing up a bit."

"The good times will always be there," Donnie philosophized. "You have to learn to pick your spots. This year more than ever I stayed in on a number of Friday and Saturday nights. I didn't have to. You play so much hockey now, and the traveling, it's nice just to stay home and watch TV, take the phone off the hook. I don't know if it's just that I'm getting a little bit older. It's probably that I've done enough. I put in the amount of partying my first year that the average person would have taken three years to do. So I'm definitely ahead of everyone else.

"I don't mind sitting home now. I enjoy just going out to dinner with a girl on a date. Buy a little wine and come home and that's it."

"That's it?" I was incredulous.

Murdoch shrugged. "Well, come home for a little plug-in

or something like that. Definitely have to have the plug-in. Don't want to waste a bottle of wine and a good meal on nothing," he said and his laughter drowned out Marcus Welby.

• SEPTEMBER 11

"Murdoch's been hitting those porn films every day. He's down to 123 pounds," Greschner joked. We were on our way out to Sportarama in Suffern, New York, an ice skating-tennis complex where the Rangers had rented some ice. It was a week before training camp was to open in Richmond, Virginia, and we were out for a quick skate. In the back seat Murdoch was trying to wake up. He yawned.

"Don't act tired once we get out there." Gresch was being paternal.

"Fuck off, Gresch," Murdoch snapped. "Take them bulbs out of your head. Shit, I only had ten hours' sleeping the last three days." Murdoch hunched up on the back seat.

"I had to go get one more beer last night," Gresch complained. "Oh, I got a stomachache."

"Me too," Murder piped up. "I was on that Perrier. Boy, is that stuff shit. Gives you animal farts."

Just then Gresch unleashed a massive sneak gas attack. Murdoch and I immediately lunged for the pushbutton windows. The perverse bastard had locked them and was cackling like a hyena.

When we got to the rink the talk was about the Swedes. It seems that they had renegotiated their contracts and signed on for another two years each, bargaining directly with Sonny Werblin, the Garden president, bypassing Shero and his assistant, Mickey Keating. Word was that they had each gotten over $300,000 a year. Word also had it that they were doing fifty laps at three-quarter speed all summer in Sweden. Word like that sobered Murdoch up.

He was bending over, putting his socks on. "Jeez." He picked at his long, misshapen bony toes. "I can't believe the hogs want to suck these." Around the room a few others were getting dressed. I pulled on my pads and, like Gresch, wore a sweat suit over the equipment. That done, I grabbed a righty stick and walked out on the rubber mat and hit the ice.

After warm-ups we divided off into two teams. I was playing with Ulfie, Don Maloney, Steve Vickers, and Hedberg. We were facing Dave Maloney, Greschner, Murdoch, and Ray Markham, a rookie. We were playing in only one zone, shooting on Dougie Soetaert.

I scored a minute into the scrimmage. It was off a standard scramble in front of the net. Ulf had made a beautiful move in front, stickhandling around Maloney and backhanding a shot at Soetaert from ten feet out. The rebound came right to my stick and I slammed it between Soapy's legs. He seemed pissed.

He seemed more angry when I scored again, off a beautiful pass from Ulfie. Two goals my first practice. I began to think that I should pack my skates for the Richmond trip. After a few minutes we took a break.

"Where's JD, that fat cunt?" Dave Maloney wondered. "He played good in the play-offs last year and he thinks he doesn't have to show up."

"Hey, Murder, you lost it," Carol Vadnais snapped.

"Yeah," Ulfie smiled impishly. "He left it in the Studio."

After a few more minutes of scrimmage, we called it a day. And after a sauna and shower, we headed back to the city. In the car Murdoch was strangely dour. "That fucking Markham." He scowled. "He thinks he's gonna take my spot. I'll skate right around him."

Steve Vickers, the Rangers' left wing, who was getting a

ride back to Manhattan with us, looked up from his cross-word puzzle. "He's strong, Doc. He can lift a tractor, but he can't start it."

Murdoch laughed. "I'm assistant captain now," he boasted. "I'm the representative of the perverts and the drunkards. I speak for me and Doog. We're voting to see if we let Gresch in."

"Hey, JD won't be ready for another month," Gresch said.

"When they opened his knee, they found Michelob caps," Murder cracked. We drove by Ward's Island. Murdoch stared at the huge institutional buildings with their barred windows.

"Hey, boys," he yelled toward the building. "I was almost over there with you guys. Better watch my ass. She's still tight, boys. There's been a few fingers up there but not much else."

When we got to the city, Greschner dropped Vickers off, then drove Murdoch to Lenox Hill Hospital, where he was taking therapy for a shoulder that had been operated on earlier that summer. We stopped on Lexington Avenue, and Murdoch jumped out into the midday traffic, paused in front of the car, bent over, and slowly pulled his red gym shorts down. It was the best shot he'd gotten off all day.

• SEPTEMBER 14

By the end of the week the pace had increased out in Sportarama. I decided to hang up my skates. After practice Murdoch and Vickers and I went back to Gresch's house to eat some Chinese food and prepare for a night of partying. It was the last night before they would leave for the secluded confines of Richmond, Virginia, and training camp.

Tonight was somewhat special. After all, it was an honor to have Steve Vickers hanging out with the bachelors again.

Vickers was one of the original Ranger swingers, and his exploits with Gilbert and Derek Sanderson have taken on all the qualities of oral history, passed from generation to generation of city-dwelling Rangers. But last summer Vickers married his longtime girl friend, Joanne, and in no time flat, Joanne was pregnant and the Vickerses were shopping for a house in Westchester. But Sarge was still revered by his teammates. As Wayne Thomas said one night in Oren and Aretsky, "Sarge's nose is about as brown as the tablecloth." The tablecloth was pure white.

We were sitting around watching the newlywed game, finishing off the Chinese food. "What people won't say for a washer and dryer," Vickers mused sagely. Then he started telling jokes.

"What's a Jewish definition for foreplay?" Everyone shrugged. "Twenty minutes of begging."

"How does a Jewish girl eat a banana?" he continued. He held one up, unpeeled it, opened his mouth, put his hand behind his head, and pushed his head down onto the fruit.

Murdoch was amused. He began to relate some stories about his friend, Yankee ace Goose Gossage.

"One time we were watching films of the series together at the Goose's house at six in the morning. It was after Studio one night. Goose took me out to his house in Jersey and we're watching the tapes and his wife is yelling at him to turn it off and go to bed. Then we went out in his backyard and had a catch. No shit. Goose even gave me one of his gloves."

"Did he tell you how he hurt his hand in the fight?" I wondered about the Cliff Johnson incident.

"He said it was the last time he'd ever hit anybody in the head," Murdoch laughed. "Next time, he'll kick him in the balls."

It was getting late. Nearly eleven o'clock. The city lights beckoned from Greschner's twenty-seventh floor apartment.

Oh, to be young, rich, famous, and unattached. Murdoch picked up the phone and dialed a number.

"We'd like a limo sent over," he said, giving Gresch's address. But then Murdoch thought a second. "Better make it one of those extension ones," he added, "in case we have to lay someone down."

- SEPTEMBER 18

Why were we in Richmond, Virginia? That was the litany here and for the life of me I still can't come up with a good answer. Perhaps it was to pump some life into the Richmond Rifles hockey franchise, now affiliated with the Ranger organization. Perhaps it was to get a respite from the temptations of the big city. Maybe it was just because nobody had had the foresight to arrange for an ice facility in the New York area. At any rate, we were here in Richmond, a town known for tobacco and transsexuals. The tobacco got processed here, the transsexuals got operated on. Neither procedure seemed to interest the hockey players.

Murdoch was the hardest hit. He was sitting in a downtown bar the second night of camp, in the throes of terminal culture shock. "Take me home to New York," he moaned. "Bring me to Studio. Bring the girls from Studio."

"Bring anyone over twelve," Duguay joined in, in mock anguish.

I was sitting with Molly, a friend of a friend, and a local, a college professor. Molly had promised to round up some of her nubile students for these poor suffering lads.

"Where are they now?" Murdoch pleaded. "Old one-eye wants to introduce himself. The little guy gets sick a lot. You know, throws up."

Molly was finding the hockey players "delightful" and "refreshing." She was muttering something about "joie de vivre." She was mainly staring intently at Anders Hedberg. She thought he was a Swedish charmer.

"Just tell your friends we're energetic and we like oral sex," Murder summed up. Molly giggled.

It was a strange camp. As Greschner put it, there were "eighty guys out for two positions." So many guys that they had to divide up into four colored teams and run two separate sessions, making it a bit hard to stand out in the crowd. But something else was making it hard to be noticed. It was the second day of camp and nobody had seen Coach Shero.

"I think I saw Fred once, in the stands," Anders reported.

"We put out an all-points bulletin on Freddie," Murdoch told me.

"Yeah." Duguay smiled. "He was last seen talking to a bartender."

FRED SHERO

The man who returned tradition—and winning—to the New York Rangers . . . Quiet and soft spoken all the time, he's earned the respect of players and fans alike . . . Highly respected throughout the hockey world for innovative and successful coaching methods . . . Became most publicized coach in NHL history . . . Calm and placid behind the bench, but always seeking—and finding—new ways to motivate . . . Lives in Hartsdale, New York, with wife Mariette and two sons, Jean-Paul and Rejean.

—New York Rangers Yearbook, *1979–1980*

I would have loved to have caught that conversation. Even after a year in New York, under the scrutiny of the sharpest media around, Shero remained as enigmatic as ever. He hardly ever talked to the players, leaving that task to his two assistants, Nykoluk and Keating. Behind the bench he would do the oddest things. Like try to send out onto the ice someone who was already in the penalty box. Or bench someone who had scored a flurry of goals because they might have been "lucky." Of course, his erratic behavior had a method. He was testing his players, throwing them back on themselves, building up their self-confidence. They hoped.

"I don't want them [the players] to think I'm God," Shero once told a reporter. "I want them to humor me, to kid me, even if it's very embarrassing at times. I want them to know it's not like Russia, that they're allowed to assert themselves. I don't want robots. Championships are won by those not afraid to dare."

Case in point, Mike McEwen. McEwen was one of the few Rangers who ever got up the nerve to approach Shero for a talk about rushing tactics. One day on the road Mike went to Freddie's room, where Shero was watching TV. The young defenseman then began a complicated exegesis on why the wing should cut to the net when he carried the puck into the offensive zone. Shero looked bored.

"I don't care what you do," he told the startled Ranger. "Make sure you carry the puck all the way in and if you're gonna go in, stay there. Guys'll cover for you. If they don't cover for you, it's their fault, right?" Shero then turned back to the TV, engrossed in the fights.

"I was still talking to him," McEwen remembered, "but he didn't care, he'd said what he wanted to say. And that's the first time I ever had anybody say, 'Do what you want' as far as rushing was concerned. It's always been 'What are you trying to be, another Bobby Orr?' But with him, it was 'Do what you want, fuck, don't bother me.' "

Which is not to say that Shero is disinterested. *Au contraire.* He lives, eats, breathes, and dreams hockey, making him a virtual stranger to his wife and two children. "If you had to open his brain, you would see a little hockey rink there," his better half once said. "That's all he thinks about." Which may explain some of the more bizarre Shero stories that circulate around the NHL. Stories like the time the coach was so deep in thought, planning strategy before a road game, that he walked right out of the rink and into the parking lot, where he patiently remained, locked out, until he was discovered just minutes before the game.

When he coached in Philly, he would often drive to the rink at 3 A.M. to work out some theories. Then there's the classic story of Shero's encounter with visiting Russian hockey coaches. It was cultural exchange time as they swapped systems, talking far into the night in his hotel room. By the end of the evening Shero was on the carpeted floor on his hands and knees, using empty beer bottles to diagram plays. He searches everywhere for inspiration and knowledge —even to pop psychologies like José Silva's Mind Control Method, a mixture of alpha-wave technology, Eastern meditation, and good old American pragmatism. In Shero's copy of Silva's book, he dutifully underlined:

> *During meditation before going to sleep, review a problem that can be solved with information or advice. Be sure that you really care about solving it; silly questions evoke silly answers. Now program yourself with these words: "I want to have a dream that will contain information to solve the problem I have in mind. I will have such a dream, remember it and understand it."*

In the margin Shero had scrawled "Power play."

It's all grist for the System. Ah, the System. Shero was famous for his System. Problem was, hardly anybody could tell you what it encompassed. On one level it was quite simple. A way to move the puck out of your own end, starting from possession behind the net, utilizing the rudimentary theory of numerical superiority. On another level the System was part metaphysics, part industrial psychology, using the latest in motivational techniques culled from everything from Zen Roshis to post-est fad therapies. Shero claimed the System was born back in Winnipeg, Manitoba, when, as a child during the Depression, he was responsible for weeding and watering his family's vegetable garden. "I soon realized that nature had a system," he wrote in one of his books. "If I didn't water or weed the garden, the results were disastrous." Zen and the Art of the Body Check.

And if nature taught him the importance of approaching things orderly and systematically, he learned another great lesson his first year of coaching with the Shawinigan Falls Cataracts of the Quebec Hockey League. The team had played with as much vision as its name implied, but when Shero took over in 1957, he tried a new tack. He refused to threaten the players or point out their obvious weaknesses. Instead, he appealed to them at their first meeting, asking them for their help, since he was a novice at coaching. Miraculously, it worked. The Cataracts finished second in the play-offs. And Shero had a better idea. Not only would he refine his System, but he would extend his psychological strategy. Next time he wouldn't ask his players for help. He'd have them coach themselves.

So here we were in training camp and Shero had pulled a disappearing act. A brilliant psychological strategem. Pure Zen. If a player falls during warm-up, who will hear it? It was like the time last year when Shero had come to practice and instructed the three defenders in a five-on-three situation to play holding their sticks upside down—by the blade. It turned the game upside down. Tweak those noses, keep 'em hungry. Satori in Richmond. Of course, maybe I was reading too much into all this. Maybe Shero had shown up. Maybe he just took a stroll and locked himself out of the building.

Murdoch was complaining again. It was about noon and he was stone-dead tired, curled up on his twin bed in the Holiday Inn. On the other bed Greschner was playing with his roommate, alternately turning the lamp on the nightstand on and off.

"Cut it out, you cunt!" Murdoch screamed. "Banana nose. You look like the Midtown Tunnel from the bottom up. Sometimes it looks awful crowded in there too."

Greschner left the light off and feigned sleep.

"I don't want to go back. I'm fucking beat," Murdoch said. "That was an easy skate compared to the first two days. Gresch, where do we get our expense money from?"

Greschner didn't move. "Talk to my ass, my head's tired."

Murdoch leaned over and stripped Greschner's sneaker off. "Look at these runners, will ya. He makes two hundred thousand a year and he wears dollar ninety-eight runners."

"I only paid eighty-seven cents," Ron corrected.

"Look at those fucking things," Murdoch went on. "There's life in them fuckers, they got a heartbeat."

"You're about as funny as a cactus saddle," Greschner said. "You're about as funny as cancer."

"You know what would be funny?" Gresch rolled over. "If I shit right in your fucking face."

"You know what he does?" Murdoch turned to me. "He sticks his ass up, farts, and fluffs the sheets right in my face." The right winger looked hurt.

Greschner smiled. "I was talking to him when the lights were out and I gave him this one. 'What you say? I can't hear you.'" Greschner leaned off the bed and farted.

"You're worse than a bad case of hemorrhoids. Kiss my ass

and lick it." Murdoch was mock livid. "Tongue me to death, you fucking whale."

"I told you"—Gresch pulled the pillow over his head—"talk to my ass 'cause my head's very tired."

Murdoch fell silent, absorbed in the game show on the tube. "Richmond's a fucking psychiatric ward," he complained. "Instead of sending me to Bellevue send me to Richmond." He grabbed a pillow and held it to his body. "Get on top of me for a while. Here, let me tickle your ass. You got her, Gresch." Murdoch threw the pillow to his roommate.

Greschner sent her back. "I don't want to hurt her."

After a while, play period was over. Duguay came to the room and we left for the rink. On the way out of the lobby, Doog gave an obligatory moon, pulling his beige jogging suit down past his buttocks. But he is the shy one. He didn't pull his underwear down too.

At the rink there was good news. Freddie was found. He was sitting high up in the rafters, alone. Within seconds of discovery he was surrounded by the press. Down on the ice the teams scrimmaged, then stayed on to take shots. Off in the corners of the rink the Rangers paired off to do sit-ups, each partner holding the other's ankles. After some blue line-to-blue line skating exercises, the practice was over.

• SEPTEMBER 20

Light workout today. That was because everyone was preparing for this evening's game between the Rangers and the New Haven and Richmond squads. Intramural madness, designed to sell tickets to a cold game in a hot town. In fact, the only one who worked hard was Josh Guevremont, the defenseman the Rangers had picked up from Buffalo last year. He worked hard because he was told that the management didn't like his play so far. Guevremont was big, 6 feet 2 inches and 210 pounds, but he had a reputation for refusing to hit. In order to keep him, the Rangers had left Fotiu unprotected in the draft. So Guevremont better learn how to hit and like it.

After the practice Rod Gilbert invited me for a skate. We cruised the rink in tandem for a while, passing the puck back and forth, talking about Pat Hickey. Hitch was a protégé of Gilbert's, one of the first players to defy the previous John Ferguson administration and move from the Rangers' Long Beach, Long Island enclave into Manhattan. But now that a handful of others had followed him, Hitch had seemed to withdraw a bit from his teammates. Gilbert was concerned.

"Hitch got hurt a little bit last year." Gilbert took a slap shot on the empty set. The puck hit the pipe and caromed all the way down the empty ice. "Fergie didn't want him in the city and he challenged it because he was confident enough. Some of the other players had to wait till last year to come in. So when Hitch did his things all the guys used to criticize him. This year he sort of pulled back on them a bit. He gave up on them, I can understand why."

We took a breather by the bench. "But he's so fucking stubborn." Gilbert was sweating hard. "He played with the two best last year, the Swedes, and he wouldn't fucking change his style. He would have had fifty goals, but he was too stubborn."

We started talking about violence. Gilbert laughed ironically. "I remember the time Roger Crozier, the goalie, gave me a two-hander with his stick and broke my ankle. I had to come back at him. So next chance I got I took the puck and skated to about here." He glided over to the corner, an impossible angle for a goal. "I wound up and he wasn't expecting me to shoot, eh, and came back at him with a slap shot from the corner. Right to the neck. It knocked him out.

Jesus, was my heart beating! I felt terrible about it but I had to do it." Gilbert drew his stick back and slapped the puck again, whistling it by the far post. "Stupid fucking game, eh?"

We started skating. "But you gotta give back to the game, you can't just take and take. Just by things like visiting hospitals. Going to see the veterans." Gilbert dropped the puck to me and I slammed it high into the net. "I was in the Bronx once, in the Veterans Hospital, and one of the vets there was a kid who was nineteen years old, just back from Vietnam. I was there with a few football players and we were passing the beds. They recognized and identified with the football players, but hockey wasn't so well known, this was ten years ago. So one of the kids that was sick asked to talk to me. I went back to his bed. It made me feel good, maybe I could share some ideas with him, and he asked me what I did for a living. So I said, 'I play hockey.'

"He said, 'That's a great hobby.' I said, 'It's not exactly a hobby for me, it's my profession.' 'Oh,' he says, 'I still think it's a great hobby.' Then he said, 'Want to know what I do for my hobby?' I said, 'Sure,' thinking maybe he was a writer or an artist. He pulled the sheets off his body and he didn't have any legs and he said, 'I step on mines for my hobby.'" Gilbert whipped the puck in the net and we skated around in silence and then we called it a day.

That night 3,612 fans packed the 12,000-seat Coliseum and saw the Rangers defeat the minor league team. But the star of the game was rookie goalie Steve Baker, who made splendid save after save and shut the big team out for the first half of the game. After they switched goalies, the Rangers came back to win by a goal. One of the 3,612 admissions was Molly, who never did round up those nubile things for Murdoch. She did manage to bring a transsexual, though, who used to be a male barber and was still a barber. She enjoyed the game immensely. "Gee," she sighed after the Rangers left the ice, "I wish I was a fly in their dressing room."

• OCTOBER 2

The Rangers were back in New York and hosting the Islanders, their cross-county rivals, in an exhibition game. And last year's upset victory in the play-offs hadn't been forgotten by the Islanders.

Both teams came out hitting. Hard. In the first period Dave Maloney lined up Islander defenseman Dave Lewis and fused his elbow into Lewis's cheekbone. There was an audible snap, a sickening sound, and Lewis departed for the dressing room with a huge welt under his eye.

Later that game Pat Hickey and Islander rookie Bryan Sutter met along the far boards. Hickey got his elbow up a bit high and then started skating away from the play. But Sutter grabbed Pat from behind and spun him around and landed a tremendous sucker punch right to the eye. Hitch left the game seeing out of one eye. Sutter left the game at the referee's request.

Later, Mario Marois, a hard-nosed young Ranger defenseman, left the game too—with a towel wrapped around his bleeding hard nose, which somehow got right in the way of the speeding puck. Both Hickey and Marois wound up in Lenox Hill Hospital.

In the locker room Greschner was pissed. He was staring at a copy of the new *Penthouse* and cursing to himself. "You can only take so much bullshit before it gets to you, Rats," he told me. Gresch was upset because management had just informed him that he would have to go to Philly for the next exhibition game. Nobody liked to play Philly at home, in front of their rabid fans. But more important, if he played in

Philly he would have to break the date he had with the centerfold that he had in his hands.

Murdoch was truly empathetic. His eyes were on the centerfold, but his heart went out to Gresch. "Look at that," he marveled, "that could be you. Bam bam bam."

"Imagine laying on top of that." Gresch shook his head.

"Phil came over and told me to go talk to you," Murder reported. "I told him, 'What can I say? I don't blame him.' I told him you're pissed off. Every other guy's sitting out. You've been in the league for six years. Phil says, 'They figure he's not in shape.'"

Gresch turned bitter. "Yeah, and everybody else is in really good shape."

"Phil told me to tell you to call him if you want to talk to him," Murdoch said.

"Talk about what? There's fuckall to talk about." Gresch straightened his tie.

"As if they're not happy," Murdoch said. "Fucking Vad's missed every game." Duguay walked by. "Look at those shoes." Murdoch pointed to some garish wheels that clashed with Duguay's smart suit.

"That's like buying a Mercedes and putting steel tires on it," Greschner cracked.

Murdoch summoned both his teammates for a huddle. "I got some dirt for you, you're gonna love it." He sounded gleeful. "I got some in the shower and the back room. Fergie's trying to get a hold of me for Winnipeg. But the Rangers were asking for too much. Sarge told me it's great to know someone else wants you if they try to get rid of you." Both his teammates nodded.

But Murdoch didn't heed Vickers's advice. He was still bothered by the trade rumor on the way up to Oren and Aretsky, where the four of us were having dinner. Wayne Thomas, who had played splendidly in goal, was along for the ribs.

"You could see the bone in Mario's nose," Thomas offered without anyone asking.

Murdoch frowned. "They'll probably offer me to Winnipeg for six broken sticks and boxes of white tape."

"Marc can't hang around with us this year. We got the word from management," Duguay said. He was referring to Marc Benecke, who held one of the most important jobs in New York. Marc was the one who stood outside Studio 54, deciding who could get in. Whenever a Ranger came up to the red ropes, it was like Moses leaving Egypt. But some of the other players, especially the ones that lived in Westchester, were a little resentful of the Manhattan Rangers and their Studio-tinged life-style. They decided that Marc was a floater and they didn't want any floaters around.

"What did Marc do?" Murdoch wondered. "But then when they want to go to Studio, they sure like Marc. Or Steve Herlihy. They sure like to go to his bar."

The waitress brought us a round of drinks. There was no game tomorrow and it looked like the warriors were settling in for a while. "Are we getting gunned tonight?" Murdoch smiled. It was a rhetorical question. Everyone lifted his glass. "Here's to getting up and feeling brutal," Murdoch toasted. He looked around the back room. Little clusters of models and would-be starlets met his eye. His eye settled on something red. "Oh, bam bam. How bad do you like it? How fast do you want it? And how many times?" Murdoch was singing to himself. "I think we should give me three hundred thousand dollars a year. Let me be the captain and everything'll run smooth," Murdoch announced.

"Wayrarawara." Gresch was slurring his words in mimicry of Murdoch past. "He hasn't talked like that yet since he's been living with me," Gresch said proudly. "We had a long talk, me and Murder one day. He hasn't walked into practice once this year going warrghrgrh . . ."

Everyone laughed.

"He will tomorrow, though," Gresch added.

"Who cares?" Murdoch shrugged. "None of the browns'll be there anyway."

• OCTOBER 11

The Rangers opened their season on the road and beat Toronto 6–3, thanks to the acrobatic goaltending of Wayne Thomas. Hickey, who was still seeing double and feeling depressed about it, watched the game at home in New York. He was cheered somewhat by the fried chicken he cooked, using his sister's recipe.

• OCTOBER 14

The home opener and the crowd was going wild. By the end of the game they were a little more subdued. The Rangers lost 5–3, with Capital supercenter Dennis Maruk getting four goals. Greg Polis also achieved a goal. He didn't score, but he managed to sucker punch Carol Vadnais in the first period. Polis is a very mild-mannered guy. Polis is also an ex-teammate of Vadnais'. The attack seemed to fall somewhere between instinct and premeditation.

In the locker room the real talk wasn't about the game. It was about the trade. John Davidson was the first to rush up to me. "It's a big one, baby. Beck's coming here within two or three days."

"For who?" I asked.

"Two defensemen who were here last year. Two wings too."

Bucchino was next. "Something's gonna happen soon." "I heard," I told him. "Beck." Bukka rolled his eyes. "We'll get the Cup if he comes."

Greschner was less sanguine. "Do you hear they're trading for Beck?" "Yeah, who is it?" I asked. Gresch frowned. "I could be out of here."

Gresch and I decided to go to Il Vagabondo, where there was a party for Gilbert. Dave Maloney came along. We took a table that was diagonally across from Andy Warhol, who was a friend of Rod's and was turning into a Ranger fan. His favorite, judging from his stares across the room, was Ron Duguay.

Maloney stared back at Warhol. "I feel better already just looking at that guy," he cracked. "Hey, Gresch, somebody told me they saw Sorkin at the race track. He must be out."

Gresch shrugged. Richard Sorkin was Greschner's former agent, a glib New Yorker who scoured Western Canada for promising, talented young hockey players, wooed them and their parents, and signed them up to Richard Sorkin, Inc. As their agent, Sorkin collected all of their salaries and bonuses, paid their bills, and deposited the rest in their own bank accounts. Theoretically. What actually happened was that Sorkin comingled all the money from his forty or so clients, and ended up blowing a cool million of it at the track and in the market. The scam fell through when too many people asked for cash.

Gresch got taken to the tune of $150,000. It was a quick education. Accounting 150,000. A course with a surprise ending. "I went to buy a Corvette one time and I had no money," Gresch was telling us. "I threw my wallet away 'cause I didn't need a wallet then. I owed thirty-five thousand dollars cash. I remember the beginning of my third year, every check was going to bills. I learned, though. Now if I want money I go to my bank and I have it in my own name and everything's cool."

Maloney cursed Sorkin out. Gresch was silent. "I'm not pissed off, though," he said. "He paid for it. He went to jail for eleven months. He's a little guy, five foot three inches. I feel sorry for him in a way."

Next stop was Herlihy's. Herlihy's was owned by Steve Herlihy, a male model, who was a friend of Gilbert's. It was a jock-model hangout and was the last stop of the Rangers' postgame circuit. Tonight was the home opener at Herlihy's.

But in the corner by the jukebox, Greschner and Soetaert were ignoring the models. Soetaert because he was married, Greschner because he was preoccupied. Both because they were scared stiff.

"What do you hear about the trade?" Soetaert was worried. He was the third goalie, a young man with a lot of promise. But somehow he never really had gotten his shot at the Ranger nets.

"Four for Beck." Gresch was succinct.

"I'm gone," Soapy said.

"Did you sign a lease?" Gresch asked.

"Fuck, yeah."

Gresch turned to me. "You gonna come visit us in Colorado?"

"I don't want to leave here," Soapy moaned. "I'd hate to leave here."

Gresch downed his beer. "If they trade me, I'll leave half my heart here."

- OCTOBER 16

Good news and bad news. The good news for Hickey and McEwen was that the Beck deal was denied by Mickey Keating.

The bad news was for Duguay. It started when Assistant Coach Nykoluk was standing in the lobby of Sportarama at 10:15 watching the guys stream in for practice. The Swedes strolled by. Davidson and Eddie Johnstone. Gresch and

Murder, the odd couple. Hitch, carrying a gift from a fan—a cute little Ranger doll, complete with black eye. The phone rang. "Must be Duguay." Nykoluk laughed sardonically. "Late again, eh?"

After practice the coaches met with the assistant captains. Over lunch Espo laid down the law. "No jeans on the road. No being late for the bus. Fine. You're late to ten-thirty practice, fine." At the meeting Duguay was chewed out by Captain Maloney. Espo concurred.

Duguay is very sensitive. All day long the chastisement had him brooding. It reached a head that night in Oren and Aretsky, over a hamburger.

"I had it with you." Greschner cornered Doogs. "I was always on your side but not now. You have a responsibility to the team. You're fucking up. You'll be in Colorado."

Duguay frowned. "I'm different."

"Sure. They're not here to cater to you. They pay you a hundred thousand dollars," Gresch said.

"I'm not like them. I get my own room on the road. I asked the coach. Keating said it was okay, he likes his privacy too. Anyway, I'm paying for it." Duguay ignored his beer.

"What about missing the plane?" Greschner reminded.

"Okay, I missed a plane," Ron admitted. "Doesn't seem like a big deal to me. These are all little things. What about Maloney missing Sonny's dinner? He missed the dinner to make money on a promotion."

Greschner got up to go to the bathroom. Duguay nibbled on his hamburger, then put it down. "I can't win," he said morosely. "I try hard. Vad says, 'Why is he trying hard?' They tell Nykoluk, he won't listen to my side anymore. Is that all they have to do, sit around and talk about each other? The best thing for the team right now would be if Vad got traded. Look at Espo. They got on his case last year in the play-offs. And me and Mud. They told Nykoluk we were both drinking."

Duguay paused. "I'm sure Josh won't be here next year. I won't even make it through this whole year. Jesus, why are they on my case? I try to get along with everyone. I asked Davey last year when I first realized. Vadnais had Maloney and Murdoch over for dinner and he didn't ask me. I was in the same building as him. I asked Davey why Vad didn't like me. I'm sure that Davey went right to him and they had a laugh about it." Duguay shook his head in resignation. "There's a lot of politics going on here."

• OCTOBER 18

Dave Maloney

The epitome of the current Rangers . . . Young, talented, exuberant . . . Team captain and a leader, on the ice and off . . . Youngest captain in team history . . . Rugged, strong and aggressive . . . Shares Ranger record for most penalty minutes in one game . . . Extremely poised and confident player . . . Good sense of humor . . . He and younger brother Don became the latest in long line of brother combinations to play for Rangers . . . In fact, each time the Rangers have won the Stanley Cup, a famous brother combination was on the squad . . .

—New York Rangers Yearbook, *1979–1980*

Maloney and I were eating lunch. We were in a back booth in Charlie O's, and the captain was rushing through his steak so he could go across the street to the Southgate Tower Hotel and get in a few hours of nap time before tonight's game against Vancouver.

Of all the Rangers, Maloney was one of the more well

informed. Not through a formal education, because Dave was standing on Garden ice in a Ranger uniform when he was barely eighteen. But he reads a lot—novels and nonfiction and newspapers—and is probably one of the few Rangers who could name the current Secretary of State.

But we weren't talking about politics. We were talking about hockey. "It means a lot to me now," Maloney began. "It's the main focal point in my life. It's my whole existence."

"What's the attraction for you, though?" I wondered.

"For a male it might be that aggression we all take pride in. The male animal thing. The instinct that's allowed to become evident without having your hand slapped, except by the referee." He mused, "There's not too many other sports or jobs where you can feel an integral part of the end result and get recognized as the person. The supposed adulation you're receiving, well, we all have a bit of ham in us."

I asked him about the New York scene and the vagaries of stardom. He frowned. "That storybook thing. Young kid coming to New York. Too much, too soon. That's what you would expect all of us would turn out like, if the clichés and the stories were all true. You would expect that Murdoch was not an exception to the rule. But there are different personalities. My father's a construction worker, my uncle's a construction worker. My dad's friend works in a brewery. Society doesn't say it's a glamorous thing. I haven't been exposed to anything else, other life-styles. I'm not impressed that a person will fall head over heels because I'm a hockey player. I realize someone else is going to be wearing my jersey when my time is up. I'd rather lie on an even keel than come up here and fall off. That's me, that's my personality. Some guys need the adulation. They need the entourage to walk into Charlie O's. They have to go to be seen here and seen there. Fine, if you can deal with it."

Maloney chuckled. "It used to be for years the players weren't allowed to expose themselves in New York City. Like the NHL Security Office has a list of bars in every city in the league that players should not be seen in. When it comes to New York, they throw the whole *Yellow Pages* at you."

"You sound pretty fatalistic," I observed.

"I could do anything." Maloney wasn't boasting. "A lot of things. Write stories for *Playboy*. I'd be a professional student probably, a bum. I don't know. I could find something. I've thought of it somewhat. I expect to play till I'm thirty. Maybe. When I first turned pro it was twenty-five."

The bill came and Maloney grabbed it. I looked around the room at the businessmen eating lunch and remembered last year and the insanity that prevailed in here after the Rangers beat the Islanders. The thousands of people outside on Thirty-third street, cheering and kissing each other and pissing on the Islander bus as it left. I reminded Maloney.

"There's an empty feeling when you finally achieve what you wanted," he said softly. "The best part was getting there. Like bowling a perfect game. I read in the paper where Potvin said the Islanders would win this year and then keep the Cup. What fun is that? That's naïve. You gotta put things in perspective. We only beat the Islanders. Hey, I felt super but I got home, the world didn't stop. The next day, there was still crime in the subway. It's not the be all and end all, winning." He got up and we made our way out into the afternoon sunlight. "Hockey's a child's game," he concluded. "But still I hate to lose. More than anyone else."

He didn't have to worry against Vancouver. In fact, he scored on the first shot of the game, a low slap shot.

• OCTOBER 21

The Rangers beat Pittsburgh tonight to go one game over .500. Hitch scored his first goal of the season, breaking his long slump, on a nice setup by Greschner. But Shero's words could not have pleased him. Or McEwen.

"Is the defense more offensive-minded than you'd like?" one reporter started off the postgame conference.

Shero dragged on his Chesterfield. "That's our biggest weakness. Always has been. Overhandling the puck. Nobody should ever beat a defenseman dekeing you. They're not thinking defensively."

"Can you change their habits?"

"Some things can't change," Freddie muttered ominously.

"It must be frustrating," one reporter sympathized.

"Sometimes it might be better unloading some, right? I think we have too many that overhandle the puck."

"Is that a clue?"

Shero scowled. "That's not a clue. That's what I'm saying. I have a right to talk. We have too many nice players." He laughed. "Talented—but too many nice guys. They start reaching for the puck with the stick when all they have to do is get the body in the way. You don't have to knock anybody down. The whole secret I guess is to get one person on each line who is strictly a hitter and a digger and give up talent for a type of player like that."

But in the locker room the players weren't listening to Shero. They were listening to John Gfeller, who lately had more contact with them than their coach. Gfeller was a slick, almost sinister-looking man whose job was to get Ranger players' endorsements. Last week he had circulated the final mix of the *Hockey Sock Rock*, an authentic novelty record, starring Phil Esposito, Pat Hickey, Ron Duguay, Dave Maloney, and John Davidson. The boys had cut it one day last summer when they had a few spare hours in LA before taping the *Dinah!* show.

Tonight Gfeller was lugging around press proofs of the Sasson advertisement, which also featured Hickey and Maloney. It seemed that Gfeller visited some players more than others. To remedy that Mickey Keating had placed a typed letter on the players' bulletin board. It read:

To all Ranger Players from Mickey Keating:
RE: SPONSOR LUNCHEON ON MONDAY, OCTOBER 22

The Sponsor Lunch will be held at the Hall of Fame Room at 12 noon. The fact that the sponsors are spending $3.5 million dollars on us means as many players as possible should be at attendance to make this lunch a success. If you are available to attend, please write name below.

Mickey Keating

NOTE: IF YOU ARE INTERESTED IN DOING COMMERCIALS THESE ARE THE PEOPLE WHO MAKE THE DECISIONS WHO SHOULD MARKET THEIR PRODUCT, THEREFORE THESE ARE THE PEOPLE I SUGGEST YOU MEET.

In the corner of the room, Vadnais was pontificating to a reporter. This was an extremely rare occurrence because most regular-beat journalists kept a wary distance from Vad. Part of it was his thick French accent. Part of it was simple fear. A few years back Vadnais was not the most pleasant guy in the world to be around. He was getting booed unmercifully by the hometown fans, and his favorite record was Johnny Paycheck's "Take This Job and Shove It." Consequently, the reporters picked up on his body language and let him be. Part of his body language consisted of sending up huge billows of talcum powder whenever any reporter made the mistake of coming too close to him.

But now things were different. Vadnais had weathered the fans' disapproval. Last year, after the play-offs, at the Lone Star Café, he had even joined Paycheck on stage, singing the chorus to "Take This Job and Shove It." His demons had been exorcised, but still the reporters were reluctant to venture near his stall. Often when Vadnais was showering, Mario Marois would peek into the showers and bark, " 'ey, Vad. Come on out, the reporters want to interview you. Hahahahaha."

But tonight someone was talking to Vad about practical jokes. They were talking about water fights and cutting ties, and a strange ritual of shaving, in which a rookie is removed from all his hair, especially the short ones. Vad relished being an expert.

"Den you got your water on top of your seat. You get up and it falls all over you. It's nothing really to talk about because dere stupid tings. People outside of hockey dey'll say, 'What's so funny bout dat?,' but when you've been around and all dat . . ." Vadnais shrugged and dragged on his fat cigar. "I'm de instigator of a lot of shaving guys. I used to do dat a lot, I don't do it anymore. I start de damn tings, den I go sit down and relax in the corner. I let dem go at it. I don't hold dem down."

Vadnais picked at a piece of lint on his expensive suit. "In a way it's wrong, because I don't protect dem. I'm the first one dat wants to see dem on de table, but I tell all de rookies, 'Don't worry, I'll be on your side. Nothing's gonna happen,' stuff like dat."

The journalist was taking it all in. With his Sony mike. Vadnais puffed contentedly on his cigar. "Er, anything you'd like to say . . .?" The reporter ran out of questions.

"I gave you my life story," Vadnais concluded, straightened his pants, and walked imperially out of the room.

• OCTOBER 24

I'm in the yellow seats, sitting next to Diana Davidson. Tonight was hubby John's first start, coming off his knee injury. Diana was everyone's favorite wife, a vivacious, cute little brunette. Her nickname was Beaver. Apparently it had something to do with Western Canada where she and John are from.

Beaver is usually very vocal at the game, moaning and clawing and shrieking, especially when her husband is playing. And she's also very superstitious, wearing lucky clothing and lucky jewelry. Tonight she did both.

On the ice the players were going through warm-ups. Beaver was only half-attentive. "What preparation do you make on a day of the game for John?" I wondered.

Beaver blushed. "Ratso, what is this, an interview? You're gonna make me laugh. It's spaghetti, spaghetti with a special kind of meat sauce."

"What brand?" I was being perverse.

"Buitoni. Always Buitoni."

"You mean if you'd slip in Prince, he'd know the difference?"

Beaver laughed. "No, he wouldn't know if I threw crap in there."

"What if he loses? Do you change next game?"

"Sometimes I'll give him something else, like an English muffin. He eats twelve-thirty on the nose. Then he goes to bed, about twenty-five to one. He inhales his food."

"Do you ever go on the road with them?" I wondered.

Beaver smiled. "Only if we sneak."

Down on the ice the game was about to begin. The Rangers clustered around Davidson, each one giving him a ritualistic tap on his big goalie pads. Maloney, as was tradition, was last. Play began. A few minutes into the period, Edmonton threatened and Davidson moved way out of the net to challenge a shooter. "Oh, no, no, no, no, no," Beaver screamed and buried her head in my shoulder. "Get back in the net, John," she mumbled into my arm. Davidson made the save. "He was nervous before the game," Diana remembered. "He said to me on the way out the door, 'Don't get upset if they slip in a few goals.'"

The period was half-over and the Rangers had pumped four goals into the net. Edmonton, for its part, had only four shots on net. The fifth one went in, eluding Davidson, who was screened by a big Edmonton forward. "Shit," Beaver cursed. "What was that guy doing standing right in the crease? I hate it when they get only four shots on goal, that's not enough for a goaltender to stay sharp."

"He's got to stand up more, right?" I hit on what was, to many, Davidson's only real weakness.

"The junior coach used to make all the guys fire shots at his head to make him stand up," Beaver said matter-of-factly.

They met in juniors in British Columbia. Diana was an usherette who was in charge of opening the gate to let the players on the ice. One day the big goalie noticed her ("he liked my body") and asked her boss for her number. The rest is hockey history.

"I was going out with a guy for two and a half years and John asked me out and I figured I needed a change," Diana remembered. "Now my old boyfriend owns a construction company. He's filthy rich." She laughed. "Me and my sister and my girl friend used to stand there at the rink and see who was the cutest. My sister went, 'I like number twenty-two.' I remember going, 'John? you like *him*?' That was when he had a pig shave, you know, his hair was real short."

By now the score was 6–1 Rangers and we were still in the first period. I asked Beaver if John brought the game home with him.

"Sometimes, it depends. He always asks me about the game after it's over. How I think he did, if he had a good game. I never have to tell him anything if he had a bad game. One year I used to sit right behind the goal. I was very critical then too. I criticized too much, I saw every little mistake that he made. One thing I learned in juniors though. When they lose, don't speak first. Wait for them to speak first."

"How about the night before a game?" I raised my eyebrows.

"Oh, he sleeps." Beaver laughed. "That's it. Seriously, sex before a game? I'm not saying it's good, but it doesn't hurt him one bit. The first six months we were married in St. Louis, there was a period where . . . "

"He didn't give up a goal?" I interrupted.

"No, it depended on how many times we did it that afternoon. If we did it once, he'd let in one goal, twice, he let in two goals. It got to the point where we couldn't do it anymore."

I asked Diana how she felt when St. Louis traded John to the Rangers. "It was horrible. I didn't know anything about New York. Didn't I ever tell you about our place in St. Louis? We had five acres, way out in the woods, had a riding arena and a horse and chickens, rabbits. John was traded two days before our anniversary. We were in Canada and I came home from shopping and my mother answered the door and by the look on her face, you would have sworn someone had died. I said, 'What's the matter?' and she said, 'You gotta phone Sid Solomon right away,' he was the owner of the team. So I looked at John and he said, 'We've been traded.'

"So John phoned and I remember I was sitting right beside him and I said, 'Where are we going?' and he said, 'New York.' I was mad, I thought I'd cry but I was mad, and I sat there cursing at the phone. But now we love it. I mean I'm just a little girl from Calgary and I get to meet all these people. Like Joni Mitchell and Kinky. And when you introduced us to Kris Kristofferson, I died. The other girls didn't have the guts. Finally I had to ask him for a kiss. I

74 ▪

mean, it was a once-in-a-lifetime thing, you gotta do it." Beaver sat back, in rapture at the memory.

"Ever get in fights with the fans?" I said.

"Never," she said. "They're paying our salary. They can say what they want. The only time I ever swore at a fan was when John broke his leg two years ago against Toronto. A guy was standing here yelling, 'I hope he's dead.' I screamed, 'Don't ever wish that on anyone, that's my husband.' The guy said nothing, but I didn't really stick around for an answer, I was running down to see how John was."

Down on the ice Greschner had just passed the puck in his own end, then looked up to see Dave Semenko flatten him with an elbow to the side of the head. Play was called, and after shaking the cobwebs out of his head, Greschner stayed on for the rest of his shift. On the bench, when he realized that he didn't know where he was, he relented and left for the hospital. Semenko escaped without a penalty.

Davidson escaped with a laugher, 10–2. Since tonight was getaway night to Philadelphia, the Rangers' bus was waiting in the rampway off Thirty-third Street. Along with a motley crowd of about twenty-five fans, waiting to catch a glimpse of their heroes. But one stood out. He was short, about twenty, dark-haired, wearing a Ranger jersey with the number 17 on his back, Eddie Johnstone's number. He was carrying a portfolio stuffed with hockey magazines and the NHL *Players' Guide* and legal pads full of scribble. His name was Robert Marcus and he was a fanatic.

This became evident as Murdoch and I stepped off the elevator and went out toward the bus. A furry little ball of energy wearing a Ranger jersey came running up.

"Donnie, be careful tomorrow night, Donnie," it was shouting. "Stay out of 54." I was intrigued. "I love the Rangers," Marcus was telling me.

"Sure," another kid piped up. "This guy thought Talafous

was Wayne Thomas and he rushed up and said, 'Wayne.'"

"So, I made a mistake," Marcus barked. "I'm sorry. Look"
—he turned to me— "anything you want to know, I've stud-
ied the Rangers for twelve years. I'm only twenty. I loved
Gilbert. Ferguson ruined him. I'll give you a fan's point
of view."

Just then Vickers came out and walked by toward the bus.
Marcus swooped away. "Stevie, what are running for? Give
me an autograph, Steve." Vickers paused to sign the legal
pad. "Steve, you gotta kick some ass."

"You bet," Vickers grunted.

"C'mon, man." Marcus was insistent. "You haven't lost a
fight yet. You gotta defend the boys, you're a tough guy."
Marcus escorted Vickers to the bus. He came back. "I like
Steve. Oh, there's Mario." And he was off again.

"Mario, Mario, Mario. Give me your autograph. Mario,
you're a little light, Mario, but you're tough. When are you
gonna gain some weight?" Marois gave Marcus the ol'
fisheye, but France, Mario's attractive girl friend, seemed
amused. Marcus picked up on it. "She's very pretty, Mario."
The dynamo gave his blessing. "Keep an eye on her during
the games."

"Who is dese guy?" Mario asked me, but Marcus was off,
after his uniformsake, Johnstone. "Eddie, you're a good man.
Eddie, you got a haircut." I interrupted and pointed to Vadnais. Marcus did 180 degrees. "Carol, you're a nice guy, but
you carry your stick too high. Carol, let me have your
address and telephone number."

Vadnais stared at Marcus. "Telephone number?" They
were streaming out of the elevator at a brisk pace now, and
it was all Marcus could do to keep up with each player. Now
it was Nilsson's turn. "Ulfie, Ulfie, Ulfie. Come over here,
Ulf," he commanded. "Ulfie, I'm your main man. Where's
Talafous? Where's Anders? Carol, take care." Marcus dismissed Vadnais as if he were yesterday's fish wrappers.

"Lucien, you had a damn good game." He was walking along with his arm around DeBlois. "You shoulda had a hat trick. You got a damn good shot, you're gonna kill a lot of guys with that shot." Marcus released Luc and paused. There was nobody to be had. "All these guys got such nice shoes, except Sulliman. Where is Sulliman? Where is Sulliman?" And Marcus went off looking for the first-round draft pick.

Instead, he found Anders Hedberg. Ecstasy. "Anders, I love you! I love you!" Hedberg froze in his tracks. "I told Ferguson to get you. Wait, wait, promise me you'll stay with the Rangers. You love New York, don't you? Don't you love us?" Anders was amenable. "Certainly, certainly." He smiled and slapped five with Marcus. Anders and Ulfie headed for the bus. Marcus reached up, grabbed Ulf's face, and planted a wet kiss on his cheek. Then he ran after Guevremont.

"Guevremont, Guevremont," he was trilling, "I know you. Nobody else knows you but I do."

I was standing off to the side with Davidson and Beaver, observing a clinical case of mania. "What a find," I told Beaver. John was gingerly touching his chin where a puck had snuck in under his mask. Marcus ran back.

"I'm great," he told us. "I want to be a writer. Seriously." Suddenly he spied Davidson. "John, I got to talk to you. Wait one second, let me get my composure." Marcus wiped his brow and rearranged his load. "Let me touch you." He grabbed Davidson's sports jacket and ran his fingers down the front. "Your suit. John, it's too wide a lapel, John. Pat Price, Pat Price." He realized that the man standing next to Davidson was the Edmonton defenseman. "I'll get your autograph, what the hell. You're a good man. Wait, wait, you guys are so quick. Put it right here." Marcus slapped the paper on Davidson's shoulder and thrust the pen at Price.

"Where's everybody else?" Marcus was complaining. "Where's Espo? Is Gretzsky a good guy? Oh my God, I'm freaking out. I can't believe this, this is too much, I never did this before." Davidson kissed Beaver and headed for the bus. "Wait, JD." Marcus was off. "Don't go, don't go." He ran off after the goalie.

But soon he was back. "Who else we got next? Take care, Pat, there's Mario again. Where's Doog? That's who I really want. I'm gonna rip him apart. I love Ron. Why are you so tough, Mario?" Mario, who was standing a few feet away, shot Marcus a dirty look. "Were you tough in juniors? Did you start all the fights? What a game. What a game. Did you notice that the European, Ulf, let me kiss him and Davidson wouldn't?" Marcus told me. I gave him a quizzical look. "I'm totally straight," he said. "I love women, but I love hockey players. They're tough."

Marcus opened his portfolio and showed me his memorabilia. He kept detailed notes on every game, shots on net, men on ice for goals, and complex records of each player from the opposing teams. When he went home to Long Island, he would write up little stories from his notes. One day he would be a hockey writer like Stan Fischler. Of course, he'd be the best. Duguay interrupted his career plans.

"Doog!" Marcus nearly knocked the orange juice out of the winger's hands. "Right here, my man." Marcus steered him away from the crowd. "I'll give him a break," Marcus announced, then checked out Duguay's attire. "Doog, those boots are for studs, check those boots he's got on. Sign this, Doogs, make it nice. I like your hair." Then Espo. Marcus smiled like they had saved the best for last. "Espo." He stretched the word out like molasses, throwing his arms wide open to embrace the somewhat shocked center. "Espo, you're wild. Espo, you're rejuvenated. You're a kid again. Wait a second." He chastized the others swirling around for autographs. Espo signed Marcus's pad. That was it. They were all on the bus. The crowd broke up and slowly made their way away from the Garden. Marcus ran back to where I was standing. "Now what?" He tucked his pen back behind his ear. "Your place or mine?" I looked at him like he was crazy. "C'mon, we got to start writing this shit up." I declined politely. "Okay." He shrugged. "But do me a favor. Tell Davidson to get himself a thinner lapel, okay?"

That was the first thing I told Beaver when I joined her in Charlie O's. She was sitting at a Ranger table in the back, along with Mrs. Eddie Johnstone and Mrs. Josh Guevremont. With their husbands steaming down the turnpike toward Philadelphia, the girls decided to stop for a few beers.

"I asked JD how he was playing and he said he was going down a little too soon," I reported.

"See, Ratso." Beaver smiled. "What did I tell you?"

"I could have told you that," Sue Johnstone said. "Whenever Eddie makes a mistake, I go, 'Hey, dummy.'"

"I don't like it when somebody else criticizes him, though," Josh's wife added.

"No, no, just us," Sue agreed.

After a while the wives left, to drive back to Westchester, and I headed to the phone. I called Lenox Hill Hospital. On the third ring Greschner answered.

"They won't let me eat, Rats," the defenseman was complaining. "I'm okay, though, I like it pretty good."

"How's your room?" I asked.

"It's not a private room," Greschner sighed. "I don't make enough for that."

• OCTOBER 25

Ron Greschner

Stardom has arrived for Ron Greschner . . . Outstanding puck carrier and playmaker . . . Excellent skater . . . Served as Captain of his junior club . . .

Grew up in Saskatchewan farm country, where at just 12 years of age, he played against senior players in their 20's and 30's . . . A regular at Madison Square Garden rock concerts . . . Makes home in Manhattan . . . Not married . . .

—New York Rangers Yearbook, *1979–1980*

Thursday morning. I called the hospital. "Get me out of here," Greschner moaned. "They keep coming around, feeling my ass, the back of my head, my feet, looking down my throat. My throat's not hurt, it's my head."

I marveled at the stoicism of the guys. And their humor. Last year Gresch had also been injured when Dave Schultz hammered him into the boards in Buffalo. Davidson was the first Ranger over to Gresch, as he lay helpless on the ice.

"Gresch, Gresch." Davidson leaned over the prone body. "Can you fart?" Greschner mumbled something. Davidson smiled. "In that case, can I have your yellow seats for Sunday?"

Today Greschner wanted out. "I gotta get home by two," he worried, "or else I'll miss my soap." He made it. When the doctor dragged his feet to discharge him, Greschner packed up and left the room and took a cab home. And watched the soap. Then he called his parents, like a good son. "It's okay, Mum." He was very reassuring to the folks back in Goodsoil. "They took an X-ray and checked to see what's in there. They said it was all right, I only scratched one of the rocks."

That night the Rangers lost to Philly, 5–2.

• OCTOBER 26

I was on the phone with Gresch again. The team had flown out to Minnesota, but Gresch was laid up for the weekend.
ME: They must have found some evidence of a concus-

sion. Why would they tell you not to play? Didn't the doctor give you any instructions on what to eat or drink, or not to smoke?

GRESCH: Nothing.

ME: Didn't he tell you to sleep a few hours, wake up, sleep, and wake up?

GRESCH: No.

ME: That's ridiculous. What kind of fucking medical attention is that? Nobody called? Keating? Or Nykoluk?

GRESCH: No, I'm not one of the browns, you know. They only like me between 7:30 and 10:30 at night. That's the only time they fucking appreciate me.

Greschner told me something else too. He had finally signed his contract—a three-year job, with an option year. With the bonuses, he was making over $200,000 a year.

• OCTOBER 28

The *Post* headline screamed it out: "FOTIU TARGETS TWO RANGERS IN GARDEN HOMECOMING," and Nicky's return was the topic of conversation on everyone's lips. Especially Murdoch and Hickey, who had been labeled the two would-be victims in the article. Out on the ice Vadnais and Dave Maloney went through their warm-ups. "They don't know," Joey Bucchino whispered to me as we gazed over the glass at Fotiu, who was skating in little circles, nervously shifting his stick from hand to hand. "Maloney and Vadnais don't know that Nicky's after them." Fotiu skated by us and Bukka waved. "I love that guy, I feel bad for him." The trainer looked down at the Ranger end of the ice. "Something's going on this week," he whispered. "Soapy thinks it's him, but he's paranoid anyway. If you say boo to him tomorrow, he'll jump."

The buzzer sounded and the teams headed off the ice, to

allow the Zamboni to put down a fresh curtain of water. Fotiu paused by the Whalers' bench. The visiting team's bench. "Hey, Nicky," one kid yelled, "throw me a puck. That's all you're good for." That may not have been all he was good for, but that's what he was known for. Nicky always threw the last practice puck over the boards to the eager kids. It was a ritual that he had gleaned from Hickey. Nicky also made sure to throw two pucks into the faraway blue seats. This was his own inspiration, to remind himself of his origins. Tonight this ceremony took on a bittersweet aspect.

But suddenly there was Nicky skating around the empty ice with a whole goddamn box of pucks, throwing them out two, three, four at a time! The crowd went wild as he slowly made his way around the entire rink, paying a small tribute to the fans who loved him so much. The kids were ecstatic. Nobody even seemed to care that they were Whaler pucks he was tossing around.

After the game, an uneventful 2–2 tie, I headed straight for the Hartford locker room. Along with everybody else. It was complete chaos, more media people than players inside. Gordie Howe, who was past fifty, strolled out of the showers with a towel wrapped around his waist and spied the horde. "Hey, Nick," he yelled back, "call them off."

Nicky came out to meet his public. It was good to see that familiar pie face, especially with a big grin on it. Tonight's 2–2 tie for Nicky was a moral victory. "Who wrote that horseshit article in the *Post*?" Nicky began by asking a question. The reporters fell silent.

"Did you buy that box of pucks?" one asked.

Nicky smiled. "Yeah, I get a discount."

"Before the game, did you talk to any of the Rangers?" someone else wondered.

"Phil, he's a good friend of mine," Nicky said. "Walter, Wayne Thomas, JD."

"But you hit Phil." I smiled.

"Yeah, I know. I laughed too. I have a lot of respect for Phil. In my opinion he's the leader of that club. I think they should give him the 'C' back. He is the leader. I don't care what anybody says."

"You gave Vad a pretty good check too."

Nicky frowned. "Oh well, it's part of the game. I gave Phil a good shot too. I'm wearing a different color jersey out there now. I'm not gonna give him a kiss, right? I don't know who made up that article in the *Post*. I never said I was gonna get two. I said I don't like two. Everybody thinks I'm gonna start killing guys. I just said I didn't like them, in my opinion, I didn't like something they did to me, that's all."

In the Ranger room everyone was subdued. "Talk is cheap." Captain Dave was toweling himself off. "No, I respect Nicky, he's got a job to do. He's a grandstand performer, he comes to please the crowd and that's fine. He's an individual and I'm an individual too."

On the other side of the room, Murdoch was relieved. "Nice fucking article, eh?" he said to me. "Fucking asshole guy said to me, 'Why is Nicky after you?' I said, 'Ask fucking Delano.' I come up in the elevator with Nicky tonight, he said, 'You know I didn't say that.' The press built that whole thing up. I got him in the corner and he came back at me from behind, so I went back at him and he said, 'Doc, what are you doing?' I said, 'Fuck, Nicky, what do you expect me to do?' "

"What's wrong with this team?" I asked Murdoch.

He shook his jead. "Too much individual shit. We're not playing as a team. Everybody wants to look good so they can get a commercial."

Gresch had wandered over and heard the conversation. "It's all gonna come out tomorrow. I'm gonna get loaded at the Halloween party and say something. We gotta start sticking together, being closer."

"You should say something," Murder agreed.

"I'm the only one who can say that without getting jumped on," Gresch said.

"I'll jump on them too," Murdoch said.

I followed Greschner into the bathroom. Espo and JD were blow-drying their hair. "Something's happening," I yelled over the din.

"There's a trade," Gresch screamed back.

"Either tomorrow or by Thursday," Davidson chipped in. "It's a big one, I know a goaltender, for sure."

• OCTOBER 29

Last night Sue Johnstone, Eddie's wife, gave me a great description of a hockey wife after I mentioned that my girl friend was becoming one since I was hanging out with the Rangers so much.

"Oh yeah?" Sue said. "Is her hair out? Does she have pimples on her face? Does she have the shakes?"

• OCTOBER 30

The sweat and the pancake makeup had combined to give Esposito a ghoulish visage. Tomorrow night it might be appropriate, but tonight it was just surreal. But then again so was the sight out on the ice in Sportarama. There were scores of little kids all over the ice in varying sizes and shapes and colors. And interspersed among them, like Giants on the Earth, were Esposito, Greschner, Murdoch, and the two Maloneys. Esposito was making more money.

Tonight's hockey clinic was a Phil Esposito Production and his teammates were hired guns. For the kids on the ice, it was a chance to skate with one of their heroes. For the hundreds in the bleachers, some vicarious thrills and a snap-shot or two for the family album. For Dave Maloney it was torture. A far cry from the fun on ice he and Espo had this morning. Then they were scheduled to shoot the Sasson jeans commercial where he and Phil and Hitch and Doogie got to skate around wearing designer jeans and their uniform tops, and to kibitz with pretty models. Only they waited for hours while the technicians tried in vain to fix the ice compressor. Standing around and posing for some New Rochelle four-teen-year-old's Polaroid paled in comparison. Maloney skated over to me by the boards and frowned. "Remind me to do this again, will you?" he said and rolled his eyes.

Phil Esposito

Greatest modern-day goal scorer in hockey . . . On verge of career goal 700 and career point number 1500 . . . Was team leader in dramatic Team Canada victory over the Soviet Union in 1972 . . . Acquired by Rangers on November 7, 1975, that deal considered one of biggest in NHL history . . . Five times winner of Art Ross Trophy as league's top scorer . . . Still holds all-time league mark for most goals (76) and most points (152) in one season, 1970–71 . . . Very active in charitable endeavors . . . Married, wife's name: Donna.

—New York Rangers Yearbook, *1979–1980*

Give Phil Esposito his due. After all, he had paid his. Going into the season he had 676 goals in only 1,161 games. If it weren't for that modern-day Methuselah, Gordie Howe, Espo would be first in all-time goals and points. He was hockey's equivalent of Reggie Jackson too, charisma pouring off his broad shoulders. It was very difficult for him to walk unmolested through the streets of Canada.

And he also had been traded twice. These were his crosses, the traumas that nurtured his deep-grained Italian fatalism, that fueled the lucky-rabbit's-foot fetishism and thin-skinned defensiveness. And who could blame him? Leaving Chicago hadn't been so bad, he was still young, still peaking, when he went to Boston to join Mr. Orr and terrorize the league for eight seasons. But when Boston traded him to New York, New Fucking York of all places, hockey hell in 1975, the sensitive paisan went into shock. Then he cried. His Boston linemate, Wayne Cashman, was even more demonstrative. When he heard that his buddy was gone, he got so furious he grabbed the color TV in his hotel room and shot-putted it out the window without bothering to open it first.

It wasn't easy for Phil in New York. He had that big price tag and he was playing hurt at first, and the New York fans are a demanding lot. For the first time in his career, Espo hated work. And he bitched. And bitched. There were cockroaches in the hotels, there were no lounges for the wives, the showers were designed for seven-foot Negroes who throw balls through hoops. He was right.

Werblin changed all that. He also changed coaches. Espo was captain under John Ferguson and for all intents and purposes, he was co-coach. But Shero liked to keep his players nervous, and everyone knew the new coach hated Stars. Before Shero coached his first game, Espo resigned his "C" and started to worry. But he had less to worry about this time. He had the fans behind him, as he did in Boston. But he also had another confidant, fellow by the name of Werblin. Werblin would never trade Espo, anybody with half a brain could see that. Werblin respected tradition, one of his first moves was to bring back the old jerseys. He appreciated charisma, it was he who urged the Rangers to become latter-day Namaths, slap-shot celebrities. And he recognized loyalty, didn't he? Tell it to the Meadowlands.

So it was a few days after last year's Cup finals and we were sitting in Cronies, one of Espo's haunts on the Upper East Side, and we were talking about him being traded again.

"I think Freddie likes me," Espo said. "A lot of people say, 'He doesn't like you' and all that stuff, but I disagree. He knows I give a hundred percent, that's for sure. Maybe he didn't like me at the beginning, maybe he heard some bad stuff about me being a shit-disturber, which I am. I always have been and I always will." Espo enumerated the changes they had instituted at his behest as if he were a union leader, which, as Ranger representative to the Players Association, he was. "I know when I become a coach, and I'm going to, there's going to be things like they have here in New York; I'm going to employ all the things that I know make a player happy. You have a happy player and you have a good player."

Espo paused to sip his beer. His thoughts strayed back to Shero. "He doesn't talk much. But he gives guys pats on the back, which are terrific. Honest to God, I've been playing sixteen years, but when he puts his hands on my back and he sort of rubs it a little, it gives me a feeling like I want to go through the wall for him." Espo closed his eyes and savored the memory.

"I thought all that trade talk last year was to keep you on edge," I said, "and it seemed to work. You scored forty-two goals."

"They're still talking trade," Espo protested. "I wish they would stop, but that's part of the business. I know that I was traded last year to the Black Hawks and they shook hands and everything. I think at the beginning Freddie thought I was a troublemaker. Maybe I just was too old for him to play his style. I hope it doesn't happen, but I'm sure they're trying to trade me right now. I don't think Freddie likes players that are almost his age. One time he told me, 'Jesus, you keep playing and you'll be too old for the Old-timers,' then he turned around and walked out. Jesus, figure that one out.

"Everyone thinks an athlete's life is so glorious and so fantastic, glamour, public eye. But we are puppets. Totally and there's no denying it. We can be pulled on the whim of one man. Maybe two. If Freddie Shero takes a dislike to me suddenly, he can just pull one string and I gotta be someplace else."

Espo laughed. "Sport is a cruel business. Number one—if you don't believe that there's always somebody around to take your job, then you're in trouble. And if you're so vain as to think that maybe you're never gonna get injured, then you're really crazy because sooner or later you'll get hurt."

Donnie Murdoch joined us and ordered a beer. Espo ignored him and knocked the table. "Touch wood. I've been very fortunate in my career. I've only had one serious injury. And that's what's kept me going and playing sixteen years. But I'm smart too. I don't go crazy, I don't throw myself in the corner like a maniac."

"You just set up in the slot and score," I joked.

"Let them whack the shit out of my legs and my back." Espo laughed. "That'll never bother me. Let them hit me on the head, that won't bother me . . ."

"He's got a jumbo bum, they never can move him," Murdoch interjected.

". . . but don't let them touch me feet," Espo howled.

Lunch came. And the talk turned to summer vacations. Of life off the ice. "We looked for you down in Lauderdale," Murdoch told Espo.

"I flew down to Nassau in Werblin's private plane," Phil said. "Oh, can he drink. He had me right under the table, laughing his balls off at me. Vodka on the rocks. Now and then he had a vodka and soda."

"We had a good time in Lauderdale." Mud attacked his

salad and started telling a story about one of his single team-mates. "So he's down there by the pool, second day we were there and you know what Don Maloney's like, eh?"

Shy, I thought.

"So he comes over the next day with a big smile on his face and he says, 'I just got laid.' He says he was sitting by the pool in the morning and this chick comes up and says, 'You got a room here?' And he says, 'Yeah.' So they went up there and she says she gives good back rubs, so I guess she whipped off her bathing suit and started giving a back rub and he freaked right out, so he gave her a shot.

"And he came running out of the motel and he tells me, 'Hey, there's a broad in my room, go give her a shot,' and I say, 'Yeah, yeah, right, right.' I know they're all gonna be laughing at me. So I go in there and open the door and there's this broad sitting there, so I go in there and give her a shot. I come out and get the other guys. They don't believe it, so they finally went over there. So six of us for two days, she stayed in this room, she didn't go out. We went fucking nuts. Finally he had to go over there and tell her to get the fuck out. We had some fun times there."

Espo poured another Bud. "Any scoops?" Murder wondered.

Phil shrugged. "They're trying to trade you and I."

"Are they?" Donnie shook his head. "Yeah, that's what I thought. More me than you."

"I don't know," Esposito said.

"They can throw me in with the deal." The right winger frowned.

"Some throw-in," Phil said. "They can throw me in. I'm gonna sign a lease now that I found out I'm protected. I'm gonna go find an apartment and sign a lease, and if you get traded and you signed a lease, the club's got to pick it up."

I asked them about the puck bunnies, the girls that like to body check. "When I was younger, I used to have some fun,"

Phil reminisced. "Funny, the girls then were as good-looking as the girls now and I never had a problem talking to them. Never. In fact, if I wouldn't have been so forward, I would never have met Donna and I'm really glad I met her. Am I glad I married her. Derek Sanderson introduced us. He knew I was going through a divorce then, but even before that I used to fool around."

Murdoch's eyes widened at the revelation on tape.

"I don't give a shit now. I don't care. I had a blast, let's put it bluntly. I used to have more broads than you could imagine," Phil boasted. "That was one good point about playing hockey. Then I used to wonder if it was my charming personality. Wrong. The broads would come and you'd talk to them and they wouldn't bother with you. As soon as they found out you're a hockey player, yeah. I'll never forget this. I owned a boat then. A thirty-three-footer. We were sitting in Bachelors Three in Boston, sitting with some buddies, and these Playboy bunnies came up. We were trying to pick them up. No chance. The minute I mentioned I had a boat and was a hockey player, we had to beat them off with a club. We went cruising around the harbor and three days later we took them back."

"Does that change the way you view women?" I wondered.

Espo smiled. "The most important thing for an athlete is to have a woman that's understanding. Because if you don't, it can make your life miserable and I've gone through that whole thing. My wife now is fantastic, she understands everything, she knows exactly the way I am, and I'm glad she doesn't know much about hockey. And doesn't want to, more important. To me, an athlete's wife has to be extra special. Without a good woman an athlete can be mixed up, in a lot of trouble, and not perform properly."

Murdoch agreed. "I haven't faced the problems of hockey yet. I've gone through some shitty times, don't misunderstand me, but I'm saying that sometimes when you get pissed off at night and you don't have a woman, next thing you do is go out and drink or stay out late and it'll hurt your performance, but if you got someone to come home and talk to, help figure these problems out . . ." Murder trailed off.

"You know what I hate, though?" Murdoch flared up. "Everyone thinks we're dumb from the start. If you're an athlete you're dumb. You talk to people and they say, 'Well, Jesus, you're a pretty intelligent person.' Look, buddy, what do you think, just because you get hit around you're dumb?"

"I'd like them to know how many businesses I run," Espo said proudly. "With no schooling. During the course of my career, I've spoken to all sorts of men in banquets. David Rockefeller, guys like that. I've spoken on the same dais with these guys, gotten the same ovations and, in some cases, been better than them. The people sitting out there relate to me better. 'Cause I won't use the big words. Instead of using elephant shit, I use something smaller like dog shit or turtle turd."

They laughed. The afternoon was wearing on and Espo turned reflective. "Hockey's given me a great living. A good life, not an easy life, and now that I'm thirty-seven I'll have to start thinking about what else I'll be doing. I worried about it since I was thirty. When I first broke in, I was Donnie's age and if anyone told me that I'd still be playing when I was thirty-seven, I'd say, 'Are you fucking bananas?' But there was nothing I ever wanted to do but play and I would have played for peanuts. I did play for peanuts. But hockey's given me a great living, and anybody that knocks their fucking sport should be punched in the mouth. I love it and when it's finished and I'm not gonna be there, that's the only thing that really scares me, the playing, not being able to participate. Oh, I can coach, I know I can coach, no problem. I can manage and I can manipulate players, but I'm gonna miss the camaraderie, the friendship of the guys, and I'm gonna miss playing, fooling around in practice, which I always do. When I become coach, I'm gonna get me some goofball like Murdoch here to be my assistant coach, some guy I can pick on and pinch his cheeks." He reached to grab Mud's cheeks, but the winger's reflexes were faster and all he got was air. Then they both laughed again.

At Sportarama they ran a little clinic, giving some individualized instruction to the kids, then they scrimmaged a bit before raffling off Ranger memorabilia. After that they retreated to the small, drab locker room. Bukka brought in a tray of cold hamburgers and there was beer on ice in a garbage can.

Davidson got up and grabbed a can of beer. "Well, let's go to the Halloween party and find out who got traded."

Bukka came in from the adjoining bathroom with bad news. There were no outlets for the hair dryers. The room filled with moans. "I'm going to the party like this." Gresch brightened. "As a pig."

By then everyone except Gresch had stripped for his shower. Dave Maloney looked at Murdoch and shook his head. "How come you look at everyone's knob every time?"

" 'Cause he's a fag." Espo joked. "He's been hanging out with Duguay too long."

Espo finished his shower and did his best to fix his hair, and then he handed his small toiletries bag to the limo driver. Murdoch scowled. "Jeez, Phil, at least you can carry your own purse."

They arranged for the limos to come around the back of the building, and I was sent out as a scout to hasten the departure. The coast was clear, only about fifty or so kids had figured out they were planning rock-star exits. One by one they rushed out, pausing only for a few seconds to wordlessly sign an autograph or two. Except for Murdoch, who was bringing up the rear. He waited till he was in the middle of the minimob and then turned to Greschner. "I can't believe you told that one kid to fuck off," he joked, then paused to scribble his name.

The Halloween party was a bust. Oh, it was at JD's rented house in Westchester, a real-nice, big old, ranch-style, with a bunch of curious nautical knickknacks belonging to the owners, who wintered in Florida. And a few of the guys really did it up right in the costume area, like McEwen in his gold lamé basic Christopher Street fagola outfit and Don Maloney and rook Dougie Sulliman in matching hood attire: white T's and greased-back hair. But the funniest visual of the night was Ulfie sitting and patiently feeding JD's dachshund twenty Swedish meatballs in a row. Beaver didn't take too kindly to that and proceeded to grab a can of whipped cream out of the fridge and chase Ulfie down in the dining room, spewing the thick cream all over his face. Then she grabbed a handful of meatballs and methodically counted off as she force-fed them into Ulf's reluctant mouth. Nilsson's face got redder and redder with each serving.

But there was trouble too. Sarge hadn't even bothered showing up. He was in such a blue funk over the prospect of getting traded or not dressing for the games. Duguay was another no-show and Hickey was walking around "pissed at the world," as he said. Just because the last game was the first time he had ever been booed at the Garden. And Greschner forgot about his vow to Murdoch to rally the guys at the party. But it was Halloween and after the trade talk died out, they broke out the disco albums, and Kinky Friedman's "They Ain't Making Jews Like Jesus Anymore," and the wives started dancing, and everybody got shit-faced and forgot about their problems. They even tried to get Ulfie out on the dance floor to join his wife for one hot disco number. "No." The Swede smiled and hugged the bar in the den. "I only dance on the road."

- NOVEMBER 1

The Rangers lost their fourth straight game to LA, 4–2. Every goal was the result of a defensive lapse. In a twist, Shero sat out McEwen, Hickey, and DeBlois. Of course, that didn't seem that significant. After all, Shero loves to keep people on their toes. It's called aversive conditioning, or, in hockey circles, using your bench.

- NOVEMBER 2

Wrong. They were gone. Hitch, Q, Lucien, and one more minor leaguer dispatched to Colorado for the massive Barry Beck, a 6-foot 3-inch, 215-pound defenseman. The Rock of Vancouver. It was a blockbuster of a trade. It was also a very bizarre trade.

Hickey read the handwriting on the wall. He had called a lawyer friend in New York after he was benched and guessed he was gone. In fact, he confronted Shero the next morning at 7:30 A.M. in the hotel lobby.

"Am I a Ranger?" he asked Freddie.

The Fog was staring at the carpet.

"Is it a trade . . . is it me?" Hitch pressed.

"No, not yet," Fred mumbled.

"Can I still talk with the guys?" Pat wondered sarcastically.

"Yeah, sure." Shero was still studying his shine.

But he didn't. Hickey and Q and DeBlois sat by themselves, waiting for the plane to Colorado, for the next game. Then, en route, word of the transaction leaked out. The wire services ran with it. And Nykoluk got a midair emergency phone call from the Ranger office in New York. He huddled with Shero and they decided to break the news over baggage.

DeBlois was first. "Mike wants to see you," Fred mumbled. Lucien walked over to the corner where Nyk had set up. "There's a trade with Colorado . . ." Bye-bye, Luc. Then McEwen got the call. Hitch didn't wait for it, he sauntered over to Shero and got the word. Then one by one, the guys came over and said good-bye. Then the Rangers got on their bus and the ex-Rangers caught a cab and that was that.

I spent the whole day at home on the phone.

One of the people that I called was my good friend, Cusimano, a recent hockey convert and a fanatical Ranger fan.

"They need Beck," he said. "Montreal pushed them around like rabbits during the finals. The Rangers have been pushed around for forty years, they're perpetual victims, especially now without Nicky around. But they paid some price for Beck."

After Cusimano, I called Joanne Vickers. She was happy.

ME: Did you hear?

JOANNE: Larry Rauch called me up and told me and I started crying. I didn't realize how tense I was. I was all ready to call Sarge when Larry called me. I was positive that they were showcasing Steve. Every time something happens I leave the road atlas on the table. I looked up Edmonton just when you were calling.

ME: I think it's a great chance for Lucien. They've been sitting on him. It's interesting, the whole trade is really psychologically interesting. Hitch was always an outsider, to a certain extent. He was a loner. I was amazed last year when Gresch called me and asked for Hitch's number. Pat dug that independence thing and Q blazed his own trail too.

JOANNE: You're right, come to think of it, most of Pat's friends were outside the club. Steve said Hitch had been nicknamed "Midnight Cowboy," that he was just a little bit different than them.

ME: He enjoyed it too. He liked being different. He liked being the rebel.

JOANNE: There's nothing wrong with that. Steve would say, "He's just different from the rest of us" and I would say, "Thank God, 'cause the rest of you are complete animals." The guy shows a little sensitivity and an interest in the arts and they think he's weird. I'd say, "You big galoot, you could learn something from that."

Then I made one last call, late that night. I couldn't reach Hitch or Q. So I rang Greschner's room in Colorado.

ME: I'm bummed out from the trade.

GRESCH: That's part of the game, Rats. It was pretty hard to say good-bye to them guys. You'll still be in New York writing books and everybody who's on our team right now won't be there at one time. Nobody's gonna stay here forever, you know.

ME: Q told me two weeks ago when I told him about the rumors then that he was gone, he said, "No, I'm getting along really well with Freddie, talking to him every day."

GRESCH: That's the problem. I haven't talked to Freddie yet. I gotta go, Bo Derek is on TV.

Mike McEwen

His thirteen points during the Stanley Cup Play-offs last season was an all-time record for Ranger defenseman . . . Third Ranger defenseman in history to score 20 goals in a season . . . Moves puck well and is constant offensive threat . . . Smooth stickhandler and good skater . . . Soft-spoken and likeable off the ice, he enjoys golf, fishing, camping, and reading as hobbies . . . Always gets plenty of shots on goal . . . not married.

—New York Rangers Yearbook, *1979–1980*

McEwen was a real loss. Sure, Hickey was an established star, he'd get thirty-five to forty goals a year, and Lucien was potential, a solid twenty-five-goal man, up and down his wing. But Q was special. He was one of the most exciting players in the NHL, quick, lithe, an excellent stickhandler, full of daring, a short hair away from being an All-Star.

And he was an interesting, complex kid. In some respects, his story was All-Canadian: born in Hornepayne, Ontario, a little railroad town of 1,800 people, on skates at three and a half, in first league by five. Q's father had put in forty years on the railroad and had accumulated three acres of land. And as soon as that first snow in October, Mike would be out on the makeshift backyard hockey rink with the big floodlights to mock the night, skating and skating. From October till April, day in and day out, Mike and his brother would brave the −40° weather to do their zigzags and backward skating and stickhandling drills. The family had a goal in mind, that someday Michael would skate in the NHL. So everybody pushed and pushed.

Q progressed through juniors, and joined the Rangers when he was twenty. And got a taste of city life. We talked about it one day during the summer in the dining room of his Second Avenue high-rise. "What was weird about it was nobody played hockey, there was nothing we could identify with down here," Mike remembered. "Nobody knows the game here. In Canada students of the game outnumber fans. Then you come down here in New York and it's fan capital of the world. It's crazy, the fans just go nuts."

"You think you're a celebrity?" I asked, remembering the hockey madness that swept Manhattan during the Cup finals.

"We are because we get treated that way, but I stay away from it because it's a drag," Q said. "It's like going out and have just one aspect of what you do constantly recognized. I think everybody in the public eye gets that. People give you gifts, all the time. You get weird things, man."

"Like what?"

McEwen smiled. "Quickies. Lots of quickies, heavy on the quickies. I had a girl come up to me at a Ranger Fan Club banquet saying, 'Want a quickie?' I said, sure. She was really nice. I couldn't believe that nice a girl saying that. I couldn't believe that nice a girl was a hockey fan."

What about women? McEwen was hesitant. "Look, I'm a married man, don't get me in trouble." He laughed. "Well, I'm not married, but I am committed to one person now. But I heard the other night that it was baseball players first, football second, and hockey third in New York as far as groupies go. But I guess they're the same as any other. They just want to meet you, talk to you, have fun with you, and screw you. And you want to do the same thing with them. They come after you. They come to your house and wake you up at three or four in the morning, two on ones, straight up, I'm not very kinky as far as sex goes. I don't even like the hogs that much. I go more for the quality. I'd rather get fucked once a week by nice than three times a week by brutal. Although I have to admit I've been in there the odd time."

"What about the press?" I said.

McEwen frowned. "They rape you, they rape your personality. I don't like it either, it's like I'm exposed. People know what you feel and think about things because these guys come in ten minutes after a game finished, and you might say something and maybe you really felt it and meant it at the time, but you just didn't want five million people to know about it.

"I remember once against Atlanta I had played really bad, and a guy came over to me and we talked and I said, 'Oh, was I brutal, I didn't do fuckall, I didn't skate, it was the worst game that I played.' All of a sudden I picked up the paper the next day and the opening line was 'Mike McEwen in a lot of ways personifies what the young Rangers are all about in last night's game against Atlanta. McEwen: "I was brutal." ' Oh fuck, I didn't say it like that, man. I said it in a kind of way that I had forgotten about it and that I knew I had to do better tomorrow night. So for the next week I had people coming up to me, 'C'mon, Mike, you gotta pick yourself up, it's not really that bad.' I mean, I *knew* it wasn't that bad.

"It's rough. But I think hockey's the best game played in the world today because it demands everything. Skill, speed, quickness, mental sharpness, intimidation, it demands you be very tough. And it demands endurance. It's very competitive, though. I've always felt I could do pretty well with hockey, but it's only good if you can stay in one place and make a lot of money and invest it for the future after hockey. That's what I'm playing for anyway, so I can play till I'm thirty-five and be set up when I leave the game. I'll be doing something else, I guess. I've hardly given the insecurity aspect much thought, though, I figure I'll have a job till I'm thirty-five.

"I think most of the guys felt like that though. But like JD wasn't a goalie till he was sixteen, and like Murder all of a sudden he gets eighty goals in juniors, but to me, I always thought about playing in the NHL since I was five years old. I don't know if Murder thinks about the future too much. But you can't really ever get settled. Even me, it's hard to become a part of New York when you don't know if you'll be there next year. You can be traded any minute. I was supposed to be traded three times last year, but there's always that job security in that if you're good enough then they'll be a job somewhere."

McEwen smiled. "The only reason we even think about security in our jobs is that we're going through what most men don't go through till they're about forty, as far as being at the top of their profession, making the kind of money we do. And it fucks you up. Like you're twenty-two and you want to go out and get laid and get drunk, and if you do something wrong, people say, 'Ah, he's only twenty-two, fuck him, that's too bad.' It takes away your freewheeling. It gets you to thinking very young about what you want to do in life, and what you don't really know. This is what I want to be, this is the kind of person that I want to be, whatever, instead of just going out at twenty-two and having a game of softball with some guys, then going for a few beers. Or just falling in love for a year and doing that. Whatever."

"Does it make you get cynical?" I asked.

"Yeah, sometimes," Mike said, " 'cause like sports is fairly moralistic, it has that high level of what you can do and what you're not supposed to do. It shouldn't make you cynical 'cause you get great benefits, great money. But rather than being cynical about it, you start doing something about it. Give your money to charity or whatever makes you feel better. I was cynical, I could feel it coming on, then I said fuck it. So I just stopped thinking about it. I just said, 'Hey, I'm here and I'm doing it' and I know when I'm twenty-two nobody's gonna listen to me and nobody's gonna care and anybody who does'll realize that I'm just growing up anyway. Maybe when I'm forty or fifty, with all the experience I've had then, people will listen to me and that's the time to come forth and say something. I think a lot of people in New York understand that, that you're young and not that capable. I think some others realize that, but they still come down on you. You feel a weight, you know. But it's a fantasy life, so you don't mind living it. A complete fantasy, the life we live, the money, the girls, everybody loves it. We meet anybody we want."

"When does the reality intrude?" I wondered.

"When you lose a step, that's the reality of it. The reality is going to practice and working hard every day. But it's a great life, I'm not a factory worker, I'm not riding the trains like my dad did for forty years."

"What about the other side of the dream—like what happened to Doc?"

McEwen shrugged. "I don't care what you say, for all the trouble that he gets into, Murdoch probably has the most fun of everybody. That's the one thing that you have to admire about him, that he's always happy-go-lucky. He just wants to go out and have fun and that's his top priority. He does that, that's what he wants to do. It's a great way to be, that's the way everyone should be. This whole big drug rap was 'Shit, I did something wrong,' but I mean, fuck, so what?"

"Tell that to the conservative hockey establishment," I suggested.

"Okay, it's Canadian, it's more British than American," Q analyzed. "I grew up in that, I accept it. Americans are so competitive, it's so wide open for a person to do well for themselves if they have the talent, that's the big secret here. In Canada everyone kind of accepts that they're gonna grow up, work eight hours a day, have seventeen to twenty thousand, and live a nice middle-class life. Whereas here people are striving to do better and if they don't get it that's an indication of the kind of people they are, and it's just not true. It's hard and it's cruel.

"Even the women. Canadian women, the groupies, are very down-to-earth and family and very loving, that's what comes out, but down here the American women are aggressive and they want to get laid and they want to do this and do that, but the Canadian women are happy to stay behind their man who's working at the factory eight hours a day and do what they want to do. Go to the macramé class and have a great time." McEwen paused and stared out his window, down at Lexington Avenue. The traffic was bumper to bumper and the streets were filled with people. From Q's vantage it looked like a tiny ant colony. "Here everything's wide open to you and so you grab it and take whatever you want and do it," he said, and then he got up and closed the window, shutting out the noise from the city below.

• NOVEMBER 3

The Colorado Rangers demolished the New York Rangers tonight. They got four goals and three assists between them. Hitch got two goals and an assist. Q had two assists. Hickey was so worked up he threw his guts up on the bench in the second period. After the game McEwen had nothing but praise for his new team and his new coach, Don Cherry.

• NOVEMBER 7

The Rangers came back from their road trip with Barry Beck, and the city guys immediately took him under their wing. Greschner gave him a couch to sleep on, and Murdoch took him to all the night spots, and they both took him to lunch at Rusty's for the ribs. Afterward they dropped him off at Jean Paul Germain's for some threads. At the standard Ranger discount. Then Barry went to the Garden and took off his new clothes and put on his new uniform and wiped LA's ass.

He did it by throwing his massive body against every King that had the temerity to go near him. In the corner, in front of the net, even in open ice, a rarity these days, Beck was a monster. In fact, he resembled Frankenstein's monster with his wiry, Brillo-ish hair and his almost chiseled, crude features. He looked like Cro-Magnon man on skates.

But he really won the game in the second period when he grabbed the puck in his own end and charged up ice. He deked one man at the blue line, then swooped around the last lone defenseman, building up steam, then he charged in on the hapless goalie, shot the puck viciously into the net, and then slammed into the crossbar. The crossbar survived, Beck got up, straightened himself out, and became an instant hero in New York.

But after the game Freddie wanted to talk about Vickers. Vickers had at last got his chance with the Swedes since the trade, and they were playing well as a unit. So well that Shero seemed afraid they might become complacent.

"It's too early to tell," Shero said of Vickers's performance with the Swedes. "We figured he needed a change and he's smart and he can score, but he didn't have a great scoring year last year and we felt if he couldn't play with the two Swedes, then who could he play with? We know he's got talent but just a matter of digging a little bit more."

"Does Vickers do anything for Nilsson or is it the other way around?" someone asked.

"I don't worry about the two Swedes," Shero said. "They always pull their own. Now it's up to Vickers to prove he wants to play there, and if he wants to play a little more aggressively and work a little harder in the corners, he's smart enough to make the plays for the Swedes."

"Didn't the Swedes ask to play with Sarge?" I wondered.

Shero shook his head. "I don't think that has anything to do with them. They have no right to. What the hell is this?" He laughed. "I wanted to play with Lindsay and Howe and Abel, but they wouldn't let me."

Most of the reporters started drifting off toward the locker room for their first shot at Beck. But one who stayed behind asked Shero if he had rethought his position on number one goaltender since JD's recent knee injury.

"The number one goaltender is in New Haven," Shero said, and all the reporters froze in their tracks. "That's interesting," the interrogator said. "I don't exactly understand . . ."

Shero shrugged. "I said he's in New Haven and his name is Baker. He's gonna be a hell of a hockey player, but that doesn't mean he's better than what we've got right now. In the long range, if there's one guy I'm not gonna get rid of, it's him. That doesn't mean he's ready."

Now the rest of the scribes drifted out. I collared Freddie near the door.

I remembered from his books that he hated to see players traded, and now that he was both general manager and coach, I wondered if it had been traumatic to make this big Beck trade. Actually I just wanted to look him in the eye and see his reaction. Besides, Hitch was interested in my report.

"Did it hurt to make the trade?" I blocked his way out of the room.

Shero paused and scratched his head. Then he looked up at me. "You hate to even sit a guy out a game, so imagine what it's like to get rid of people. It's even worse, like losing a son or something . . ." He mumbled and then darted past me and went into his office.

In the locker room, Beck's stall was surrounded. In the center stood the massive man-child, discreetly holding a white towel around his waist. His responses were measured, hesitant. "Because of me we should do better?" he repeated a question aloud. "How could they do better? Win the Stanley Cup, I guess, but I don't think they should expect that. A lot of things can happen, you have to be lucky and get a lot of breaks. I just hope I can add a little and do my part for the team." Barry took a sip of beer from a plastic cup.

"I'm shy," he admitted, "especially coming to a new team. I don't know if all the guys accept me. They've been good to me, though, they tell me where not to go. Don't go past Ninety-sixth Street, that's for sure. Murder, Doog, Espo, Gresch, they've been good. I feel like a burden on their backs until I get to know the city better."

"Harry Howell said it wasn't a five-for-one trade, that your value is intangible beyond numerical considerations, you can inspire others on the team," someone suggested.

Beck adjusted his towel. "I hope I can. I know I play aggressive and I know I'm a big guy and that's the way I should play. The littler guys look for that in a big guy, to lead. I'm gonna hit. I don't mind being hit, it gets me in the game. Anytime you're a big guy you naturally become not a policeman, but an inspiration to the littler guy. How does it look for a big guy if a little guy goes out there and takes a whupping and you do nothing about it? I'm a big guy, so something happens they know that I'll be there."

Over on the other side of the room, Murdoch was singing his praises of Bubba. "He helps this team, boy, let's not kid each other. Everybody plays with more confidence. How about that goal, eh? People didn't like that too much. How about when he yells at the guys to stay away from in front of the net? 'Sure, Mr. Beck.' Jeez, he didn't even hit anyone that hard. Better bring in some more red meat for the next game."

"We can use one more like that and we'll be scary," Doogie added.

I escorted Beck down to Charlie O's, as if he'd ever need an escort. And as soon as we stepped off the elevator, it started. "Here comes Barry," one shouted, and we were surrounded by forty screaming fans, waving programs and autograph books. Of course, one of them was Marcus.

"Barry, Barry." Marcus pushed his way to Beck's side. "How are you doing, Barry Beck? Get over here, I love you. Wait, give Beck some room." Marcus took charge. "He's a big man. You're a wild man, Barry."

One fan lurched up, offering a half-empty bottle of Beck's. "I wanted to save a whole one for you, man," he slurred, "but I couldn't, I'm sorry, man."

Marcus shook his head in disgust and threw his arm protectively around Beck's huge shoulders as Barry scrawled his name. "Beck, you're wild, I love you. You're an animal." Marcus was in ecstasy.

"Oh, I'm all right." Bubba shrugged, attempting to dislodge Marcus's arm.

"Beck, did you hear me yelling 'Bubba' all night?" Marcus wondered. Bubba nodded yes. "That's me, baby."

"Get Philly," said the drunk, veering near Beck as he tried to struggle through the seas of programs. "We want those bastards buried in the ground."

Marcus was a protective shield. "Don't touch him," he warned.

"How do we get to the bar here, Ratso?" Beck was getting edgy. I led him through the crowd, toward the kitchen back door. Marcus ran up for a parting shot. "Barry, all I say to you is this. Every check you throw, I'll buy you a beer. Barry, Barry, my name is Robert Marcus. Remember me. I'll be yelling Bubba, Bubba. You're wild."

Reluctantly Marcus let us escape into Charlie O's' kitchen. Inside we grabbed a table and ordered beers. Then we heard the booming voice coming from Sonny's table.

It was loud and black. It belonged to Don King, the ex-con turned boxing promoter, who was now doing business with the Garden. He was standing up at the table ogling Ron Duguay, who was attempting to exit. "Mr. Ron Duguay," King exulted, grabbing the hockey player by the neck. "Forget about Too Tall. That's yesterday's news. You're big, you're beautiful." All the people at Werblin's table seemed to be enjoying the show. "Sonny, leave me alone," King thundered. "You signed me, you can't keep me in the closet now, Sonny." Everyone laughed. No one outside of Sonny's table found any of it amusing. "Mr. Ron Duguay." King bestowed his attention on Duguay again, who was itching to bolt. "Your complexion is your protection." The promoter trotted out all his lines and Werblin's entourage tittered politely. At our table Beck just shook his head half in disgust, half in amazement. Welcome to the Big Apple, Bubba.

• NOVEMBER 10

A rare Saturday afternoon game at the Garden. More kids, more noise, less sophistication. And Vickers continued to shine with the Swedes, potting two power-play goals, the last one tying the game. Then Greschner scored with two minutes to go, and the Rangers had two points.

Naturally Shero kept the heat on Sarge. "What's Vickers doing now?" one reporter asked after the game. "He's scoring again. Is he working harder or is he in position more?" Shero scowled. "He's on a line that creates more things for him."

"Why did you put him there?" someone else asked.

"I just put him there, no particular reason. Just because I make a move doesn't mean I'm a genius. Everybody thinks you have a great plan behind it." He chuckled to himself.

"Well, isn't there a certain chemistry operating? You looked a long time to find someone for that line," another observed.

"It doesn't make any difference, the third man on a line generally isn't that important." Shero shrugged. "There's two that work and have some feeling for each other, and the third man should be a good checker and score the odd goal."

In the dressing room Vickers was uncharacteristically ebullient. That is, as ebullient as a chronic phlegmatic can be.

"The pucks just been coming to me," Sarge said modestly.

"Do you look forward to playing now?" someone asked.

"That's an understatement," Vickers allowed.

"Do you feel reborn?" Journalism returned.

"The guys keep bugging me about that rebirth thing." Vickers smiled. "I read in a magazine, 'the rebirth of Steve

Vickers.' Jesus, it seems that every game I'm supposed to be reborn. Maybe they think I was dead for a year. Maybe a lot of others do too."

"Can the helmet have anything to do with it?" Journalism was straining for a peg.

Vickers smiled slyly. "I finally smartened up. I remember getting hit a couple of times in the head last year. I thought, I protect my crotch, why am I not protecting my head? I mean, where are my priorities?"

"Is wearing the helmet, can we interpret that as a new attitude?" Journalism's last try.

"Bullshit," Sarge said. "I just value my brains for some reason. I don't know if that makes me eccentric."

The pack then turned to interview the game winner, but Greschner was relaxing in the players-only lounge, munching on a sandwich, and talking only to his colleagues.

• NOVEMBER 11

This was quite possibly the dullest hockey game I'd ever seen. The Pittsburgh Penguins lulled the Rangers for sixty minutes and won 4–1. Early in the game Ulfie departed with the flu, and Shero spent the rest of the time coming up with bizarre combinations. At one point he threw out the fourth line on a power play. No wonder those charitable to him call him enigmatic. With this loss the Ranger record stood at 7–7 with one tie.

Later Fred was asked if he was satisfied with the progress of the team. "You're never satisfied. If you're satisfied, you should quit." Well, was his dissatisfaction mild or substantial?

"Always mild," Fred said. "I'm not gonna say it's substantial. I'll tell the players that but not anyone else."

"How about Duguay?" someone threw out.

"I like him in the middle."

"Why?"

"Because I like him."

"Why?" More voices joined in.

"That's my business," Shero snapped. "There's some things I can't tell you. I don't even tell my players, I'm gonna tell you? There are some things I don't even tell my wife."

Then he told them. "You experiment. You give them confidence. You use an entire season to develop people, you put them in situations where you're desperate. You even put forwards on defensive, if necessary, if the game is decided."

"Did you ever think, 'Tonight's not their night, they're not hitting'?" someone wondered.

Fred shook his head and furrowed his brow. "You *never* say that, you just hope and pray. If you don't pray, you get out of the business, you give up. You might as well call the team off and go home. Then you got to give the people their money back. At least pray a little bit . . ."

In the locker room Duguay had some questions for me. Some advanced scouting. He was going to do a session with *Interview* magazine and he wanted to know everything about Warhol.

• NOVEMBER 13

We're on a road trip. Me and Rod Gilbert, driving out to Long Island for the game against the Islanders. The first meeting between these two rivals since the Rangers shocked the Isles and sent them home on a bus, disgraced, in last year's Cup semifinals. Tonight the Islanders sought revenge.

"I talked to Mike about putting Sarge together with the Swedes," Rod revealed. "He got a raw deal. He didn't get a chance. They tried the new kid, Sulliman, Talafous, everyone but him. Mike said he's got an attitude problem. He doesn't stay around when he's not dressed." Gilbert scowled. "What the fuck is he, a cheerleader? He's paid his dues."

So had Gilbert. Gilbert had an illustrious career as a Ranger right wing until a few seasons back when he was unceremoniously retired by Coach John Ferguson and kicked upstairs. Since then he had worked on promotion for the Rangers but had been generally underutilized. So this season they were breaking him into announcing by using him as an on-site color expert. Rod was stationed in the Ranger penalty box, with a headset and a live mike, and, from time to time, Ranger announcers Bill Chadwick and Jim Gordon would go down to the former star for expert analysis. Of course, most of the time they seemed to forget Rod was around. Then on the rare occasions when they did cut to him, Gilbert would try to get too much in and get flustered and his fragile hold on English would slip away.

Then there were the guys themselves. "I'm sitting in the box and Gresch hooks this guy, real obvious," Rod related. "Three or four times he got the stick in, and they called it. So Gresch comes into the box. 'Hey, Rocky, did you see that bullshit?' he says. 'It was a fucking dive. Rocky, tell them it was a shit call.' I said, 'Gresch, my mike is on.' Then Mario gets called and he comes in. 'I'm gonna get that asshole back,' he tells me." Gilbert rolled his eyes and drove on to the Coliseum.

Tonight Ulfie was still suffering from flu and he was scratched. His disability prompted some skepticism from some of his Canadian teammates. "We play in pain," one said. "I guess a hundred-thousand-dollar-a-year players play, six-hundred-thousand-dollar ones don't."

They could have used him. After a 2–2 deadlocked first period, the Islanders scored six times in the second period. It was as if they had the book on Soetaert; each shot beat him low and to the stick side. For the Islanders, who had been struggling as much as the Rangers this season, it was an impressive showing.

For the fans it meant free chili after Islander goal number five. When they hit nine the Coliseum announcer took the mike: "Alan Bernstein is here, the president of Wendy's, and if the Islanders get one more goal, he will authorize double chili." The crowd went wild. "This is bullshit," a stringer from the Associated Press muttered to himself. "They're gonna regret that some day." But he was drowned out by the cheers when Potvin waltzed in and put it between Soetaert's legs. Double chili.

Shero thought it was bullshit too. We were standing after the game in an unused dressing room, littered with the remains of Fleetwood Mac's occupation the night before. There were plates with half-eaten cheese, empty wine bottles, beer cans strewn all over the floor. Fred stepped gingerly around the carnage and talked about chili.

"That's just promotion," one reporter said. "This is the NHL."

"We never did that in Omaha," Fred said. "If I want a bowl of chili, I'll go out and buy it."

"Could you isolate the problem?" someone asked. "Is there one technique they forget most?"

"Don't think it was their lack of effort," Fred began. "They just weren't coming up with the puck. If you want the puck, you gotta make up your mind and want it. It's mind over matter, nothing else. It's got nothing to do with talent, really, if you're close enough."

I was still thinking about that one on the way back to the city when Gilbert started talking about Shero. I told him Fred's line about the chili. Gilbert laughed. "There's no bitterness, everything is fucking equal to him. It seems like the guy is so stabilized in his own ways. It's like he has zero for an ego. And he's the best delegator of authority. He knows how to surround himself with leaders and capable people. He detects them just by talking to them a bit and seeing how they react to certain conditions."

Gilbert shook his head. It was pouring now and the rain beat a steady rhythm on the car roof. "I think a coach has to be like Fred," Gilbert continued. "I love the mysteriousness about him. I don't know if I could handle coaching because I'm too open. I want to give to too many other phases of life, but him, he has all the time just to think about how he's going to work on one problem, one player at a time. He'll think for days about how to remedy a situation because he doesn't have any ulterior, any outside disturbance. He doesn't go to all these functions, he doesn't surround himself with a lot of other ideas. He's arrived at a comprehension for hockey, he's dedicated himself to understanding the mental psychology of the hockey player. If I could only speak English, it would fucking help."

Rod paused and collected his thoughts. "You obtain some results, some tremendous results, if you understand the level of intelligence of the players. So you can't surpass that, you've got to give on that level and you've got to think on that level, so therefore if you've put yourself up higher than them. . . ." He trailed off. "See, they don't know that he's more intelligent than them, the players, they think he's fucked up. They feel sorry for him because he's so inside. They don't want to be like him, so they know they're not entering in competition with him. You ask a guy like Ron Greschner if he would like to have Fred's understanding of life or Fred's understanding of success. No fucking way, he'll say, it's got to be the most boring fucking thing he's ever seen. So, it's like your father, it's like the guidance that you got from your parents. At one point you say, 'My father, he doesn't understand me, he's so fucking dumb.' He's dumb like a fox, eh, he doesn't want to compete with you, so he lets you go your own way if he's a good parent. Well, that's what Shero does. He's a good parent."

"He's a complex guy," I agreed, "but he seems a bit different from last year. He doesn't put the slogans up anymore. He's getting much more remote, like he's pulling away. Maybe it has something to do with his delegating all that responsibility to Nykoluk and Keating. It's like he's testing them, the same way he tests the players. What's Keating like?"

"He used to play with Freddie," Rod said. "Mickey's almost the complete opposite to Fred. Much more outgoing, much more fucking around."

"He seems to have almost a perverse sense of humor, though," I said.

"He's like a sergeant in the Army," Rod said. "What's good for the boys type thing. A rah-rah type of guy."

"The guys all imitate him and put him down behind his back, it's hilarious." I laughed. "How's your position this year? Is it solidifying?"

Rod scowled. "I don't have a fucking position. They don't want me to do fucking anything. They're afraid of me, Keating is fucking petrified of me."

"Why?" I asked.

"Because of Mr. Fucking Cool himself." Rod smiled. "He's playing games with him. Shero got all the fucking money, he brings in Keating who makes fuckall, thirty thousand dollars a year to run the fucking Rangers. So Keating goes to Werblin to talk about a raise, Werblin says, 'Well, I got Rod here, I don't need you here.' I'm Werblin's adviser. I set it all up for the Rangers. So it creates that insecurity feeling in Keating, so it freaks him out, he thinks he can be replaced at any time and when I'm around it makes him uptight."

Rod shook his head and turned on the radio, and we barreled through the rain, happy to be leaving Long Island.

The Rangers stumbled along and the fans weren't about to take it. They had gotten to Guevremont already. Every time he went near the puck, the boos would cascade down onto the ice, and whenever he headed toward the bench, mock cheers would peal out. By the third period he was skating with his head bowed and twisting his stick nervously in his hands. He looked like a condemned man.

But Murdoch was doing okay. He had scored his eighth and ninth goals of the year tonight, and now in the final minutes of the game, a cluster of fans behind the Ranger bench were yelling for a hat trick.

"C'mon, Shero, get Murder in there," one yelled.

"We want Murder." The chant started to build. On the bench Murdoch turned around and shrugged.

"Look at Murdoch," one of the fans said. "Look at him sweat."

"It must be the snow," another laughed and they slapped hands.

But Shero didn't give Murder a chance at the trick. And afterward he explained why. "I like to see new faces," he told the press. "Last year we did the same thing, brought in kids for no reason. They give us life and made the others think a bit, 'Hey, we're not here forever, we have to work.' I've done it all my life. Even if a guy scores two goals for me like tonight, he could be benched tomorrow. I may consider him one of my extra men. You gotta keep moving in your extra men, and every once in a while I get mad enough to bench one of your so-called stars. You gotta do that, they need to be shook up. But then they are the guys that you gotta look to and help constantly and pray that you give them enough ice time and don't give up on 'em and that they still feel part of the team."

Some of the Rangers reshot the Sasson commercial because Hickey had been traded and it might have looked funny. At least that's what Audrey from Sasson thought. So she picked Anders Hedberg to replace Hitch. Only Anders didn't want to do it because he didn't want to "replace" his traded teammate. After a long talk with Gfeller, Anders said yes. Today the compressor worked.

All the Rangers played Winnipeg, an expansion team, whose general manager was John Ferguson, their old coach. The way they were skating you would have thought they were auditioning for the next Sasson commercial. After nine minutes of the first period, they were losing 4–0.

Imagine the boos. They were coming from all over. You see, the Garden is divided by class. First there are the red seats, where Corporate New York entertains its clients and rewards its executives who occasionally deign to watch the action on the ice only several feet away. These choice seats for the most part are peopled by dilettantes.

Above the reds are the orange seats. People in the orange seats come from Westchester and own small businesses and write off their tickets even though these seatholders actually watch the games. Next up are the yellow seats. Yellow seatholders are middle class and they reside in Queens and they're younger and more vocal than the orange or red seats. Except for the hockey wives who sit scattered among the yellows. They all come from Westchester now.

By the time you hit the greens, it's getting harder to see the ice. The green seats are tucked in between the yellows and the overhanging balcony seats. People from Long Island and New Jersey sit in the green seats. Most of the Garden doesn't even realize there are green seats.

Everyone hears the blues, though. High above the ice, separated from the other seats by a natural balcony, are the blues. The Blue Seats originated the famous "(insert any ref's name here) Sucks" chant. The Blue Seats house the older gentleman who sits on the railing and gets on Bobby Clarke of the Flyers, a courageous diabetic athlete. Every time Clarke hits the ice, the old man's foghorn voice floats down and permeates the entire Eighth Avenue end of the Garden. "Clarke"—it sounds like the voice of God in *The Ten Commandments*—"you're a junkie. You're on the needle." The Blue Seats house the Chief, the Rangers' unofficial mascot, a skinny guy who carries his headdress in a shopping bag and between periods runs around the lower, more expensive seats entertaining the hoi polloi with his semaphoric Ranger chants. The Blue Seats also house the pot smokers (for cocaine, try the yellows or reds), who smoke up a storm in the corridors between periods. The people in the Blue Seats know and care about hockey, many having played it themselves. Everyone in the blues, no matter where they're from, is from Brooklyn. And, judging by the view of the ice way down below, they might as well be in Brooklyn.

But this is America, the land of opportunity, and Bobby Marcus was enjoying downward mobility. He was sitting in the middle of the red seats, center ice, tucked into a vacant seat along with his bagful of hockey programs and newspapers and magazines. A few rows below him sat Sonny Werblin.

Marcus gestured to me, "Sit down. These are my seats. I know the usher." Marcus reached into his bag and whipped out a Pearlcorder Olympus minicassette. For the last few games he had been posing as a reporter, interviewing the opposing teams that came into the Garden. After his first interview, with a few St. Louis players, he was surrounded and forced to erase some spicy dialogue. Incredible as it may seem, the St. Louis guys mistook Marcus for a fan.

But he had been in contact with a guy from *The Hockey*

News who promised him a reading of anything he might write. Marcus immediately called Krumpe and Werblin to set up interviews. The same day, he bought a big stuffed bull for Bubba and a small toy koala bear for Ulfie.

"LET'S GO, BUBBA!" Marcus screamed at the top of his lungs, shifting nervously in his seat. "I'll always be a fan. I go crazy during the game." We watched the action as the Rangers started pressing the Jets.

The referee threw up his hand and called a penalty on Winnipeg. Twenty-seven seconds later, Esposito scored from a scramble in front. Marcus leaped up and screamed. "We want more," he bellowed. "All right, Sonny, I'd told you we'd get them." A minute later Hedberg pushed Nilsson's rebound in. It was 4–2. "Hedberg, Hedberg, Hedberg." Marcus was up. "Sonny, we ain't through yet." Marcus pulled out his pad and scribbled on it. "Turn around, quick, we could be on TV. Wave, wave." Marcus was flapping his arms. In front of us Sonny's wife was showing her son, Bobby, how she shields her face with her bag if the puck flies near them. "MARIO, BUBBA." Marcus was getting hoarse. He was also getting stares from everyone in front of us. Suddenly there was a scramble in front of Winnipeg's net and the red light went on.

"All right, Sonny, we're doing it!" Marcus screamed. Above us the Chief was going through his routine, using his body to spell out R-A-N-G-E-R-S. Each section roared its response.

Below us Werblin started to nod, and his chin dropped to his chest. "DON'T LOOK DOWN, SONNY," Marcus screamed. "LOOK UP, LOOK UP. YOU'RE THE MAN, SONNY. WE'LL GET THEM, SONNY." Werblin's head snapped up and struggled to follow the play. "I'd do anything to be Sonny Werblin's best friend," Marcus said. "Shit, if we lose this I'll kill myself." Just then Beck checked someone at center ice, freeing Sullivan. He came in unmolested and beat Davidson, making it 6–3. Marcus was downcast.

"Bubba was on ice for three goals tonight. IT'S ALL RIGHT, BUBBA," he screamed. "I STILL LOVE YOU."

Duguay scored, but it was over. A 6–4 loss to an expansion team. At the buzzer the boos came again and the Rangers skated quickly off. Except Murdoch, who stopped to exchange pleasantries with a fan. "Fuck off, you cocksucker," Mud yelled and slammed his stick against the corridor wall, breaking it in half.

JD was able to contain his disgust, though. The big goalie sat in his stall, with his pads still on, surrounded by reporters. "I guess if I gave up six goals, I didn't do such a good job," he said softly.

"Is this a nightmarish way to come back?" a reporter asked.

"I'm not gonna worry about it too much," the huge goalie shrugged. "I can't fold up the tent. You gotta fight back."

"Does it bother you that the same ones who were cheering you last year are booing now?" another asked.

"It's their right," JD said. "This is a democracy. My job is to stop the fucking things. People are emotional, they cheer and boo. But tomorrow the sun's gonna shine. I'm pretty sure about that. Unless Iran drops the fucking bomb. My angles are a little bit off. I'm not going to fold up the tent, though. I might even request to go to New Haven and play a couple of games this weekend. I need the work."

Across the way Murdoch had cornered Tom Murray from *The Hockey News.* "You said I got put on waivers? It got my mother all excited. She cried, she called me. She reads *The Hockey News.* It said Keating said it was true. I was waived through the league and nobody wanted me."

"I didn't write it," Murray said. "Maybe it was in Fischler's column."

Murdoch shook his head. "My mother's like that, you don't know my mother." He finished dressing and called Bubba, and the three of us headed for Charlie O's.

But lying in wait was Marcus. "Barry," he said smiling, arms wide to greet the man, "tonight you were on the ice for a few goals." Bubba shrugged and walked through the basement toward the restaurant's back door. "Wanna walk?" Marcus trotted alongside and threw his arm around the big defenseman. "I'll walk, it's okay. What happened? You hit a guy in center ice and Sullivan went right by you and put the puck between the post and the left side. Are you gonna stop hitting at the center line? What goes through your mind when you get goals scored against you, when you're doing something right and it backfires? What goes through your mind?" Marcus had whipped out his Pearlcorder and was taping the conversation.

"You're not too happy about it," Bubba said impassively.

"I know that." Marcus prodded him on.

"I just think I was trying to do the right thing, if something goes wrong try to keep it out of your mind and go out next shift and make up for it," Beck explained.

"How do you like New York now?" Marcus changed the subject swiftly.

"Now I like it pretty good," Barry said. "I'm just gonna go out for a couple of beers right now, then go to Studio, have a little bit of dancing, and go home."

"You're going to Studio tonight, you dog?" Marcus's face lit up. "You gotta be careful over there, there's a lot of drugs."

"I'm not into that," Bubba said.

"I know, Barry, you're straight, and I love it." Marcus smiled. "Barry, compared to Colorado with the mountains and everything, do you miss all the outdoor life?"

"Yeah, I miss it, but I'm getting used to the city," Bubba replied.

"We have Long Island." Marcus was helpful.

"Where's that?" Beck wondered.

"I live on Long Island." Marcus was incredulous. "You're

gonna come out to my condominium, go swimming, and play some tennis during the summer if you're around."

"I won't be here during the summer, I go back home to Vancouver," Bubba explained.

"You grew up three blocks from the Vancouver coliseum, is that correct?" Marcus remembered.

"One block." Bubba corrected.

"One block. Okay, Barry. You know that I love you. Did you hear me tonight? Yelling for you?"

"Yes, I did." We were nearing the back door.

"And did you hear me say I still love you?" Marcus probed deeper.

"Yes, I did."

"All right, I still do."

"I was very happy to hear that, Robert." Bubba paused at the door. Murdoch was impatient to hit the bar. "And you'd better keep that up."

"I still love you and you can do anything you want on the ice," Marcus summed up. "And I'll still love you. I think you're a cornerstone. I think you're a man-mountain and I'll always love you. Good luck, give me a kiss, you mother-fucker." Marcus got him smack on the lips. We turned to enter the door. Marcus grabbed me. "Where are you going without me, you bitch?" he hissed.

We stayed in Charlie O's for a few minutes, then Bubba and Duguay and I headed up to Studio. There wasn't much happening there, just a few outrageous drag queens. Bubba pointed one out, a bald guy in a long black evening dress. "Put that in your book," Duguay said.

• NOVEMBER 25

The malaise had set in. The Rangers lost yesterday to Pittsburgh and again tonight to Toronto, making it three straight defeats. They were 9–12–1 now. And everyone was bitching. Gresch was bummed out he wasn't getting enough ice time. Murdoch was in a funk since he'd been pulled off the Esposito line because they'd been giving up too many goals when they were on the ice. Eddie Johnstone, about the only guy busting his hump day in and day out, hardly ever got on. Beck was hampered by a groin pull.

"Why'd you change the lines around, to snap them out of it?" someone asked Fred.

"Sometimes it's other reasons." Shero was evasive.

"What other reasons?"

"I just said other reasons," Shero snapped. "If I tell you, you're gonna put it in the papers." Everyone nodded. "Well, I don't want the players to know."

Shero did reserve some praise for Davidson. He admired the goalie's guts in sending himself down to the minors to get in shape.

In the dressing room nobody had any answers. Espo was depressed as hell, Thomas felt they weren't "coming together as a team," everyone else was stumped. Except Vadnais. He had an idea, but he couldn't reveal it. "I have to tell management first," he huffed.

Afterward Gresch, Bubba, and I grabbed a cab to Oren's for late dinner. In the cab I asked about the team meeting that had been held before the game. Greschner raised an eyebrow. "Hey, Rats, we can't tell you about that. What's said in that room stays in that room." Beck nodded gravely. "Of course," the big man said, "if you were a Penthouse Pet, I'd tell you everything."

Murdoch was already at Oren's chomping at a burger. He was sitting with his friend, Larry, who owns a rock club in Westchester, talking about the good old days at Long Beach. "Remember the time there was the blizzard," Larry said, "and you were on the phone with this guy from the Chinese restaurant telling him to deliver in eighteen inches of snow?"

Murdoch howled with delight. "Jeez, were we ever fucked up then." He laughed. "Thank God for B₁₂ shots, I would have never made it through that year."

We sat at a corner table with Richard Weisman, who had been having some late-night, early-morning parties at his luxury duplex which had been well attended by Rangers lately. Now he was trying to help Bubba find an apartment and move off Gresch's couch.

At the next table Reggie Jackson overheard. The introductions were made. "What's he need? What does he need?" the slugger asked me. I told him. "How much do you want to pay, Barry? Where? What part of town?" Reg was wearing a sweater and puffing on a pipe and acting very professorial. "This is a son-of-a-bitch town for a sports figure," he told Beck, with great gravity. Beck went back to his salad.

"How old is he?" Reggie leaned over to me.

"Twenty-two."

"Twenty-two," Reggie repeated slowly. "Twenty-two. And how big?"

I related Bubba's story to Jackson. A big grin cracked his face. "Hey, Matt," he said to his agent, "the Rangers got a superstar. The Rangers got themselves a superstar. Just like Steinbrenner, huh?" Reggie had one last question before I was dismissed: how much was Beck making? I guessed $200,000 a year.

"Why'd you say that?" Duguay shook his head later, when I related the conversation to him. "You should have made up some outrageous figure. Seven hundred and fifty thousand dollars a year. And told him it was the average salary. He would've been running into the Yankee office tomorrow asking for a new contract."

- NOVEMBER 28

Oh, did the Rangers screw up. It started like this. Shero wanted to get a look-see at his "number one" goalie, New Haven's Steve Baker. So Soetaert, who hadn't played since the Islander shellacking, was sent down to the farm team. He was pissed. And he spilled it all over the tabloid pages of the *New York Post*.

"DEMOTED SOETAERT: *RANGERS LIED TO ME*," the headlines screamed. Then Soetaert screamed, "You know what Keating had the bloody nerve to tell me? He said he tried to trade one of us, and not one other team in the league is interested in any of us. He said other teams say the Rangers have quantity but no quality in goal. What bull. Can you believe the nerve telling me that? He told me today that he never said one of us would be traded. He meant maybe one of us would go down to the minors. Well, this is just brutal."

Keating, needless to say, was quite shaken by Soetaert's banner-headline charges. But then again he was caught in a lie. Then he got caught in red tape. It seemed that the league made an administrative error and the Rangers couldn't legally send Soetaert down. And thanks to Soetaert's agent, Larry Rauch, the league and the Rangers were made aware of their faux pas. So, less than twenty-four hours after the demotion, Soetaert was back up. And Freddie's fog seemed to get thicker by the minute.

"He's back with us." Fred spoke of Soapy after the Rangers tied Minnesota 4–4 with new goalie Baker in nets.

"For how long?" Jim Naughton, the *Times* man, cracked.

"It could be forever," Shero deadpanned. "Everybody was happy when he came back. They gave him three cheers when he came back in the room. It was the shortest twenty-four-hour recall ever. We bumped into each other coming in and I told him he was very lucky. I was sent down on twenty-four-hour recall once and they called me back twenty-eight years later. That's some hell of a difference."

But I wondered about Soetaert's public criticism of Keating. "I was very happy he spoke out," Fred said, "because it proves he wants to be here in the big league. He was very sorry, he called within a couple of hours. I'm not stupid, I've been in the league a long time, I've been a hockey player. The man wants to play and he was very hurt for a while, and he called to say he was sorry. Lots of times you say something you're sorry for." Shero started for the door. "Especially when you see it in print."

Across the hall Soetaert was eating crow. Yes, he was happy to be back. Yes, he was sorry about what he said. Yes, he had been hurt, but now he was ready to play. No, he has nothing to say about who goes and stays. No, he didn't want to cause any more waves.

"After the things you said in the *Post*," Walt McPeek, a gutsy reporter from New Jersey started in, "it seems to me, an ordinary average jerk, that there's no way they're gonna keep you. All things equal, why would they?"

"Why would they give me a chance?" Soetaert was slipping. "Because maybe I'm good." He paused and caught hold again. He talked on a few more minutes, then headed down the hall to meet his wife and agent. "How was that, Rats?" he said. "I didn't say too much, did I?"

• DECEMBER 1

Now, about that movie. Remember the guys from Montreal? Well, there was damn near a run on Valium when Hitch and Q, the film's two principals, were dispatched to

Colorado. But after suitable discussion, they decided to go ahead with the filming. Which meant that the Lone Star shoot with Davidson and Kinky Friedman, who was writing the theme song for the movie, was still on. Also, the Duguay-Murdoch mock pickup scene at Oren's was still on. And the Ranger fan-atics shoot got the green light.

Which explained why I was in a car somewhere in Brooklyn with the two Bills and Martin and Glenn and their equipment. In a quiet, residential, white neighborhood, where not one but many trees grew, lived the Chief.

The Chief was New York's wholesale answer to Baltimore Oriole cheerleader Wild Bill Hagy. They were both from a long line of official and unofficial team mascots, average workaday fans who somehow lived out their fantasies by dressing up (or down) and rallying the troops behind the home team. The Garden had been blessed with another quasi-official cheerleader years earlier, Dancing Harry, who would tap-dance around at courtside during the Knick games, putting the hex on the opposing team.

But the Chief wasn't even quasi. Oh, he had written Werblin all right, even gotten back a nice form letter, but till now, after all these seasons of donning his headdress and whoop-whoop-whooping it around the Garden aisles, he was still the People's Chief. And here, in Brooklyn, in plainclothes, in the nondescript, attached two-story brick house, he was barely even that.

"You're not filming in the house." He ushered me and Bill Brownstein into the upstairs apartment as a suspicious face peered out at us from behind the curtains of the downstairs abode. "My parents live downstairs," he explained. "They're a little upset about the whole thing. They're retired people. My father was an exec on Wall Street. They don't approve of this character that I do. They're very conservative, they make Barry Goldwater look like a liberal. You know, they live their private lives and they don't understand why, uh, you see, ever since I was assaulted they just . . ."

"You were assaulted?" I interrupted.

The Chief nodded sadly. "Yeah, last year I was assaulted down the block," he sighed.

"By who?"

"By a guy that turned out to be an Islander fan," the Chief said. "No kidding, ever since then they've been even more adamant against this character that I do. But my sister is for it."

He led us upstairs and we walked around the apartment. It was like walking into the 1950's. There was an old TV, and old furniture and sports books and a few old record albums. In the Chief's bedroom the walls were decorated with icons and little signs with quotations from Jesus Christ. On the bed the Chief was gathering up his uniform and stuffing the components into an old, torn, brown-paper shopping bag.

"Do you work, Chief?" Brownstein was interrogating him with the air of an anthropologist.

"Right now I'm out of work," the Chief mumbled. "I was a salesman. Actually my last job was cashier at Alexander's on Lexington Avenue. I had to leave after Christmas. I wasn't considered Christmas help but . . ." the Chief trailed off.

"How old are you, Chief?" Brownstein again.

"I'm thirty-five," the Chief chuckled. "Physically, I'm thirty-five. People say I'm nuts."

He resumed looking for his headdress among the pile of Indian artifacts. "If you guys could pull off a job with the Rangers for me, I'd give you ten percent of my first year's salary," the Chief suddenly said.

I had been examining the Jesus iconography on the walls. "I was very sick about ten, eleven years ago," the Chief explained. "There was the Hong Kong flu epidemic. I nearly died. The whole Northeast was hit by it." He resumed his search for the headdress, coming up with a microphone. "My microphone. When I'm at the game I go like this." He pushed the plug down the front of his pants and grabbed the mike. "WELCOME TO NEW YORK RANGER HOCKEY." Instant transformation. The Chief was yapping away, a cross between Howard Cosell, Mel Allen, and Tiny Tim. "This game is brought to you by Sunsweet Prune Juice. Do as the Rangers do, drink Sunsweet Prune Juice. Hi, everybody! This is the Chief . . ."

"Let's go, Chief." Brownstein was getting impatient.

The Chief was still rummaging through his memorabilia, looking for the headdress and the letter from Werblin. He stopped to unplug his microphone. "I know it's here someplace." He was shifting the contents of the shopping bag.

"I hope you don't give anybody else my number," the Chief worried. "I told my father I gave them permission to have it. You see, they're private people and you have to understand they're retired and they've been through a lot with me." The Chief sat on the edge of the bed. "I had a breakdown, a nervous breakdown, the same year as the flu. I guess the breakdown came out of guilt or something I felt I was being unpunished for and all that stuff. I'm gonna bring the cup." He picked up large plastic replica of the Stanley Cup and stuffed it into the bag.

"I was in the hospital," he continued the narration. "I wasn't given shock treatments. I came back the slow way. Through medication. Valium, ten milligrams, but I was taking it four times a day. I stayed home and I'd take the medication after every meal and I'd be knocked out. Gee, that was about a year and a half. I couldn't even go to sporting events because I'd been so screwed up."

"Did you watch 'em on TV?" I asked.

The Chief's eyes widened. "No, I couldn't even watch the Jets win the Super Bowl. I would start crying for no reason 'cause I felt guilty if the Jets won 'cause I wanted them to win so much. So I figured I can't watch them. I figured if I didn't watch them they would win and they did. You have to understand the total situation, I figured I wasn't entitled to see them win 'cause I had some tough breaks. It's like with the Rangers. When the Rangers lose, I'll talk to the signs here." The Chief pointed to the walls. "It's like I'm talking to God. I'll say, 'Why?' or 'What is it I've done now?' I really take defeats . . ." The Chief struggled for the word.

"Personally?" I suggested.

"Very personally," he corrected, "as if God was punishing me. Really, sometimes I get so mad."

Just then the phone rang. The Chief guessed it was Marcus, because we were to meet him at the subway when he arrived from Long Island. It was going to be the super bowl of fans, Marcus vs. the Chief. He waited for the phone to be answered, and then a few seconds later, there was a sharp rapping on the heat pipe. The Chief bolted to the phone and picked it up. "Where are you? Oh no, you took the wrong train. I told you the D train. D. Listen, just stay where you are. Take your conehead off so you can hear." He turned to me. "It's bad enough I'm a nut, but I have to share the billing."

The Chief gathered up his stuff, and we jumped in the car and headed toward the train station on Nostrand Avenue. On the way he regaled us with tales of his short-lived radio career. Apparently there was a time when he was a regular on a few of the popular call-in shows. After that he treated us to five solid minutes of tests of the Emergency Broadcast System.

Marcus finally came and we set up on a corner, the Chief on one side with his stuff and Marcus next to him with his briefcase stuffed with magazines, books, and his conehead. A curious crowd had gathered around us as the camera rolled.

"My name is Bob Comas and I am the Chief of the New York Rangers," the Chief said with a flourish.

"I'm Robert Marcus. I'm from Long Island and I'm a Ranger fan, a hockey fan, and I'm gonna be a writer," said Marcus.

"Chief, show us a little of your routine," I prompted.

The Chief reached into his bag and grabbed his mike. "Okay, what I do at the Garden is very simple. I have a headdress on my head which has been sort of tarnished because I've been having several attacks lately. Anyway, what I do at my seat is a play-by-play like 'Okay, now we're at the game, down the right-hand side Eddie Johnstone, the shot—score! New York Ranger goal scored by Eddie Johnstone, and now we pause for station identification.' Now when the Rangers score a goal, I run down the aisle and I go uhohohohohwhowwhowhowwhwo, just like that, and the crowd goes crazy. Don't forget our friend here, conehead, before every game he drinks Sunsweet Prune Juice. Also what I do is I go around the Garden and I see kids and if they have a pen I sign autographs . . ."

This was too much for Marcus to bear. "Who would want your autograph? Who are you?"

The two fans shouted at each other for a while.

Reid waited, then rolled the camera again. He asked Marcus who his favorite player was. "Right now my favorite is Beck. I mean he kissed me on the lips and I freaked out."

"Oh God," the Chief gasped, off camera.

"What about the trade?" Reid asked.

"I thought it was a good trade for both teams," Marcus said. "I was upset. I loved Mike McEwen. I wrote an article when he first got drafted by the Rangers. It was destiny. So I was annoyed when he got traded, but he'll never learn how to play defense."

"I disagree," the Chief shouted. "I'm sorry but you know for a fact he's a great defenseman."

"Who's smarter, you or Fred Shero? Who knows, you or Shero?" Marcus taunted.

"Freddie, I apologize." The Chief stared into the lens. "But I have to say in this case I'm smarter."

"You're hallucinating," Marcus screamed.

"What about Pat?" Reid to the rescue.

"I love him, I think he's a nice human being," Marcus said. "I think he's lots of fun to be with and he said he couldn't wait to be a cowboy. He'll be an asset anyplace he goes."

"What do you know about the way these guys live?" Reid asked.

"Pat, as far as I know, is a playboy," Marcus decided. "I wouldn't know for sure, I never lived with the man. Mike McEwen is really quiet, his nickname was Bambi."

"Yeah, but he's also a swinger," the Chief chimed in. "I would say from the impressions I've gotten. All the bachelors from the Rangers are swingers the last couple of years. And for those of you ladies out there throughout North America, you can address mail to the New York Rangers, Four Penn Plaza, New York."

The Chief began whooping and doing a strange war dance. "Testing, testing. If this had been a real test, he would have thrown me on my head," he babbled.

"He's too much of a groupie for me." Marcus sneered at his counterpart. "I was gonna take his job away as mascot of the Rangers, but I decided I would be a writer. Sonny Werblin's a dynamite guy."

"I like him too," the Chief chimed in. "If he would only give me a job."

"It's your fault, Chief," Marcus said. "You had a job offer from the Islanders. He should have taken it, they offered him a hundred and fifty dollars a game. Harley Chester offered it."

"I thought he said it as a joke." The Chief shrugged. "I would have had to wear an Islander jersey, though. I turned it down. I'm too big of a Ranger fan."

"I would have done it," Marcus said.

"I know *you* would have done it." The Chief sneered. "I think it's the moral of the thing. I couldn't come to the Garden as the Chief anymore. But then again there are some sections that yell, 'you bleep you' when I go past."

"Do you say anything to piss them off?" I said.

"No," the Chief said.

"What are you talking about? You're a nut," Marcus screamed. "When I first met you, I almost wanted to beat the shit out of you. Just because I said I would take your job you were sticking your fingers in my face."

"I never did that now, c'mon," the Chief yelled. "You were going to take my job away from me."

"But you don't have a job, Chief." Marcus smiled triumphantly.

"Well," the Chief admitted sheepishly, "it's unofficial."

"When I speak to Werblin, I'll mention your name," Marcus sneered and Martin turned off the camera.

They loaded the equipment back into the car while the Chief danced around, whooping a bit. Marcus was reveling in the memory of his kisses.

"When you kiss these guys, it's on the cheeks, right?" The Chief was concerned.

"No, Ulfie was on the cheek, Beck was on the lips. You saw, Ratso—Beck leaned down and kissed me on the lips."

"You're joking around, aren't you?" the Chief said.

"No, I swear to God, my knees melted. He melted me."

"I don't believe this." The Chief held his head.

"Was it a sexual experience for you?" I said.

Marcus smiled. "He could definitely seduce me. I was thinking what hotel we could go to." The Chief was in anguish now and I was shocked and Marcus broke up laughing. "Ratso, I could fake you out anytime." Marcus grabbed his tape recorder from his bag and started playing back some of his interviews.

Marcus's voice floated out of the recorder. "Okay, now

we have twenty-two-year-old Steve Baker. Steve, how do you think you played tonight?" Robert was all smiles listening to the replay.

"Well, I gotta be happy with the game tonight, at least we didn't lose, eh?" Baker said.

"Last shot, what happened?"

"It was tipped," Baker said.

"I think you have an excellent glove hand," Marcus said. "You're great on angles, your only deficiency I can see right now is your stick. Do you agree with that?"

"Yeah, I guess so." Baker sounded disappointed.

"Steve, this interview is short, sorry for you, sorry for me." Marcus cut him off and found Beck. "Bubba!" Marcus's voice was sheer joy. "You don't look too happy tonight."

"I'm not happy tonight, Robert," Bubba said. "I missed that guy when I went to put him into the boards in the third period. I missed him. I'm not happy," Bubba deadpanned.

"I know, Bubba, you've been hitting a lot," Marcus commiserated.

"I'm not happy, I'm not happy," Beck repeated.

"You almost went into the penalty box yourself on that check." Marcus laughed.

"I'm not happy, Robert, I just can't talk about it. I can't relate to it," Bubba said.

"BUBBA!" Marcus suddenly screamed. "All right. Listen to me, Bubba. I love you, did you hear me yell for you tonight again?"

"I heard you yell. I hear you yelling every game, for Christ's sake," Bubba said, "but not too much tonight, though."

"I sat up in the yellows tonight," Marcus explained. "See, you're honest, a lot of guys wouldn't say that. You're right. But at the end of the game I snuck down and I said I still love you. Remember that, going into the locker room?' "

"Yeah, oh yeah," Bubba remembered.

"You didn't look up at me, you bastard."

"I remember that well," Bubba said. "I don't look up at anybody when they yell at me."

"Nobody, not even me?" Marcus was heartbroken.

"Never, nobody."

"Don't you like me?" Marcus worried.

"I love you, baby." Beck laughed.

"I told Warren Miller that you kissed me on the lips, and he looked at me like you were crazy," Marcus said.

Bubba laughed. "Is that right? I am crazy."

"I know that you're gonna come visit me on Long Island this summer. I already asked you that and you said you couldn't during the summer, but how about during the winter?"

"If I get a couple of days off, I can," Bubba promised.

"We'll play some tennis, eat some dinner, meet some Long Island females." Marcus was social director.

"I don't know about playing tennis," Barry hesitated.

"Barry Beck, I want to see Buffalo embedded into the boards." Marcus finished, then he turned to the others. "Murdoch, say good-bye to me." On the tape you could just about hear Murder following orders. "Rocky" Marcus was on to the next case, Rod Gilbert. "How do you feel about the way Steve Baker played tonight? I thought he played a very good glove game, a good pad game, but his stick work could use a little improvement."

"Well," Gilbert started, "as a reporter you seem to be the expert. You ask me the question and answer it at the same time." In the back seat of the car, Marcus was in seventh heaven, reliving each question and response. But up front the Chief was still very concerned.

"Is he for real?" The Chief leaned over and whispered in my ear. "I mean if I kissed Barry Beck, I wouldn't go around bragging about it."

- DECEMBER 2

Ulf Nilsson was pissed at me. Or maybe it's his wife. At least that's what everyone's telling me. It was all because of my *Playboy* article on Shero. I had a section on the Swedes, and the offending passage went like this:

> "This is for PLAYBOY?" Ulf Nilsson leans toward the recorder. *"I get a hard-on when I score a goal."*

To me, a line like that shows wit and self-awareness. To the guys on the team, it was shocking.

- DECEMBER 3

A moral victory. A 3–3 tie with the awesome Canadiens. Everyone seemed happy, but Murdoch seemed especially happy. He was back on the Esposito line after a few games' banishment. So he held court in front of his locker.

"I felt the excitement this afternoon," he was telling an enthralled group of reporters. "I couldn't sleep. I went out and did some shopping for my apartment. Then Phil called me to come with him in the limo to the game. He said he had to get loose for the game, so I went with him and talked dirty to him the whole way."

Murder dressed quickly and we went out for a drink. Murdoch stopped briefly to chat with a woman in her forties who took pictures of the Rangers. He grabbed a manila envelope full of blown-up color prints, and we hailed a cab. Murdoch immediately pulled out the pictures.

"That's nice. How much did you have to pay for those? I asked.

"This one's nice, eh? Must be from the finals last year," Murdoch said. "Pay? Oh, I fuck her."

"Huh?" I wasn't hearing right.

"Yeah, I fucked her for two years now."

"Why?"

" 'Cause I get free pictures." Murdoch laughed mischievously.

"I don't believe you," I scoffed.

"Ask Beck." Mud was serious. "I won't say nothing. Ask Barry. Look at the free pictures I get." Murder held the photos out.

"You're a sick fucking bastard." I smiled.

"Thank you." Mud laughed. "I fucked her in Atlanta, I flew her down. Ask Gresch. Somebody's gotta fuck her."

• DECEMBER 4

Soetaert was sent down today. Without having been given another shot in the nets, because of Baker's hot hand. He and JD and EJ commiserated his fate by getting shit-faced at the Mug and Ale, a bar in Westchester. At the same time, Keating told Wayne Thomas he had no future with the team. Or, in JD's words, that he was "chopped liver." All this is known as solving your goaltending problem.

That night I called JD:

ME: In third period, Islanders one, Vancouver five.

JD: Isn't that disgraceful? You don't know how much I love this. I was sitting here trying to make myself a tuna fish sandwich and I got a hard-on. So what's up?

ME: You're a sick fuck.

JD: Potvin's hurt. They say he'll be out six to eight weeks.

ME: I heard that.

JD: Ain't that a shame?

ME: Yeah, I really feel bad. Fuck the Islanders.

JD: I remember, no bullshit, three or four years ago, before I knew you, we averaged for a whole year thirty-seven shots against per game. I remember Smith and Resch saying, 'Well, Davidson doesn't do this.' They're averaging twenty-five shots a game now and they got five goals against. Hey, it was the best practice I had all year today.

ME: Really?

JD: Fucking shined. I'm gonna stick it up some people's asses. First time this year I've had legs. 'Cause of all those games I played. I'm like a fucking horse with a big carrot in front of him. I'm just chomping at the bit.

• DECEMBER 5

Another tie, 3–3 with Chicago. But nobody was happy. Maybe Vickers. He got his 200th career goal, his eleventh of the season. Since he had been paired with the Swedes, the line had been unstoppable and the fans had suddenly started cheering their new hero.

So now they were booing Greschner. For the first time in his Ranger career, the boobirds had turned on the slick defenseman, and every time he touched the puck, the disapproval wafted down from the stands. But it wasn't Gresch's fault, tonight everyone could be blamed for blowing a 3–0 lead going into the last period. The last goal, especially, seemed soft. Mulvey had skated down the right side and unleashed a fifty-foot slap shot from the boards that somehow hit Baker's blocker and bounced in.

After the game Greschner, despite the boos and his shyness with the press, stayed to face the music. "We don't see your face around here much," Lawrie Mifflin of the *Daily News* said. "Glad to see you."

"I'm all right," Gresch mumbled.

"You're not supposed to carry the puck as much in Fred's System," one reporter noted. "Isn't that a big part of your game?"

"They just want us to get the puck up to the forwards right away," Gresch said. "So that's the way he wants to play, that's the way we do it."

"Are you pleased with your start?" A perverse question.

Gresch grimaced. "No, not really. I think I put too much pressure on myself. I have to relax more and not worry about things that are gonna happen all the time. Every time there's a goal against I get down. Maybe it's because last year's team had a good year, so we want to do better this year. We've been playing fairly well of late. We just let down four or five minutes every game and they get a couple of goals. That's what beats us."

The press drifted away to get more quotes, and Gresch called me over. "Why don't you talk about the difference between the two coaches, put that in your book?" he whispered to me. "Nykoluk is just brutal. At least Shero gives me ice time. He puts me out on the power play."

"Don't worry," I said. "You know Shero likes to experiment. He knows what you can do. Watch, by the end of the season, come play-off time, you'll see who's out there."

"We'll see," Gresch said and headed for the showers.

Anders came over. "Very, very good *Playboy* piece. Congratulations," he said. I looked at his face and noticed a large red welt over his left eyebrow. "What happened to your face?"

"A stick." He shrugged.

The opposition around the league had been taking runs at the Swedes ever since they had jumped from the World Hockey Association to the NHL. There were many explanations offered, but it seemed to boil down to a simple one: chauvinism. "They're still taking cheap shots at you guys?" I said.

"No, no." he frowned. "It was unintended. He apologized. Fuck, that ref pissed me off. I don't mind taking the hooking, that's good when they call it, but nothing. It was unbelievable, no calls."

"They seem to carry their sticks higher around you," I said.

"They never call hooking," Anders said. "That's a terrific way of not having to skate. They just get the stick up here from behind and carry you along. There's too much bullshit in this league."

"I remember last year when you were playing Boston, you were in the corner going for the puck and you jumped to dodge a check, and on the way back up ice, Cherry jumped up on the Bruins' bench and started yelling 'Yellow Swede' at you."

Anders smiled ironically. "I remember that. Some guys play tough against everyone, but some guys, if they see a European name on the sweater, they think they can take advantage of you. It takes you a while to find out who are the bullshitters. In the WHA I knew who the fucking bullshitters were, here I didn't. It takes time."

"What do you do when you find out who they are?" I asked.

"You slash back," Anders said. "Anything. The guys that play tough against anybody, that's fine, you accept that, that's their style. But if guys play different games for different guys, those are the ones you give it back to."

It was time to leave. Tonight was the Lone Star shoot, with Kinky singing, for the first time anywhere in North America, "Skating on Thin Ice," the theme song of the upcoming movie. My job was to chaperone Gresch and Doogie. JD, EJ, and Mario were coming on their own.

But Gresch was in no mood to go anywhere. "I feel like Mr. Boobird," he said morosely as we walked out the front of the Garden, headed toward Seventh Avenue. "I'm getting out of here."

"Don't worry, they'll be cheering their asses off by the end of the season," I said.

"When I come back here with another team, I'll beat the shit out of them," he muttered. "Fucking stick it right to them."

We hailed a Checker cab and piled in. "If I ever did anything here, it would never be for the fucking fans. I'd do it for one person: me. I told a guy, I don't play for fucking guys like you." Gresch was still fuming.

"Don't say that to the press," I moaned. "I hope they don't use that. Look what happened to Seiling." I remembered the Rangers' defenseman who was traded after he criticized the fans that were getting on him.

"So they'll trade me." Greschner shrugged.

"Yeah, but that was Seiling," Duguay said.

"Seiling said the fans here suck, and Gresch just told the press that he hopes the ones that boo him die." I rolled my eyes.

"What do you want me to say?" Gresch pleaded. "A guy asked me what I thought of the fans that booed."

"Fuck, you go out and score a goal next game, they'll love you," Duguay said.

"I'm gonna give 'em the finger," Gresch barked. "Fuck 'em."

"Cut that out," I said.

"Even our best fans don't cheer us on when we're down," Duguay admitted. "Even the ones in the balcony don't cheer."

"I made enough money this year." Gresch was cavalier. "Over a hundred thousand dollars. I can quit for the year and live, eh, no big deal."

We pulled up to the club and went straight upstairs to Kinky's dressing room. Kinky was resplendent in high cowboy drag. He had his Nudie Jesus coat on, the one with the large heads of Christ on the front vents and the sequined cross on the back. Bob Dylan had bought that coat for Kinky, back in 1976, before he had been born again. Kinky was spreading the rumor that now ol' Bob wanted it back. Besides the coat he had on some sequined pants, some two-toned boots made of "fine brontosaurus foreskin" with some gaudy toe-tappers. He was chomping on his ever-present cigar.

"How are you, boys?" Kinky drawled, giving Gresch and Doogie his famous LA finger-snapping handshake. "This here is Chinga Chaven, you'll probably like him, he's a very perverted person. You guys know Corky Laing? He's a world-famous drummer. Ron is probably very heavily into world-famous drummers."

JD and EJ and Mario were ushered in, and the cameraman was set, so the room was hushed up. Then they turned on the kliegs and started shooting.

"I want to check on my lyrics here, see if it rings true, if it's real." Kinky was tuning his guitar. "You might think this song is all bullshit. If you like it, though, maybe I'll make two or three hundred dollars on it."

"Did you write this one with the Eagles or Jackson Down?" JD said.

"Wait a minute, I got to adjust my tampon here." Kinky tightened the capo. "I never practiced this before in my life now. I want to know the truth, though." He turned to the hockey players. "I don't care if Americans love it, I want to hit you guys where you live, right between your nose. Okay, this is a sensitive moment now, it's called 'Skating on Thin Ice.'"

"Is this the song I helped you with?" Gresch asked.

Kinky frowned. "Cute, Greschner." Then he sang:

They say that even Jesus hates a loser
And when you die you go to hockey hell

And when your soul gets sent down there'll be
* the devil skatin' round*
And an interview with Howard Cosell

And Lord you keep on skatin' on thin ice
Just six inches from Paradise
Livin' on the ice, boy, lovin' on the run
And you keep on skatin' on thin ice
Just six inches from Paradise
Written in the stars, boy, meltin' in the sun

Some say he's a jet set gladiator
Some call him a soldier in a bloody silver war
But he's a helluva warrior, he's got a good
* lawyer*
And everytime he crosses that line you can
* hear that Garden roar . . .*

Well he scored again last night out in Vancouver
You might say that it was on a Power Play
He came in close, he shut the light, before
* his teeth came out that night*
In the morning, it was hard to break away . . .

Through Northern lights and Southern lights
* there's someone*
Who warms your heart as you shiver from the cold
But every gypsy, every lover, every dreamer must
* discover*
What you win out on the ice you're gonna lose
* out on the road . . .*

And Lord you keep on skatin' on thin ice
Just six inches from Paradise
Livin' on the ice, boy, lovin' on the run
And you keep on skatin' on thin ice
Just six inches from Paradise
Written in the stars, boy, meltin' in the sun.

"Unbelievable," JD cheered. Everyone was applauding.

"C'mon, Kink," Gresch urged. "Do 'Old Ben Lucas.'" Then the defenseman broke into his favorite Kinky song:

> *Old Ben Lucas has a lotta mucus*
> *Hanging right out of his nose*
> *He'd pick and pick till it made you sick*
> *But back again it grows . . .*

"Well, we certainly have enjoyed this little interchange between the athletes and the musicians this evening." Kinky had switched from his shit-kicking drawl to his effete English accent.

"We're trying to find out which one is which," Gresch said.

Kinky scowled. "I'm still trying to figure out who to fuck to get out of this movie."

• DECEMBER 6

I made two observations the other day. The first was that every time Shero meets the press, while listening to their questions he closes his eyes and touches his thumb to his first two fingertips. According to José Silva, author of the Silva Mind Control Method, this is the emergency method of "going to alpha," for those times when you can't bother with twenty minutes of meditation.

The second observation was that Steve Vickers's pad on his locker-room stall was missing. Everyone else sat on a nice cushy red one, but all Vickers got was hard wood. Was Shero trying to tell him something?

"Sarge doesn't like to be too comfortable between periods," Tkaczuk explained to me. "Didn't you know that? That's why he took the cushion off. He likes to have a hard seat because if he gets too comfortable he gets too lazy on the ice. It's like being in an easy chair. He says, 'Give me something that's hard, then I know I gotta go back and work.' "

If you're wondering whatever happened to good old-fashioned rabbit's feet, don't. Espo's got three of them hanging over *his* stall.

• DECEMBER 8

The hard-on line in *Playboy* was still a hot topic of discussion. Tkaczuk had come over to me after the last game and said he heard that I really "got" Ulfie in *Playboy*. Ulf's wife, Barbro, told me she wouldn't read the article, and every time I saw her lately she gave me the ol' fisheye. But then I heard from the voice of enlightenment: management. The word came from Jack Krumpe, Werblin's right-hand man. They loved the article, hard-on and all. In fact, it was quite useful to a Garden executive's wife. It seems that there was a scramble in front of the net the other game, and it was uncertain whether Nilsson or Vickers had touched the puck before it went in. But the executive's wife knew.

"It's not Ulfie's goal," she told her husband. "I checked his pants."

• DECEMBER 9

The Rangers beat the Islanders 5–4 on a phantom goal that never went in, credited to Anders Hedberg, but the biggest hand of the night was for a banner. It was unfurled at 9:34 of the third period, up on the Eighth Avenue side of the Blue Seats. Its message was short but eloquent: "IS-LANDERS EAT SHIT."

A few people saw it first, then more, and the roar began. In front of me a father turned around and pointed it out to his young son. The kid read it and his eyes lit up and he stood clapping and laughing. On the Ranger bench the guys turned around and cracked up. In fact, the only people who didn't seem to enjoy the banner were the Islanders' GM, Bill Torrey, and the New York press, who scurried home to write articles denouncing the vulgarity of New York fans. Oh, the Garden cops didn't like it too much either. They removed the offensive banner, to a chorus of boos.

But at the buzzer, all there was was cheers. Murdoch was one of the cheerleaders leading the guys in, shouting praises. Bukka brought up the rear. "We want chili, get the chili," he was shouting. And in the press room, Shero was threatening.

His threat stood 5 feet 10 inches, weighed a solid 200 pounds, and went by the name of Frank "Seldom" Beaton. Beaton was a journeyman wing who had been called up from New Haven to provide some sorely needed muscle. Last season, in the Crabapple, Beaton had amassed 319 penalty minutes, which is quite a high total. He also had spent a night in the slammer once, for coldcocking a wiseass gas-station attendant. Beaton was here to protect the Swedes.

At least according to Shero. He dropped the word while answering a question about the abuse the Swedes had been taking.

"It's still about the same," Shero said. "I may be putting Beaton on that line. Then let's see how tough these guys are. The officials aren't going to do anything about it, but I think Beaton could."

"Would Beaton be a deterrent?" someone asked.

Shero seemed to savor the word. "Deterrent, yes, he's a deterrent. He don't have to touch anybody. Nobody went near him in Hartford the other night."

"Ulfie had a pretty good collection of slash marks after the game, though," a reporter said. "Gordie Howe went after him pretty good."

"Well, Beaton might be able to straighten those things out. Listen, when they see a guy who's a known fighter, willing to fight, and he doesn't care if he wins all the fights, then they start thinking twice."

Shero was asked why the refs didn't seem to call penalties against the Swedes. "Well, if we went and played in Sweden and Russia, we'd get the same treatment," he speculated. "I imagine the world is the same all over. Nobody likes a foreigner. What can you do? When it comes to foreigners playing here, we got to almost murder them before they call something."

Naturally the press ran from Shero straight to Beaton and the Swedes. Ulfie, for one, was singularly unimpressed. "I don't know if it's going to solve any problems," Ulf said slowly. "I think we played some good games with Sarge." He paused and stared at my recorder. "I'm afraid of Ratso's tape." Then he went on, "I believe if we go out there and score goals they're not gonna care how much shit I'm taking out there 'cause I like it when I get hit. Then I get mad and play better." He smiled impishly. "But don't hit me *too* hard, just a little bit."

But over on the other side of the room, Vickers was finding the wood harder than ever. "I heard that rumor shit," he said. "Where does that leave me? I'll be sitting again, shit, just when I was starting to get in shape."

"Why do you think Freddie's spreading the rumor?" someone asked.

"I don't know." Sarge was testy. "What am I gonna do, worry about it?" He was.

"I think he wants you to be more aggressive, protect them more," someone suggested.

"I think they're quite capable of defending themselves," Vickers said.

"The press is making this big thing about . . ."

"The press is always trying to make shit," Sarge snapped. "What the hell am I supposed to do? Why did he trade Nick? Nick could have played up with them."

But Nick was gone. Leaving Beaton, who was entertaining the press in the far corner. He was sitting at his stall, wearing only a blue towel. He had his teeth out, revealing a large gap between whatever teeth were left. The impression was one of harnessed ferocity. If he was called, he'd be there, he said, and then we'd see about people roughing up the Swedes.

The press left. I went over to say hello.

"I been watching you on your infrequent shifts," I said. "Nobody goes near you. They give you lots of room."

"Yeah." Beaton smiled, showing the gap. "You noticed that, eh? I wasn't sure if that was the case."

"Freddie said that tonight too."

"He did?" Beaton was proud.

"Yeah, he's been talking to the press for days about you playing with the Swedes," I said.

"It's been scaring the shit out of me." Beaton's eyes widened and he leaned over and whispered, "I can't fucking eat, I can't sleep. Holy fuck, what the fuck am I gonna do if I do get there? Really, two of the most famous players in the world and me struggling along and to hear him say that." Beaton rolled his eyes. "What the fuck, what a pain in the ass."

• DECEMBER 10

Mario Marois has been spending time this season trying to perfect his atrocious English. Whenever he had the chance he and his lovely fiancée, France, had been going to the Berlitz School. To supplement that Nykoluk had given him a

146 ▪

small book of one-liners, and the defenseman was getting dangerous.

"Wat has long 'air and four purple feet?" he asked everyone at his table last night at Charlie O's. "A lion dat makes its own wine." He roared with delight.

"What's two tousand pounds on a stick? A hippopsicle. What did Christopher Columbus say to his men before dey boarded the boat? Men, get on de boat." He was in seventh heaven. "How do you know when you're not wanted?"

Guevremont, who had been quiet, spoke up, "When they put you on waivers."

- DECEMBER 11

The Rangers won in Detroit tonight. Without Murdoch. Oh, he was there but he didn't play because he was suspended. He was suspended because he missed the plane. He missed the plane because he partied all night at Richard Weisman's house after the Islanders game. Of course, a few other Rangers partied that night too, but they made the flight. They just had a faster cab driver.

Guevremont missed the plane too. He was last seen driving to New Haven.

- DECEMBER 16

The Flyers were at the Garden tonight and Dom always gets up for the Flyers. Dom is the mayor of the red seats, a squat, balding hockey fanatic who squirms and stamps and bellows and spends most of the game yelling out insults at the ref and the opposing players. Dom sits by the bend on the Seventh Avenue side, which is just as well because if he sat between the blue lines in Drydock Country, he wouldn't go over too well with his corporate neighbors.

But in his section everyone loves Dom. He kisses the ladies and fusses over the babies and glares at his three big sons anytime one of them crosses the lines of decency and includes a curse word in his verbal barrage at the enemy. Dom is a considerate man. He even brings along Kleenex to wipe his paw marks off the glass whenever he jumps up and sticks his nose through the crack to get within eardrum range.

Which is where he was as soon as Lewis blew the first call against the Flyers. "What about that pig, Daley?" he was screaming at Lewis, his anguish fogging up six square inches of glass. He wiped it off and sat back down. "You're a dope, Bridgman, you pig," he yelled and bounced around his seat like Jello in a windstorm. In front of us Greschner took Clarke into the boards. "Get Clarke, thataway." Dom was up with encouragement. "Hit that pig in the head."

"This is good for me," he said as the play moved up ice. "My wife doesn't allow me to talk at home. But I gotta watch out for cursing. I never want to give them a chance to say, 'Now get the hell out.' I tell my sons not to curse or throw anything. Yell, scream, ridicule them, but don't throw nothing."

Dom, longtime Ranger fan that he was, usually reserved his wrath for the refs or the opponents, but every once in a while he would zero in on a Ranger. "Huckleberry Hodge, we were on him for two years, every game," he said, without taking his eyes off the action up ice. He punctuated the anecdote with a few oohs and aahs and one or two "you pigs." "Every game we'd yell, 'Hodge, how can you play, Huck? You're asleep.' He would just skate past smiling. Then one day he wasn't playing and I said, 'Huck, what the hell is it with you? When you were in Boston with Cashman, you used to hit everybody in sight.' He said, 'You can't do it by yourself.' Then he said, 'Merry Christmas,' and shook my hand, and he told us he was being sent down. I felt so bad, I almost cried for him, what a classy guy.

"And Vickers, ah, we love Vickers. He don't even come near here when we're going good. He takes a look here and his moustache falls off." Dom laughed with delight.

Tonight Dom had a lot to shout about. Bryan Lewis was calling a lousy game, which meant that the Swedes were eating their share of lumber, courtesy of Bridgman and Dupont and Kelly and Linesman and Clark and all the other nice guys that the Flyers ice. Which went a long way toward explaining a twenty-six-game unbeaten streak that the Broad Street Bullies were enjoying, which was just two short of the all-time NHL record.

So Dom was ready for them when they wound up in the corner. It started when Gresch and Kelly tied the puck up in front of him. Moose Dupont, a stubby French-Canadian defenseman, skated in over to them as the whistle blew for a face-off. But Dom was already poised to strike. "Hey, Dopey." He was kissing glass again. "Dopey, c'mere, you too, Kelly, you pig."

Dupont fumed and measured Dom and then spat at the figure behind the glass. But he was sweating too much and he was too dehydrated and he couldn't glob anything up through his gap, so all he could do was resemble a gasless engine sputtering.

Dom was ecstatic. "We got Dopey, we got Dopey." He did a little jig in the aisles as his sons slapped fives. "He tried to spit, Dopey couldn't even spit. I thought Gresch took Kelly's head off. It couldn't happen to a nicer pig." He gloated and sat down. When the play went back up ice, he sprang up and dutifully wiped the glass with his soggy Kleenex.

- DECEMBER 19

Santa came early for Marcus. Tonight the Rangers won, with Gresch and Murder scoring two each. And after weeks of trying, Marcus had finally gained admittance to Charlie O's, disguised in a three-piece suit, and he was making the most of it, hopping from table to table, schmoozing with his heroes. The ultimate lounge lizard.

- DECEMBER 20

At Greschner's house the other night, as we were watching him score his two goals again and again on videotape, and as he was extolling playing with Bubba on defense and Donnie Maloney up front—"the most valuable Ranger"—he also issued a warning. "This team is gonna blow up in a month," he said darkly.

- DECEMBER 22

The Rangers were in Pittsburgh, but I was at Greschner's apartment watching the game with the Greschner family, who were in for the holidays. There was Mum and Dad and his sister Linda and her husband, Don, and her children and his child from a previous marriage, and we were eating cold cuts and wrapping presents and drinking beer and Canadian Club and having a swell time. These were nice people. Salt of the earth.

But one thing was marring this holiday celebration. Ron, the apple of everyone's eye, wasn't getting enough ice time.

And now, when he was on, he got a penalty. This was not pleasant.

"Greschner got a penalty," Dad said, from the couch. Gresch's mum was sitting at his feet on the floor. "C'mon, guys, we gotta win this one," she said, clapping her hands. "I'm a tremendous fan. I'd just die for my son. C'mon, Gresch." She clapped some more. "Do something special for the holidays."

On the screen Pittsburgh was breaking, a two on one, with Vadnais caught up. Faubert scored and Greschner left the penalty box. "Ronnie wasn't on for that one," his mum said. His dad shot her a disapproving glare. "I feel bad for Ronnie," Mum sighed. "He gets blamed."

Mum was finding it hard to recognize her son on the screen. Whenever a defenseman with a small number came on, she thought it was Ron. Dad always managed to correct her. And each shift that Gresch seemed to miss, she was getting more and more morose.

Pittsburgh meanwhile kept swarming, and finally in the third period with ten minutes left, Anderson got around Maloney and scored. "You donkey." Dad was cursing the captain. "Darn right, that's what happened." Mum was fuming.

"Take it easy," Don said.

"What's Gresch supposed to do on the bench, whistle?" Mum said. "That's bullshit."

"Gresch has gotta sweat, they should double shift him," Don said. "We found that out in the juniors."

"My parents used to go two thousand miles to see him play," Linda recalled. "But if his team lost, he wouldn't go to their room to see them."

"They miss Nicky," Don said. "Nicky was good for the team morale. Once after Ron stood up for Nicky, he told Ron he'd always back him up. But I don't like what Shero's doing here. You should go with your best. Freddie's doing a lot of monkey business. Either he's looking at a lot of people or he's playing games."

"He's got to get two goals." Mum was worrying about her son. "He asked us a while back what we want for Christmas and I said seven goals, one for each of us. He's got five since then, he needs two more."

Santa never came. But Gresch did pick up two assists, and Warren Miller converted a Beck pass with four minutes left to eke out a 4–3 win. So later that night after his present, the portable TV, had been wrapped and put under the tree, when he got back from the airport, Gresch was in a good mood. And everyone talked and drank till the wee hours.

• DECEMBER 23

Boston was in, which meant another chippy game. And combined with the benign neglect of referee Greg Madill, who kept turning his back on what appeared to be penalties, all the ingredients for a donnybrook were brewing. But there were no major fisticuffs, just the usual slashes, and trips and hooks, and high sticks, a small percentage of which were being called.

And, as usual, the Swedes were bearing the brunt of many of these minor infractions. Every time Hedberg or Nilsson picked up speed and tried to freewheel, one or another of the Bruins would give them the stick in the ribs or the elbow in the face.

By the middle of the third period, Ulf had had enough. So, as he was skating off the ice deep in his own end on the way to his bench, he passed Secord, a Bruin forward, lined up for the upcoming face-off. With Madill preoccupied with getting the puck from his linesman, Ulf had his chance. With a quick jab of his stick, he sent Secord sprawling ass first to the wet ice. By the time anyone noticed, Ulfie was already sitting. But Secord knew. He had jumped up and shaken off the moisture and looked back to get the perpetrator's number, and then he shook his head in disgust.

Ten minutes later he got his revenge. The buzzer had sounded and the Rangers had fallen short, 4–3, and Nilsson was heading back to console his goalie before the trek to the dressing room. Then, thanks to Secord's leg, he was eating ice chips. But one thing Secord lacked was subtlety. Seconds later, Davidson was flying across the ice and pouncing on the hapless defenseman. It was now an altercation and the fans were going wild and they were pulled down as if by magnets to the boards, watching the fracas.

As altercations go, this was lame. Some pushing and shoving, lots of verbal abuse, a glove or two dropped but no punches. Until Stan Jonathan, a fireplug of a player, ventured too near the sideboards. Suddenly a fan reached over and punched him on the side of the face. Jonathan's stick flashed up and someone grabbed it, and then all hell broke loose.

Terry O'Reilly was the first to go over. Then Peter McNab and Mike Milbury and soon all the Bruins had hurtled over the sideboards and were skirmishing in the stands. It was the height of surrealism. There was O'Reilly pinning down a guy in a suit and Milbury beating him over the head with his own shoe. In the background the chant, "BOSTON SUCKS," had reached deafening proportions. Garbage was streaming down from the upper stands. The Garden security cops were dragging fans past, blood pouring out of gashes onto expensive suits. In the corridor, smoking a Camel, Shero waited patiently.

"I didn't see it," he told the assembled press minutes later when some semblance of order had been restored. What about Secord tripping Nilsson? Didn't see it. Wensink kicking JD earlier in the crease? Didn't see it. Surely he saw the flare up at the end of the game? "I didn't see it. I can't help it if I didn't see it," Fred protested.

One reporter ridiculed the slow response time of the Garden security force. "We have so many security people here it's unbelievable." Shero was a good company man. "You go to the other buildings you see nothing. We threw fifty people out of our dressing room last night. Fifty people! They had no business there. They just walk in the room. They were all bombed out on drugs. And they weren't reporters either." Everyone laughed.

But inside the room Maloney was close to tears. The captain had protested Ulf's mugging to Madill, who was calmly watching the fracas as the game ended, as if he were a spectator. The only penalty Madill finally called was on Maloney, a game misconduct, when the captain slammed his stick on the ice, breaking it in two and brushing the referee in the process.

Dave was sitting at his stall with his head bent. "We both got pretty emotional," he said, his voice cracking. "I tried to question him when EJ went off cut. He explained to Mike that Eddie had been cut before the play, but at the time he put the blame on me and he just didn't treat . . ." His voice trailed off. "You know, name-calling and swearing. It seems like a trivial thing, but it's my job to question him and when I'm told that I don't know what I'm talking about and that I'm an asshole and if I'm right he can kiss my ass, that's not right."

"What happened at the end of the game?" one reporter asked.

"I just questioned him and lost my head," Maloney said.

"Did you have any problems with this ref or others before?"

Maloney laughed ironically. "I've had my share of problems with all refs. I can understand if he made a bad call, but it's no reason for him to call me an asshole." Maloney shook his head, then buried it in a towel.

But JD was still livid. He was standing in front of his stall, wearing a towel, declaiming. "That's the problem with hockey," he boomed. "You got a cheap-shot artist like that and have guys with some finesse that put people in buildings, like the Swedes, and a guy with no class, like Secord, and he just floors him with no reason after the game's over. You tell me, does that make sense? That's brutal. He just suckered him right on his can. Ulfie didn't even see him. Now you tell me, for the betterment of hockey . . . is this All-Star Wrestling or something?"

Davidson had attracted a large audience, including his next-door neighbor, Vadnais, who was watching the proceedings with curiosity, a big cigar dangling from his mouth. "I'm sorry they got in the stands there, I mean what can I do? I didn't start the fucking thing. Secord started it. The Swedes are not gonna take a dive. They'll do anything in hockey but take a dive because everyone thinks the Swedes aren't tough."

Well, Davidson may have gotten lost on his way home off the ice, but the entire Bruin team was now holed up near their dressing room and there was no telling when they might go home. The problem was the three thousand fans, who had spilled out onto Thirty-third Street and were chanting nasty things and blocking the exit ramp, lying in ambush for the big bad Bruins bus. The first reports were that the situation was getting ugly outside and everyone started worrying. Especially Duguay. He was worrying about Cheryl Tiegs, who had been his guest. He had met her the other night at Weisman's, and he told her to come to a hockey game because they were "interesting."

As soon as I heard about the fans, I rushed outside. There were a thousand or so left and they were massed outside

Charlie O's, drinking beer and chanting "BOSTON SUCKS." Across the street another contingent was screaming "LARRY BROOKS SUCKS." Brooks, a *Post* writer, whose specialty was the Islanders, had recently written a snotty column condemning the "obscenity" of these fans.

I crossed the street. The Chief was there with his headdress and he was doing some ritualistic step in tune to the chant. As soon as he told a few of them I was a writer, I was surrounded. "Those reporters are full of shit," one kid said. "I work in that building. Those refs suck. Every game it gets out of control. You see what they've been doing to the Swedes lately? Punching the shit out of them, elbowing them, and nothing gets called." Everyone shouted approval.

"I want to defend the fans," the Chief screamed. Suddenly they were chanting his name. "CHIEF, CHIEF, CHIEF." They dragged him up the steps and stood him on a marble overhang, and the Chief spoke.

"The game was fixed tonight," he said in a shrill voice, one finger punctuating the night air. "THE GAME WAS FIXED, THE GAME WAS FIXED," the masses echoed.

"They let the Bruins climb over the wall like that into the stands there," another kid said with disgust. "Our guys just watched. They're a bunch of faggots. If the Rangers went into the stands in Boston, they would have gotten their asses kicked. Our fucking security goes and beats up on the fans. What the fuck is Terry O'Reilly using his stick on the fans for? Let him and McNab come out here and try that shit." Everyone echoed approval.

"What wrong with the Rangers?" his friend said. "We pay their living. Man, the Rangers didn't do shit, they suck."

Just then, four police cars took off with their sirens blaring and tore the wrong way down Thirty-third Street. "That's a ruse to get us away so the bus can come out," one kid screamed. "It's bullshit."

"BULLSHIT, BULLSHIT." They were ecstatic now, the

Chief leading them in the chant from his perch. "Is this America or Nazi Germany?" he screamed to the crowd below. "What are we gonna do about the refereeing? We should write to John Ziegler, the president of the NHL. Madill should be fired. Every policeman here should be fired," the Chief paused dramatically, "and the Mayor of the City of New York should resign." He waved his arms with a flourish at the end.

"JUMP, CHIEF, JUMP," a new chant went up. After a while the fans wandered away and I headed for Charlie O's. And there was Marcus, calmly sitting at a window table, wearing a suit, munching delicately on a hamburger.

Amazingly enough, Marcus had in the past few weeks befriended Krumpe and his wife, Kitty. And the young fan had been visiting the executive in his office, getting scoops on what's what with his team. In return, Marcus had done small things for the exec. Like running over between periods of the game after Soetaert had returned precipitously and asking him for an autograph. "He's depressed, it'll boost his morale," Krumpe told his soldier. "But don't let on I sent you."

This was too much. Two weeks ago Marcus was a maniac, wearing his EJ uniform, banging on the window of Charlie O's like an extra from *The Night of the Living Dead*. And now he ate while his brothers and sisters were in the streets, dealing with the Man's injustice.

I called him out. "You sellout," I fumed. "You're not on the street anymore. Go ahead, eat, you pig. You'll be just like the rest of them, asskissing management, contemptuous of the true fan, sipping designer water with Sonny, writing bullshit. You've turned into a monster, Marcus. If Hunter Thompson were here, he'd poke your eyes out with a salad fork. You're a sellout. And at your age too." I shook my head sadly. "You've lost it."

"Shhh." Marcus silenced me, glancing furtively over

toward Sonny's table. "I'm not going out there." Marcus turned and looked out at the whooping fans. "You're not gonna get me in trouble with management." Then he turned his back to the window and resumed eating.

• DECEMBER 27

Shero hadn't been seeing much lately. He didn't see tonight's exhibition game against the Russians. He didn't see this game because he didn't see a shoe on the floor of his house the other night. He fell on the shoe and tripped and hit his chest against the side of a table and fractured some ribs. That's what he got for Christmas.

The Rangers got a drubbing. They scored first, a typical Vickers goal. He was parked in the left of the crease, and the puck shot from the point hit his leg and tricked in. But then it was all Russkies. They were amazing, throwing the puck around at will, crisscrossing on the wings, snapping shots before the disk seemed to even reach their sticks. They romped.

But this was an exhibition game and it was interrupting the guys' holidays and nobody on the Rangers seemed to give a shit. Espo was the first to walk off the ice, and he was singing. Maloney was the last, and he was whistling "Silver Bells."

Later I met Gresch, and we went to the Hall of Fame room to pick up his folks, then we all headed to Little Italy for dinner. I suggested Luna's, a modest, family-type restaurant on Mulberry Street, and everyone loved the food and Louie, the Mexican waiter who was once with the circus. We drank a lot of house wine and ate the delicious garlic bread, and everyone told their favorite story about Ron in juniors.

"Not a bad day for the Russians, eh?" I said. "They won the game and took Afghanistan."

"Smell this hand." Gresch suddenly put his left hand out. "Now smell this one." He offered the other. I couldn't tell the difference. "This is the one I used to shake hands with the Russians. Smell the difference? I'm just glad they're Commies, though. If they came over here, they'd put two hundred people out of a job."

Gresch's mum was making plans to videotape all the Rangers' games, and she asked me to clip articles for her complete Greschner scrapbook. Ron had been clipping but lately he was getting derelict. However, Gresch was too busy singing the praises of Bubba to hear.

"Is it great playing with him?" Gresch gushed. "If anyone goes near you, Bubba cruises over to them and says, 'Touch him and I'll take your fucking eyes out.' He's not too big, eh? That was a great trade, getting Bubba."

Speaking of trades, Murder's name came up again. "Murder might be better off being traded," Greschner said softly. "Vad and Maloney are on his case all the time."

• DECEMBER 29

Hitch got traded again. This time he was going home to Toronto.

• DECEMBER 30

The Chief was getting ready. The second period was almost over, so he reached in his shopping bag and began to pull his old Ranger jersey over his head. I strolled over to say hello.

"Welcome to the Blue Seats," he announced. He pulled a Wise potato-chip bag out of his shopping bag and offered me some. "We don't use profanities in this section," he assured me. "Did I ever show you that picture of Walt Tkaczuk?" He reached down into his bag and pulled out the shot. It was a picture of a naked woman, with Tkaczuk's face superimposed. The Chief chuckled and filed it.

We walked down the stairs through the upper press box, the Chief en route to his appointed duties, me to visit with Beaver. She was stunning tonight in a chocolate-brown leather jumpsuit. "Can you believe this, Ratso?" She smiled seductively. "John got me this for Christmas. I couldn't believe it, that's not him. He's got pretty good taste, though."

"Good game, eh?" I was content with the 4–1 lead over the Capitals.

"It makes me mad," Beaver flared. "They play so damn good now. They play like shit when John's in goal."

But less than three minutes into the third period, Lehtonen scored a soft goal and suddenly it was 4–2. Vadnais skated back to the bench in disgust. "What's he trying to do, get them back in the game?" he bitched about Baker. JD told him to shut up.

The Rangers hung on and Vickers got number sixteen and everyone was happy in the dressing room. Except for Vadnais, who was moaning about a statistic he felt was inaccurate. "This fucking ting suck." He threw the stat sheet back on the table. "Every fucking game, it's the same story. Here's the Rangers' tird goal, they got three and twenty-six on ice, both guys play the same fucking side. They can't be on the fucking ice at the same time. Dere's no fucking way. I'm on the ice with Dave dere and this one here. I just got off the fucking ice and Gresch was coming on, but I lose the plus. What the fuck is that guy doing up dere? I wish I'd meet that cocksucker one of dese days."

Duguay was upset too. Nykoluk had just informed him that he would have to go to all the optional practices from then on in. "He said it seems like I'm not working," Doog said sarcastically. He was also miffed because they had forgotten to add an assist on one of the goals.

In Charlie O's, though, everything was right with the world. The groupies were clustered around the bar, sneaking anxious looks into the dining area, trying to cop a glance at a Ranger. Sonny was at his table, with his happy entourage. And Marcus, sitting with me and Anders and his wife and the Krumpes, was in seventh heaven. "This is unbelievable," he whispered to me, waving at the same time to Baker's wife, Rosie, at the next table. In front of him were the remains of the thirty flowers that he had brought for each Ranger wife and girl friend.

"I broke up with my girl friend." he said, without a trace of sorrow. "She told me it was her or the Rangers." Just then a lovely young thing paraded by in Sasson jeans. Anders smiled. "Do you have an open marriage? Do you cheat on Gun-Marie?" Marcus was all over him.

Anders smiled again. "You have to appreciate what God created," he laughed.

"Hedberg," Marcus trilled, "Hedberg, Hedberg." He went back to his cheeseburger. "I had the strangest dream last night. I dreamed my girl friend was naked in bed on the top of the sheets and Beck was sleeping over at my house. I was changing the sheets for him. There's something called gestalt, it's like my girl friend represented Bubba. I think I wanted to have sex with him in the dream. That's all I can figure."

We finished eating, and then I took him to Oren and Aretsky, then to Herlihy's till closing. He was staying at a hotel tonight so he could catch the Capitals in their hotel in the morning before they left town. He had his microcassette all loaded. But first he had to get through this night. He did it by talking to the one with the one black glove, and three others. They routinely made the circuit from Charlie O's to

Herlihy's. So they were all sitting together at a side table in Herlihy's, oblivious to the models, actresses, lawyers, and stockbrokers surrounding them. Oblivious even to Bubba, who had strolled in at about two with Gresch and Doogie. At three forty-five Glenn threw the lights up and Marcus blinked. "This place sucks," he decided. "I can't believe this." He looked out at the bar. "They can't be Bubba's people." The girl with the black glove agreed and nodded her head gravely.

• DECEMBER 31

JD, Doog, and Murder were sitting on the trainer's table in the big room at the practice rink, gossiping. Beaton came over, nude from the waist up, and flexed his stomach muscles.

"Look at these ripples," he said, striking a Mr. Universe pose.

"That's ugly," JD said with mock disgust. "There's no stories there. No beer halls to bullshit about."

"Doogie used to look like that," Murder cracked. Ronnie blushed and pulled his stomach in.

"Did you hear about Nicky the other night?" JD began to talk about his friend, Fotiu. "It was four to two Philly after two in Hartford, and Nicky came into the room and he started throwing sticks, saying, 'You gutless bastards,' stuff like that. They go out and score two and tie four-four. After the game Keon and Howe went up and shook Nicky's hand and said, 'Thanks for the point.' He's the best." JD paused and looked around the room. "Right here, he's the best. He's the best in airplanes too. Airplanes are a real drag now."

After a while Doog, Murder, and I headed back to the city. Tonight was New Year's Eve and they wanted to do some last-minute shopping for their outfits. There was a team party to go to, out in Westchester, but that was only a token appearance. They would stay there a few minutes and then limo it back to the Apple for the main event, a $150-a-couple gathering at Oren and Aretsky.

"Did you hear that Bubba was turned away twice at Herlihy's by the new doorman?" I said. "I wouldn't want to be that guy if Bubs got mad."

"How about Gresch at Studio?" Doog said. "He went there the other night with his dad and mom and Marc wasn't there and Rubell threw them out. Wait till I see that little jerk off."

"Yeah, but the next day he sent Gresch a bottle of Dom Perignon with an apology when Marc told him what he'd done." I laughed. "What a schmuck."

"Did you see that ring Maloney gave Vicki?" Murdoch said. The captain had announced his engagement to his girl friend, and the wedding was set to be in June. "It had to be five grand."

"That's a lot of money," Doog said.

"Fuck, he doesn't spend any money." Mud shrugged. "He told me he's got over four hundred thousand dollars saved. Hey, how about Cheryl Tiegs at Weisman's the other night? You should have seen the slit dress she had on, Ratso. Fuck, when she got up I wanted to eat her seat."

We arrived at Murdoch's apartment, parked the car, and took a cab to pick up their tuxedos at Jean Paul Germain's.

But on that same block, they ran into their girl friends, who were on their own shopping spree, carrying the boys' plastic. Murder was quick to check.

"Sure, I used the card." Murder's girl friend smiled. "There was no problem. I just signed your name. You're gonna kill me when you see what I got, but it was on sale. Look, isn't it beautiful?" She pulled a garment out of her bag, and Doogie's girl friend admired it anew. Murdoch seemed uninterested. "What can I do, I have a hole in this pocket." She patted the plastic. The girls giggled and went off to spend more money.

"I can't figure out how women shop," Doogs was puzzled. "They start with the big things, then they forget the little things. Like shampoo. Then they tell you what they bought when you're home, in bed, just ready to come." Ron shook his head in awe.

We entered Bloomingdale's. Murdoch was looking for accessories and Duguay had an appointment with his hair stylist. As we entered, three gays sashayed out. Doogie hesitated. "If I get attacked just once, I'm leaving," he lisped petulantly.

Inside Murdoch grabbed a down vest, on impulse.

"Not bright enough," Doog counseled.

Murder scampered back with a corduroy one. "That one looks really good," Ron screamed, and Murdoch shook his head and joined the line at the cashier.

"Hey, Donnie," Doog shouted across the room, turning heads, "anybody know you're here? Don Murdoch." Just then, a tall, striking black woman walked by wearing a chic padded-shoulder outfit and a small bellhop cap with a strap beneath her chin. "She looks like the little chimpanzee that collects money on the corner." Doog laughed.

He pointed out some more gays who giggled by us. "Fuck me, there's so many fags in this world," he marveled. "That's good, though. More girls for us, Rats." Murder returned and we started off to find the hair salon. "I need a good conditioning." Doog patted his curly locks. "So I don't look like a deadhead."

But Murdoch couldn't keep his eyes off the women. "There's lots of dirty-looking ladies here," he whispered under his breath. "Look at that one. I'd like to put my finger right up her ass." He looked somewhat incongruous wearing his new vest and carrying his new shoes in a little plastic bag. On the escalator we passed the lingerie level. "Here's where I'd like to hang out," Mud said longingly.

We left Doogie in the salon with the mannequin heads with the neon hair and the High Tech baskets that masqueraded as chairs, and bolted. "What a zoo," Murdoch sneered as we hit the midday traffic on Lexington.

"What you think of the *Voice* article?" The current issue featured an article on the single Rangers which had caused much controversy in the parochial ice hockey world by suggesting that some of the single guys might get laid from time to time. Murdoch, being one of the single guys, was featured prominently. Especially in the section that contained verbatim dialogue from the women's room in Charlie O's.

"How about that part with the chick in the bathroom going 'I want to fuck Murdoch'?" Mud said. "Do lots of people read *The Village Voice?*"

I nodded yes.

Murdoch smiled. "I wanna fuck Murdoch," he repeated, and then went upstairs for his power nap.

• JANUARY 1

Everyone had a good time last night. The Westchester Rangers had a good time at their New Year's Eve party and the NYC Rangers made a brief stop in Westchester, then got convoyed back to the city and had a good time at their party. Such a good time that a few of them just plumb forgot to go back to Westchester this morning. For practice.

• JANUARY 2

The Rangers were in Quebec. The game ended up tied 3–3, but the big story was the premiere of the Sasson commercial. There was Anders and Phil and Davie and Doog cavorting around, doing a Rockette leg-pumping chorus line, shaking their denimed tushes. It was very bizarre. "Jesus, is that embarrassing," my girl friend said. "What is this world coming to?" I shrugged. "I bet the Canadiens are laughing their asses off," she decided.

• JANUARY 6

All was not well. Freddie was still holed up in Westchester with his cracked ribs and his return was uncertain. What's worse, Ulf Nilsson was in the hospital suffering from an undiagnosed neck affliction. According to Dr. Liebler, the Rangers' medicine man, he'll be laid up in the hospital for four or five days to get rest and "possibly traction" for a sprain that has been bothering him for some time now.

Then, to make things worse, at 14:40 of the second period of the Atlanta game, JD stuck his head in front of a fierce shot from Gary Unger. He fell to the ice like he was shot. Hedberg was the first to reach him, then trainer Nick Garen ran out on the ice. Baker leaped over the sideboards to cheers.

"Stay on your feet, you won't get hurt," someone yelled. After a few minutes, Davidson was helped up, but he was too woozy to get off unassisted. Maloney and Beck each grabbed an arm and they slowly skated off. Up in the yellow seats Beaver ran down to check on her husband. Apart from an awfully sore jaw, he was all right. "Too bad," Mario said later. "JD won't be able to kiss his wife for a couple of weeks."

So the Rangers were lucky to get away with a 5–5 tie. They traded hat tricks too—Don Maloney for the Rangers and Kent Nilsson for the Flames. Nilsson was another flashy Swede. For Anders it was a reunion as the two walked down the corridor after the game on the way to Charlie O's for some beers.

Anders introduced me to Kent. "Ratso here is the guy that wrote that article in *Playboy* on Shero," Anders smiled sagely.

Nilsson laughed. "I get a hard-on too," he said.

Later, in Charlie O's, the Chief cornered me. It was almost three now and he was standing by the bar, looking sad. "What's wrong, Chief?" I asked. He was in plainclothes, without his headdress, and he was balding. He looked very frail.

He talked at my tape recorder. "It's 1980 now, a New Year, and I just want to say that most of the fans that I come in contact with are very nice, I'd say nine out of ten, but there's one in ten, I want the lady here to close her ears when I say this." Francesca, the hatcheck girl turned modestly away. "They can go . . . well, do some things to themselves. First of all, I'm always hit with objects like pretzels or beer containers or ice-cream cups. My feathers are always being plucked, somebody's always trying to grab them."

"Why?" I wondered.

"Because they're either trying to be funny or are trying to hurt me, and when I fell tonight everybody was laughing . . ."

"You fell?" I interrupted.

"I hurt my back tonight." The frail Chief rubbed the spot. "I slipped on a beer in front of 127. One foot went one way and the other went the other way, and I twisted myself and I landed on my right hip, and, I don't know how I did this, I also landed on my left, what is this bone here, on the base of my left hand? Anyway, so when I fell . . ."

"I'll get you, Chief," a tough-looking kid sauntered over and then walked out. The Chief sighed. "That guy. I'm going to have to start lifting weights. So, when I fell several people were laughing. I went to the medical room just to make sure."

"Ranger fans were laughing at you?"

"Ranger fans," he nodded sadly. "I really don't need that. Ranger fans. I don't care what they are. I've been doing this for eight years. This is my twenty-fifth year as a Ranger fan. Eight years I've done this. I had a small headdress when I started out. And now I think the time . . . well, maybe another year or two. Right now, I'm interviewing prospective successors. Someone that has to meet my criteria. The character will continue."

"You mean you're hanging up your headdress?" I couldn't resist.

The Chief smiled. "I'm going to step out and become the Chief Emeritus. I'm serious. I haven't found anyone yet. No two people are alike, you know. Finding a carbon copy of me would be difficult. I think when I'm forty—I'm thirty-five now—I'll give it up." He gave Francesca his claim ticket, and she handed him his shopping bag. The headdress peeked sadly out of one corner.

"Unless I'm paid by that time," he added and then he waved good-bye and headed for the A train to Brooklyn.

• JANUARY 7 AFTERNOON

I called Ulf in the hospital.

ULF: I feel the same, Rats. When I move my head down, I get like electric shocks. They got me in a brace. I'm going to get more X-rays. Wayne's right across the hall, so it isn't too bad. And Kent came up and visited me yesterday.

ME: They miss you out there.

ULF: You think so?

ME: There's a lot of problems.

ULF: You know, none of the city guys have come up to visit us. That's bad. I don't really care, but you think they could at least stop by with a six-pack. John Davidson called, he said he's coming by. That's the problem with this team. We don't care enough for one another. You have to help one another.

• JANUARY 7 EVENING

Maybe I was paranoid, but it seemed to me that everytime the press asked Nykoluk about when Freddie would be back, Nykoluk made a veiled reference to Shero's "drinking problem." Tonight, after the Rangers beat Nicky and his Hartford teammates 5–2 in a ho-hum affair, the assistant was asked about Fred's return.

"Like he says he's most comfortable when he's crawling around on his hands and knees," Mike said, biting on a fat cigar. "So you can all get down on your hands and knees and talk to him." The other night, when asked the same thing, he said Fred was still "staggering" around.

Shero's alleged problem had been whispered about all year. It was well known that Fred liked to imbibe. Last year, when I interviewed Maloney after the Cup finals, he told me he'd seen Shero "sneak into the odd gin mill there in the morning." He also told me that Keating loved to relate the story about the time Shero was coaching in Winnipeg. He told the owner that he was there to teach the players how to play hockey. And if they wanted to discuss their problems with him he'd be available every afternoon. In the bar across the street from the rink.

There was also a bartender in Cherry Hill. New Jersey, I ran across once who claimed that Shero used to frequent his bar every afternoon when he was coaching in Philly. He'd sit around in silence and drink beer till it got dark and then he'd depart, but not before leaving a twenty-five-cent tip. In my *Playboy* article McEwen recollected the first time he had seen Shero show any real emotion. It was coming home on the bus from a game in Philly. Shero was furious. He was furious because there was no beer on the bus. Fred checked every niche for beer, and when he couldn't come up with a can, he ordered the driver to stop and fill up.

They were also whispering about Murdoch. Of course, labels are hard to live down, and every time the kid would mess up on the ice, or in practice, the rumors started flying. And although Donnie had been scoring lately, including his twentieth goal tonight, there was still the speculation that he was backsliding. Of course, missing planes and coming late to practice don't do much to scotch those rumors.

But tonight Murdoch was ebullient. Scoring twenty goals is like hitting .300 in baseball, and there was still time to shoot for forty. At any rate, it was better than sitting out. "I'm not panicking around the nets." Murdoch was standing in his long johns, sipping on a beer. "I'm starting to get a couple of two-goal games. It was hard tonight, though. These guys put us to sleep. We were joking on the bench. I had to put up with listening to Bignose there." He pointed a bony finger at Esposito.

Just then Boxcar walked by. Hospodar was rapidly gaining a reputation around the league as a tough hard-nosed fighter. But it didn't seem to jibe with his sweet off-ice disposition. I asked him about it.

"I'm a nice guy, Ratso," he said ingenuously. "I don't know. I just play a rough style of hockey. Sometimes something happens, it certainly is some sort of change. I'm not afraid. I've never been afraid in my life, why should I start now?" He straightened out his cowlick.

"I shouldn't say I'm not afraid, though," he mused. "Every game I play I'm afraid. I'm afraid 'cause you never know what's going to happen. But I never backed down from anybody and I'm not going to start now."

"What do you mean you're afraid every game?" I asked.

"I'm afraid of the game," he said, "what can happen. Afraid of losing."

"Are you afraid of other players?"

"Sure. I hear everybody. Even my winger going up and down. In that way I'm afraid, I don't want him to score."

Bubba came by and we went down to Charlie O's. The big defenseman was in one of his black moods, and after a beer he left for home. Marcus was concerned.

"Does Bubba still like me?" He was worried. "I know Murder doesn't. But Bubs used to kiss me. I haven't been over once yet to his house, I'm proud of myself. Hey, Frankie, Mrs. Beaton. How's the house?" He waved across the room.

"Did you give Ruby a quickshot the other night?" I was talking like a hockey player.

Marcus's eyes widened. "What shot?"

"You know, put the bone in her."

"I'm not that type of person," he protested. "What do you take me for? I won't take advantage of a girl."

Marcus caught the train to Long Island and I went up to Herlihy's. Tonight there was a large turnout. There was Murdoch and Greschner and some Westchester singles, Don Maloney and Warren Miller. And there were some other rather large *homo sapiens* there too. About half the Hartford team. Which did not exactly please most of the Rangers.

Greschner wasn't complaining, though. In fact, he was standing in the front of the bar, having a great time talking to a Hartford player. Of course, the Hartford player happened to be Nicky Fotiu.

"I'm coming back," Nicky told Gresch. They were both feeling no pain.

"It's dead without you," Gresch said. "I go to practice every day, it's the same thing."

"I'd shake it up." Nicky smiled, a huge smile. His face was so big and round that the guys called him Pieface. "I was gonna pie JD in the warm-ups."

"Jesus, with you and Bubba, nobody would go near me." Gresch was savoring the thought. "Hell, I'd score forty."

"You should have seen us play Philly the other day," Nicky said. "Holmgren wouldn't go near me. Listen, get rid of those two guys and I'll be back."

"It wasn't them, it was the management," Gresch said. "They made a mistake and they know it."

"I'll be back," Nicky repeated. "I hope before the play-offs."

"We got a tough kid," Gresch said. "Hospodar." "They said I took too many cheap penalties. I only got twenty-four minutes this year," Nick boasted. "I'll be back. Krumpe and Werblin call me all the time. The other night I got home, Leslie said that Werblin was trying to get me all night. I'm either three weeks or a season away from coming back."

"I hope." Gresch bought a round of beers. "You don't seem happy out there."

Nicky frowned. "My uniform's too small. I'm playing like I'm dead out there. But tonight I kept telling myself, how could I hit these guys?"

• JANUARY 8

I told Murdoch about Ulf's complaint, and he went to visit the center in the hospital the other day. As he was walking toward Ulf's room, he saw two nurses leaving. One was shaking her head. "I can't believe it," she told her colleague. "That patient told me that if I would only jump on his bones, he'd be a lot better."

• JANUARY 14

Some people find Colorado Rockies coach Don Cherry delightful. He's glib, he dresses with as much care as a Detroit pimp, and he has a cute bulldog named Blue that he lavishes much attention on. McEwen had been singing his praises ever since the trade because Cherry was more demonstrative than Shero, more emotional. His charisma extended to the local press too. Word had it that whatever Grapes wanted, Grapes got printed. He would not only answer questions but suggest them. He was a character, in a sport that lacked many of them.

Others found him boorish. Arrogant. Provincial. Everyone would agree that he was highly opinionated. Tonight he had some very vocal opinions. His Rockies had just tied the Rangers 6–6, and he was standing in the dressing-room corridor natty in a three-piecer, exchanging some good-natured words with Vadnais and Esposito as they trouped into the room to change. Grapes waited for an audience and then he began his press conference right in the hall.

"I want to know first if we treated the Swedes all right. That's the big thing, treat the Swedes right?" He began by asking his own question. Sarcasm dripped off each word. "Tim," he addressed Moriarity, a longtime, well-respected hockey writer, "did we treat the Swedes okay?"

"I guess so." Moriarity was embarrassed.

"Acceptable to New York standards?" Cherry continued. "We all got to know, we don't want to be chastised like the Bruins."

"Only one was playing tonight," someone pointed out.

Cherry ignored him. "It looked like we had a bunch of Swedes there," he said in a mock sing-song Swedish accent. "That's all I want to know. The big thing in hockey today" —he was declaiming like a barrister now, holding his thumbs in his vest pockets—"is when you come to New York if you treat the Swedes right, you're a wonderful club. I thought we treated them rather fairly tonight. You wouldn't want to be like the big bad Bruins? I think the Bruins have lost here once in the last four years, is that right, Tim?"

"I guess so." Moriarity didn't relish his role.

"Well, all I want to know, and nobody's answered me, if we treated them well tonight by the standards of New York writers. Maybe the guys that write that aren't here. We got special rules for nationality and others, a bunch of crap but . . ." Cherry paused and jettisoned his act. "It was a nice comeback anyway," he said softly.

Dead air. "Eh, c'mon, what am I, Rudyard Kipling here?" Cherry protested loudly. "Ask me a question, c'mon."

"What was the ruckus at the end of the game?" A voice floated up from the rear of the press pack.

"Well, I think that someone said something disparaging to one of the Swedes." Grapes was bitter. "And I'll chastise him as quickly as I can, because everyone knows there's two sets of rules in North America. One for the Swedes and one for the Canadians and Americans, and I'll chastise him severely for even thinking of saying anything or taking them out like the big bad Bruins. I just went through this routine, but I'm polishing it up." He smiled sweetly.

"Somebody said something to Beck."

"Someone said something to Beck?" Cherry raised an eyebrow. "I don't know why they said it to him. I thought he got a hell of a goal. He's gonna be a dandy."

The questions died down. "I thought it was a stroke of genius putting Sheehan on the left wing. You guys never mention anything I do right," Cherry prompted. Sheehan, the former Ranger who was the throw-in on the Beck deal, set up the tying goal. "He's a good little guy, and as far as that problem he's supposed to have, I've never seen it since I've been here and I guess the problem was drinking and maybe I'm in the bar with him half as stiff and I never notice it. When two guys are drunk, they never notice the other guy's drunk, maybe that's it." Cherry shrugged.

"He hasn't fallen down and broken any ribs, has he?" Norm MacLean cracked. Everyone snickered.

174 ▪

"Ooohoh." Cherry laughed. "I won't touch that with a ten-foot pole."

"Have you developed the same camaraderie with this club as the Bruins?" a radio man asked.

"Well, I gotta weed out a couple of more guys and it'll be just the same thing. The only trouble with this club is they can't drink like the Bruins. But neither can I anymore, I'm getting old. Okay, everybody get the Swedish thing?" Cherry opened the locker-room doors to the waiting deadliners.

The pack scurried in and searched for ex-Rangers. DeBlois, a massive bull of a guy, was leaving the shower, dripping wet. McEwen was already pulling on his street clothes.

Someone asked the inevitable question about Cherry. "We got really great communication," Q said. "Cherry's probably one of the best coaches I've had in my lifetime. With Grapes there's a lot of communication and a lot of emotion. He's always behind you, trying to pick you up. He gets pissed off at you if you're not doing well, happy for you if you are."

"Could you get pissed at him?"

McEwen smiled. "No, every time I do I think about how much I love him. Of course, when he yells and screams you might, but thirty seconds later you're thinking about how great the guy is. That's just the way he is and he should get pissed off at you if you're not doing the job."

In the Ranger locker room, Duguay was also rapidly dressing. He was hurrying because jet-set photographer Peter Beard was waiting for him in Charlie O's. Peter had a nice collage that he and his girl friend, Cheryl Tiegs, had made for the superstar, vintage Beard with elephants and Tieg's leg, and it was signed "Best Wishes from Africa, Peter and Cheryl, fans forever." In return, all Doogie would have to do would be to sign Peter's diary book.

Duguay signed. "I wish I would have scored a fucking goal."

The shit was hitting the fan for Murdoch. On the ice he was the hottest Ranger. Nine goals his last eleven games, twenty-two goals in forty-four games to date. But off the ice he was messing up. He was coming to practices too wasted to tie up his skates. Last night he got to the Garden during warm-ups, and he kept getting everyone's name wrong. Then early in the game he injured his back and was sent to Lenox Hill Hospital.

Gresch and Doogie and Bubba had all been talking to him, trying to get him to drink less and hang out less, but maybe it was the loneliness, or maybe it was the pressure, or maybe it was the trade rumors, but, whatever, he'd still make the bar scenes and then after bartime, more likely than not, he'd hunt up an after-hours club. By then he was a lone Ranger.

People were talking about getting him help. It was all talk, of course, but I had broached the subject with Kenny Aretsky, and Aretsky was going to talk to Esposito. When I suggested professional help, Aretsky blanched.

"You've got to understand, Ratso, that you're dealing with a mentality. They're all the same mentality. And that's what you're up against. It's a big thing to be up against. I spoke to Murdoch about going to see a shrink, and he looked at me like I was crazy. If he ever told anybody he went to see a shrink, they'd think he was a fucking lunatic. So you're dealing with a very difficult mentality."

I talked to Joey Bucchino, the trainer. He felt Murdoch was gone.

ME: Bukka, what are we going to do about Murder?

BUKKA: Oh man, he's history, you know. No one wants to help him anymore. They stopped helping this kid. They gave up.

Ron Duguay on Broadway. Note the cover boy in the background. (BRUCE BENNETT)

Coach Fred Shero (BRUCE BENNETT)

Ron Greschner (BEVERLY CUSIMANO)

John and Diana "Beaver" Davidson (BEVERLY CUSIMANO)

A wary Sonny Werblin confers with Phil Esposito. (RAY AMATI)

Nick Fotiu meets his public. (BEVERLY CUSIMANO)

Steve and Joanne Vickers (BEVERLY CUSIMANO)

Don Murdoch (RAY AMATI)

Mr. and Mrs. Dave Maloney share a laugh. (RAY AMATI)

The goaltenders: Steve Baker, John Davidson, Doug Soetaert (BEVERLY CUSIMANO)

Ulf and Barbro Nilsson
(BEVERLY CUSIMANO)

*Anders and Gun-Marie
Hedberg* (BEVERLY CUS-
IMANO)

Mario and France Marois (BEVERLY CUSIMANO)

What'd she say? Espo and wife Donna in Sasson drag (RAY AMATI)

(Top left) *The Chief in costume* (PHOTOGRAPH COURTESY OF BOB "THE CHIEF" COMAS) (Top right) *Barry Beck and Penthouse Pets cavort off the ice at a lingerie fashion show at Magique.* (BRUCE BENNETT) (Above) *The defense: Tommy Laidlaw, Ron Greschner, Barry Beck* (BEVERLY CUSIMANO)

(Top left) *Pat Hickey and then-girl friend (now wife) Debbie Page* (BEVERLY CUSIMANO) (Top right) *Bubba and Robert Marcus in the Ranger dressing room. Boxcar adds his two cents.* (LARRY SLOMAN) (Above) *Don Maloney* (BEVERLY CUSIMANO)

Ron Duguay and his sweetheart from Canada (she's the one on the left)
(RAY AMATI)

Dave Maloney scores at the Electric Circus. (RAY AMATI)

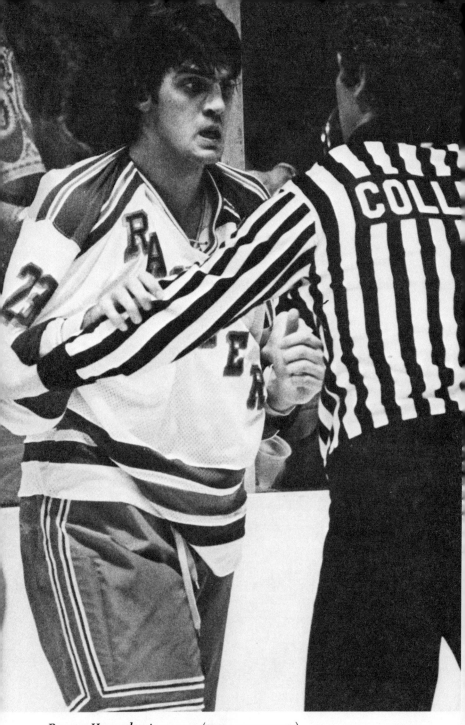

Boxcar Hospodar in a rage (BRUCE BENNETT)

(Top) *John Davidson* (the goalie) *sings at the Lone Star Café with pal Kinky Friedman.* (BEVERLY CUSIMANO) (Above left) *Why is this man smiling?* (BEVERLY CUSIMANO) (Above right) *Esposito signs a fan's back.* (BEVERLY CUSIMANO)

Murdoch witnesses another Espo goal. (BRUCE BENNETT)

Joey Bucchino and Director of Operations Craig Patrick (BEVERLY CUSIMANO)

Ratso and Bubba (BEVERLY CUSIMANO)

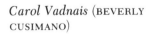

Carol Vadnais (BEVERLY CUSIMANO)

Eddie Johnstone signs autographs as wife Sue watches. Note the Chief broadcasting at left. (BEVERLY CUSIMANO)

Tennis star John McEnroe visits pal Ron Duguay in Ranger locker room. (RAY AMATI)

ME: They never helped the guy. How has the guy been helped? Has he ever been sent to a therapist?

BUKKA: He's been told. He won't go. He's been set up with the best in New York, Ratso. *He will not go.* I'll tell you one thing, he was fucked up last night. And today Dave Maloney turned around and said to a few players that Murder's gonna be history.

ME: Sure the players gave up on him. They're not professional therapists. But there are people who can help him. Otherwise, he's gonna be on the Derek Sanderson express. Shero understands. He's not afraid of psychiatrists or Ph.D.'s. Those labels won't bother him.

BUKKA: Shero does not want to know about this. Shero does not want hassles. Shero doesn't know what's going on. He finds out about this guy, he'll get rid of him as fast as you can say Bukka. Do you know when Ronnie Duguay missed the plane, and this is confidential, he got disciplined the next game not to play? Do you know what Freddie was told by Mike? That he had a pulled groin. All right.

ME: What would have happened if Freddie had been told he missed the plane?

BUKKA: He would have been traded. I'm telling you. And with Murdoch he'll say let's get rid of him. I called the kid. I'm always calling him, I'm always pushing the fucking clock back for him. I'm telling him to smarten up, because these guys, not only management, his own goddamn players, are trying to give it to him. But this kid cannot be controlled. Ratso, let me tell you something. I would go out on a limb for this kid. I would lie, I would cheat, I would steal, everything to get him honest. I defend him to the utmost. But it's not fair. I'm not talking against the kid. But you got guys on this team working their ass off, for example, Eddie Johnstone. Straight guy, honest, honest to the game, and then he sees a guy like Murdoch playing more than him, getting treated better than him, getting more money than him. He'll say, 'What the hell is going on?' These guys got legitimate reasons to be this way. Because this is not something light. I mean, Murdoch came in the dressing room, his lips were twisted, he had the shakes, he's calling everybody by different names. Then he pops in last night ten after seven. I called him. I made the operator interrupt on an emergency. I couldn't get him on the line 'cause the phone was off the hook. He came in ten past seven. He said there was traffic. I went up to him and said, 'Murder, tell everyone your phone was disconnected for a month.' That's what he did. Was he fucked up. He didn't know what he was doing. Don Maloney came off the ice and said, 'I can't play with this kid' to Phil, 'he's screwing me up.' He's had it. Phil could see it too. Phil said he couldn't take it. What am I gonna do?

ME: The guy needs help.

BUKKA: Ratso, you want me to tell you another suggestion? I would stay clear of it. It's a very touchy subject. Let me feel this out and let me be the one to say it. I'll bring it up to Walter and Espo. They're the big mature men in the club. I couldn't bring it up to Vad. Vad wants to bury the kid. It's a sad thing. This whole thing is taking everything out of me. I feel so bad. I know the kid's wrong, but I feel bad for him. He's a good kid. I love him, he's unreal, he's been super to me. He wants something and he can't find it. He's escaping with this stuff. But I'll feel it out, I'll do that tomorrow. But I won't be surprised if tonight he gets fucking gassed.

• JANUARY 16

Marcus might get a job. For the Garden, doing research on the opposing teams for the broadcasters. Up in the blues the Chief was keeping his fingers crossed.

• JANUARY 17

Ulfie's neck was still hurting. The tests showed nothing, so today he went to an acupuncturist, Dr. Choy, on Lexington Avenue. Dr. Choy stuck nine needles into Nilsson's body. It seemed to help for a little while, but in the evening it was the same feeling again. Tingly.

• JANUARY 20

After the Rangers' 2–1 loss to Chicago tonight, Mickey Keating was holding court. Since the Beck trade, he had been infused with a good dose of arrogance, even though the conventional wisdom had it that Werblin had made that trade in concert with the Rockies' owner.

But to talk to Keating you'd get the impression that he masterminded the deal. His attitude had many of the general managers around the league shaking their heads in pity. He was not well respected. Nor was he well respected by the New York press. For some reason Keating felt that he would get away with treating reporters with disdain. Maybe it was Shero's influence; Freddie had a remarkable facility for playing with the press. But whenever Freddie fibbed it was to protect one of his players from the scrutiny of the press. Keating seemed to get some perverse pleasure out of sticking it to the Fourth Estate. As a result, the press hated Keating and undermined him every chance they got. And they loved Nykoluk, who had enough intelligence to play up to them.

And because Nykoluk and Keating were at each other's throats, having the press on your side was a great strategy, since they had a direct pipeline to Werblin, who was always anxious to hear about the politics of his Ranger organization. The politics were getting more and more Byzantine daily. With Freddie off contemplating his navel, his lieutenants had a field day backstabbing each other.

Tonight Keating was standing with a foot up on an empty stall, pontificating about a possible trade.

"This time of year teams start to fade, eh? and players get expendable, eh? You know we're out talking, we're out talking." He ran a hand over his balding head. "We could use a center ice man, but there's not that many good centers around, eh?"

I asked him whether the Rangers had been ostracized by the other GM's, since they had pulled off such a steal getting Beck. Keating puffed up with pride. "No, we're pretty friendly with the other guys. Most of us are looking for the same thing, eh? It's pretty hard to pull off a big one."

"That Beck trade was a once-in-a-lifetime thing." I stroked him.

"We talk every day, every day." He looked world-weary. "They're all afraid to make a trade, eh?" He winked.

"That's what I thought." I nodded sagely.

Keating smiled. "We're not afraid but they are, eh?"

One of the targets of the trade rumors was picking lint off his pants. Murdoch finished his grooming, and he and Bubba left for Charlie O's. "I haven't got laid now for two weeks," Murder moaned.

"Didn't you get anybody in the hospital?" I wondered.

"No," he said sadly. "Fuck, I got a hand job from a fat fucking pig, that's all."

We got to the back door and Murder paused. "Let's just go in, say hello, and let's fucking go."

"Yeah, I'm not having a beer," Bubba said.

"Mickey told me I got to start picking my spots," Murdoch reported.

"What does that mean?" I asked.

"I can't drink when we have days off, so I ain't drinking no more on days off," Donnie said. "But I'm gonna call him now and tell him I'm gonna have a beer."

• JANUARY 30

Slowly the players straggled into the airport for the trip to Buffalo. In the corner by the ticket counter, the coaches were convening. There was Freddie, and Mike, and Mickey, and now there were four—André Beaulieu. Beaulieu was an old associate of Shero's who had been running the Richmond team. Shero had summoned him for emergency duty with the Rangers.

"It's the four stooges now." Dave Maloney nodded toward the brain trust. Anders Hedberg smiled. "Hey, Mike," the captain yelled out, "you guys got a golf foursome now."

• JANUARY 31

They finally shaved someone. It was the Boxcar, Ed Hospodar, who got it the other day in Rye after practice. Hospodar's a sweet kid, and a hell of a teammate when the shit starts flying on the ice, but he had a tendency to exercise his lip a little too much around the veterans. That's why he got it before Conacher or Sulliman or the other rooks.

It was Mario Marois, a pretty yappy second-year man, who initiated the ritual. He stormed into the dressing room, pushing the trainer's table and yelling, "Shaving Time, Shaving Time." So Bukka got out a muscle man sweat shirt magic-markered "SHAVING TIME" on the back of it, and Mario put it on.

Next step was catching the quarry. To accomplish this Sarge put on Baker's face mask and JD donned his, and they grabbed Boxcar as soon as he stepped through the locker-room door. It happened really fast and Hospodar only saw the masks, so he was convinced his old pal from New Haven, Baker, had sold him out. "Bakes, I'm gonna get you. I'm gonna get you for helping out." He was screaming like a banshee. Later he told Bukka that he thought Sarge looked like Baker because he had the same fat stomach.

The masked men dragged him in and pulled him down on the table. Then they took a hockey stick and put it across his chest, pinning his arms down. Crucifixion style. By the time they got the towel over his face, they were ready. First came the shaving cream, smeared all over his massive body. Then it was Murdoch's turn.

Murdoch was the custodian of the whammy stick. It was his pleasurable task to take a butt end and wrap it around and around with cotton and tape it down, and then to get the hot stuff and saturate the cotton with the ointment. Then he'd take aim and wham it right up the Hershey Highway. In other words, anal insertion—and it hurt.

Dull razors. This was next, the scraping of the skin to remove every last hair follicle using the scratchiest, most unhoned metal edge they could find. Of course, they began by shaving his balls. Of course, Hospodar was screaming bloody murder. But this was just the start.

They hoisted his cock up like a flag, using a skatelace, until his penis head began to turn blue-line blue. When it took on the color of a puck, Bukka, with infinite mercy, cut the lace. Then they shaved his armpits and his chest, and by this time Nykoluk had gotten wind of the chop-chop job and he ordered the head off limits. They had no other choice but to free him from his cross. Mario shook his hand and welcomed him to the team. Amazingly the next day Boxcar was yapping again. So here at practice, the day of the game in Buffalo, some of the guys were plotting to shave him again.

But not everyone had participated. The shaving ritual was

a dying practice; more and more of the professionals were refusing to take part. Tkaczuk wanted nothing to do with it. Neither did Espo or Anders. Or man-mountain Beck.

"Bubba wouldn't do it." Joey Bucchino was relating the shaving story to me as we sat in the empty Buffalo arena, watching the Rangers take practice shots at Soetaert, who had been called up when JD came down with a dreadful flu. "Let me tell you something, Bubba's a guy in his own class, a hell of a guy, my right-hand man," Bukka was gushing. "He's the best thing that happened to this team. Like every time he pumps weights on our Universal in the locker room, he puts all the weights on and he pumps them about ten times. Then he puts the weights on for the one that goes up, and he says, 'Bukka, get over here, give me encouragement,' and I stand there saying, 'Do it for me,' and he lifts the whole thing up. Then every time after he lifts weights, he says, 'Bukka, want to do some chin-ups?' and he puts his arm straight out and I do chin-ups on his arms. He's amazing."

Soetaert skated over for a new stick, and Bukka sprang up. He threw the stick over the glass and sat down again. We started talking about team spirit. "We got to have a togetherness," Joey said. "I think it might be getting better now, but still there's that jealousy, a feeling of one guy getting more than the others, commercials, the outside stuff. They don't realize that if we keep this togetherness and everybody works and works and we do well at the end, everybody's gonna benefit by it and they'll get a piece of the action. But you got guys at this time, like the guy at center ice right now." Bukka pointed to Dave Maloney. "He don't help the matter out. It's a tough, tough scene."

Bubba stood at the blue line and took a slap shot right at us. The puck smashed against the glass in front of our faces. I jumped nearly three feet. "When he shoots, it's like a thousand men shooting the puck," Bukka marveled.

"What's wrong with Davey Brown?" I asked.

"Who the hell is Davey Brown?" Bukka looked puzzled. "Oh, Maloney, he's the worst guy to be captain."

"Everyone's down on Vad too," I suggested.

"The team's never been so loose since he's been hurt," Bukka agreed. By now, Bubba had enlisted Espo, Doogie, and EJ, and they were all taking slap shots at the glass in front of us.

"Save it for the game, you bunch of stiffs." Bukka was up and screaming. On the ice the guys cracked up. "I got one problem," Joey confessed after he sat down. "I get too involved with the guys. Most trainers make themselves outside the team, a group of their own. But with me, I've always been like this. Maybe because I'm a sentimental kid. I'm not sensitive to the point of crying at weddings and funerals. It's just that I get involved with the players and I get hurt when someone's hurting them. There's a few guys on this team that, if I was on top, wouldn't be here. One bad apple can ruin the bunch."

"Doesn't management know that?" I wondered.

"This is the thing that upsets me," Bukka said, and then he got up and started yelling at Espo. "Hey, double duo, you should be wearing number twenty-two. You're a duo." Duo was Ranger talk for two-faced. Then he opened the door to let the guys off the ice.

In the dressing room there was yelling and a strange chirping. Bubba and Mario and Murdoch were doing their menagerie repertoire. "That's what the Philly room sounds like when Quinn brings in the bananas," Dave Maloney said. "They got vines there."

By now Bubba had broken into a heavy metal version of "Purple Haze," and Mario was yelping along. Then it was Maloney's turn. "I'm a Ranger groupie, I am," the captain was singing to the tune of "I'm Henry the Eighth, I Am." "I won't fuck Bruins, never take an Islander as well, I'm a Ranger groupie."

They were still playing on the bus. When Halligan came on to take a head count, Greschner got down on the floor and hid behind the last seat. "There's two guys missing." Halligan shook his head.

"Hitch isn't here," Walter volunteered. "Q's in Colorado." Halligan frowned.

"Bill Goldsworthy," Tkaczuk tried.

"Rocky." Dave Maloney hit on it.

"He retired." Tkaczuk was full of revelations.

They finally rounded everyone up and the bus rolled back to the hotel. The team was staying at the historic Statler-Hilton. It was a great old hotel, complete with fading carpets, chairless lobbies, and winding, twisting, labyrinth-like corridors. It was a place where if Freddie decided to take a stroll, they might not find him until the play-offs.

Except the hotel was teeming with Secret Service agents. It seems that Rosalynn Carter was in town for a banquet at the hotel, and she was ensconced in an upstairs suite. There were two rather large men with huge rifles sitting right outside the elevator on her floor. Dispersed throughout the building were other armed suits. People like that might put a damper on Shero's nocturnal wanderings.

After lunch Bukka decided to go to a nearby mall and get some underwear for his good buddy, Bubba. Bubba was going to Detroit to play in the All-Star game, and Bukka was worrying about his friend's image. He wanted the best for Bubba, in every department. Today it was underwear. I tagged along.

"People think Freddie Shero is the Fog." We were walking outside the hotel toward the downtown area. It was a brisk winter's day, and Joey was talking about his second favorite subject, his coach. "Let me tell you something. Last year in

Westchester, every Tuesday I saw when the juice used to come in, and as Fred was leaving after practice, he'd come up to me and say, 'It's a quarter past three, where's the juice and soda?' Now what does he want to know about soda and juice coming in on Tuesday at a certain time, between one and three? So he knows what's going on."

"I don't want Bubba to go to the All-Stars with skeevosa underwear." Joey was concerned. "Bubba's my main man. He's so sincere, so honest. One night he was having a rough time, he had the flu and he was dogging it 'cause he was sick. So he turned around to me on the bench and he says, 'Joey, pull the parachute out of my back.'"

"You know who's a great guy?" I said. "Sarge."

Bukka lit up. "One of the all-time greats. Steve Vickers says to me, 'Joey, I enjoy my own company.' He can go on the road and he'll go to a bar by himself, a shabby bar, and talk to the bartender."

Over lunch the talk drifted back to Shero. Joey was telling me some Fog stories, like the time that Freddie got up to change a channel and stepped on his dessert and then sat down as if nothing had happened. Or Shero's weird proclivities, like dropping his coat on the floor next to the door when he came home, or stubbing his cigarettes out on the marble end tables in the living room, oblivious to the ashtrays. "I'll tell you one thing, though." Bukka turned serious. "Freddie Shero cares about his players. No one can walk in and say anything bad about the players 'cause he sticks by them like glue."

"So why, when I talk to his ex-players, do they bad-mouth him?"

"Freddie Shero has changed since he came from Philly," Bukka said, between bites of his cheeseburger. "He knew in Philly they wouldn't make him nothing. When he came here, this organization showed they cared, so he went all out. Why would he go all out in Philly? Personality-wise he's changed. The players never had a day off in Philly, he'd have them skating eight in the morning. With us he gives them optionals. In Philly he never walked in the room and laughed with the guys. Here he comes in once in a while and gives his war stories, he talks about hockey thirty years ago. The other day he came into the Nautilus room and he was telling Ulfie and them that the Nautilus machines were a lot of crap. He believes in the weight-lifting barbells, freestyle. He got a weightlifter friend he's known for thirty years that when he chews his food he chews it thirty-two times before he swallows. That way you don't gain weight."

I asked about Keating. I had heard that originally Shero had summoned his old comrade from Flin Flon to direct the Rangers farm team in New Haven. But there was one small obstacle. Their current coach, Parker McDonald, had a contract. Keating wound up in the Big Apple as Freddie's assistant general manager. But most people looked at him and saw minor league.

"Mickey Keating right now is a very sincere guy." Bukka was diplomatic. "He's sincere, but a lot of general managers don't have faith in him because of the fact that Mickey Keating was an international hockey league coach and all of a sudden he's general manager of the Rangers. A lot of general managers wouldn't deal with him. They say that Mickey Keating can't trade bubble-gum cards. But he loves what he's doing. He told me about two weeks ago that he would actually kill his own mother for Freddie Shero."

"But why do the guys make fun of him all the time?" I acted perplexed.

"Because of the way he talks," Bukka said. "Plus he doesn't have any personality. His intentions are good but his approach is bad. But he's all for the guys."

"He lectures them, he tells them to be very moral . . ." I said.

"Oh, yeah, he believes in God," Bukka said.

"They laugh at him," I repeated.

"See, you can't do that to a professional." Joey waved a fork in the air. "To a professional there's nothing sacred. I remember a time when I was with the Bruins and there was this kid dying. He was on his way out within two weeks, and they brought him in the locker room. His last request was to meet the Bruins. They brought him. And when I brought him out and came back in, all the guys were going like this" —Joey contorted himself—"and making fun of him. Here's a kid that's gonna die, but nothing's sacred to athletes. They'll always be there when you need them, though. If they like you, they'll be there. When my grandmother died, they got about five hundred dollars' worth of flowers."

Joe paused. "When Espo first got here, I worked for him as a chauffeur. He brought me with him from the Bruins, and I saw there was no togetherness. This team brought to-getherness. This organization, this bunch of guys, made the Rangers believe in themselves. Last year we were good potential-wise, but we won a lot on believing in ourselves. We won a lot on togetherness. When we went to the Islanders, it got so tough there that I used to walk into the room and we used to just cry. This is what we gotta get now. But a lot of guys get away with stuff on this team which they shouldn't. A lot of guys have too much power for a player."

"It's cliquey," I observed.

"Very cliquey," he agreed. "Biggest thing is you got to have trust in a coach, in a manager, in a captain. Phil Esposito is one of the classiest, most sincere guys you'd ever want to meet in your life. I've been with this guy for ten years and I've seen how people shit on him because he's got one prob-lem: he doesn't say no. When a guy shits on him and a guy comes back and tries to make up with Phil, Phil's a sucker, he goes with him. I don't care what you say, Phil is the base of this operation, the younger kids idolize him."

"Why did he resign as captain?" I asked.

"He thought it would help David," Bukka said. "It made it worse. A captain in New York is not like a captain anywhere else. A captain here is always in the limelight. It's too much for the kid."

"It went to his head," I offered.

Joey nodded. "When David skates around in warm-ups, he loves looking at himself in the glass. Watch how many times he looks at himself in the glass. Every shift he runs off the ice, yells at the guys. Bubba told me if he ever yells at him like that, he'll break his legs and drop them in Freddie Shero's office.

"But Espo's a leader." Joey returned to Phil. "Bobby Orr said if these guys went to Montreal and looked in the record book and see the records this guy's set, they'd realize this guy is playing on their team and take advantage of it. All right, he's older, but, God, the guy's putting in thirty goals a year. Who's putting in thirty goals a year on this team? Think about it. Know why they didn't pick him for the All-Stars? Because he has a bad reputation, certain players are very jealous of him. All right, Phil's making three hundred thousand a year, but he's just starting to make that. The guy gives everything. I feel bad Davey and Vad are doing a number on him. He loves Gresch and Bubba, loves Murdoch, loves Doogie. That's why they don't like him."

Bukka signaled for the check. The afternoon was passing by and there was still underwear to be gotten. But first, more talk about Shero.

"When he broke his ribs, I called him up on the phone a few days later and I asked him how it was going and he said he had to get back. He said it was the first time that he missed the game. He missed it so bad he asked the doc if he could go back."

"That wasn't bullshit with his ribs? He wasn't laying back to give Nykoluk his chance?" I wondered.

"That wasn't shit." Bukka was sincere. "I took Freddie to the doc. Freddie Shero did not want to go to the doctor. He believes in faith healing, you know. He gave me all those books on Mind Control and stuff. Freddie Shero is in a class by himself. I think a lot of the reason why he acts the way he does is it makes people talk, like we're doing now. He wants everybody to think. He told me in the summer the guys shouldn't work out, they should use their minds."

"He's a Scorpio, isn't he?" I asked. "His birthday's in October?"

"It was during the season. I remember because I gave him a case of beer for his birthday. Schaefer was our sponsor and they gave us fifty thousand cases of beer. I'd bring cases over to him. He drinks beer warm 'cause he says the warm beer is better for your stomach. He says you don't get no agita. No acid congestion. He likes Canadian Club too, but beer is first."

"How come everybody thinks he's drunk all the time?"

"He isn't." Joey shook his head philosophically. "That's his look. That's the way he is. What that man does is unreal. When the Russians came and played the All-Stars, the way they killed penalties was his invention. They took it away from him. I've seen him sitting down watching TV once, writing plays up. After he wrote the play, he would rip it up and throw it in the basket, and he kept doing that till it was perfect. He loves coaching. He lives for it, that's why he's always thinking about it. But Fred's style is hard for these guys. Beaton came up to me the other day and asked me if Freddie was mad at him. He says that he never talked to him since he'd been there. I said when he talks to you, then worry.

"But when he talks to you, it's like he's looking in your mind. Like he has your brain on the table and he's talking to your brain. Really. When he talks to you, you feel vibrations and everything from him, and everything he says has a philosophy about it. He walks away and he makes you think about what he said. Last year I had a talk with him about my future. I was pretty anxious, you know, and he told me that, say, it's Monday morning, I'm looking forward to Tuesday when Monday didn't go by yet. People told me that he doesn't have emotions. I'll tell you one thing, when we got the big goals of the game, he had emotion. It's always his right arm goes up a little and his left foot kicks."

"You plugged into his wavelength, but maybe he's too cerebral for the players," I suggested. Joey frowned.

"The players only want to see it the way they want it," he said with disdain. "They never tangled with a guy like this. Look what he did with Vickers. He played everybody with the Swedes but Steve. He played a Mind-Control game with Sarge. Steve Vickers was talking to the other players, he was talking to himself, he was looking in the mirror, saying, 'Why didn't he put me with the Swedes?' So when he got the chance, he excelled. That's Freddie Shero. I study this man, I know this man. Believe me, this is how he does it. How about the thing he pulled in Philly? I read this in one of his books. A player wasn't playing well, so he wrote a memo: I want to see you in my office. The guy comes, Shero doesn't show. Another memo. Still Freddie doesn't show. Third day, same thing. Freddie hadn't talked to this player for a couple of years and I read about this and I approached Freddie on this and his theory was he said he did it purposely. His reason was because the player was worried, he wasn't doing well, he was worried that Freddie was gonna give him hell, he didn't know what Fred would say. Right away he goes back and tells all the players on the team that the coach wanted to see him in his office and it was the first time he was gonna speak to him. So all the guys give a little more, and Freddie told me that that guy became a better hockey player within a month. And Fred never even talked to him."

Underwear time. Bukka jumped up and we walked across

the mall to Penney's. He made a beeline for the BVD's. "Gotta get underwear and T-shirts for my Bubba." Joey was pawing through the various styles and brands. "My main man. He's got to look macho. I said to him today, 'When you go in there to the All-Stars and people try to shake your hand, spit on it.' "

He finally decided on seven pairs. "Fruit of the Loom." Joey beamed as he rushed to the register. "Bubba gets the best."

He never got to wear them to the All-Stars. In the second period that night, Bubba had the puck on the left point during a power play, and he faked a shot and skated around the Buffalo defender and lost his edge and landed smack on his left elbow. Bukka had to jump on the ice and help him to the dressing room. Hypertension. Out a couple of weeks, the doc said.

• FEBRUARY 1

As soon as he hit the bus, Mario was yapping. It was bad enough that it was eight in the morning and nineteen or something below zero, but who needed Motormouth Marois? Duguay winced and leaned his hand against the window and tried to get forty winks.

"Dis is fucking bullshit." Mario's voice cut through the bus like an alarm clock. "Dis is just like the fucking juniors." Murdoch straggled on board. "C'mon, you fuck," Mario bellowed. "Who are we waiting for now?" Ranger PR man John Halligan told him it was Conacher, the rookie.

"Where is Charlie, dat fuck?" Marois fumed. "I lost ten minutes of my sleep." He carried on until the squat rookie climbed sheepishly on board. The bus pulled away from the Statler, leaving behind two Secret Service men, who were on their hands and knees checking Rosalynn's limo for bombs.

At the airport Mario was bitching some more. It seems we had at least a twenty-minute wait for the flight. Bubba and Gresch immediately broke out their *Hustler* and *Playboy*, and they got passed around, hand to hand. Mario fumed. "Fuck, shit, cocksucker, dat fucking Halligan, I'll kick his ass." He was spewing venom even as we took our seats. "Hey, Stew," Mario yelled as the pert stewardess made her first appearance. "Could I have a glass of water with ice, please?" She put her fingers in her ears and scurried back to first class.

Meanwhile, Bukka was convincing Gresch to play in the All-Star game. With Bubba injured, Al Arbour, the All-Stars coach, wanted Espo and Gresch. By the time we hit LaGuardia, Gresch was amenable. It was much easier to get Espo to go. "Am I going to Detroit?" He smiled. "Are you kidding? I get a bonus for the All-Stars. Fifteen g's. That'll pay my taxes next year. Let's see, that's about five thousand dollars a shift. Yip yip yip yip," he cackled with delight.

• FEBRUARY 2

Murder was on the rag and Gresch was rubbing it in. He kept poking the seat in front of him, annoying the right winger. "Gimme those ragtime blues, those ragtime blues," Gresch was croaking. His voice did not meet the approval of the other early-morning shuttle commuters. It was Saturday and we were off to Washington to play the Caps.

Murder wasn't talking.

On the bus to the Ramada Inn, where they'd eat the pre-game meal and snooze a bit, Sarge picked up Mud's slack. The usually taciturn forward was regaling some of the rooks with his own tales of feminine trouble. "There was this guy about three years ago who was impersonating me," Sarge told Hospodar and Conacher. "He was picking up all these ladies. He ran up a three-hundred-dollar phone bill when I was in camp. I used to get all these calls and letters from broads, 'When are you coming back? I miss you.' They finally got him."

"You snitched on him?" Hospodar was wide-eyed.

"Yeah, what if he was a bad lay?" Sarge said. "Think of my reputation."

"Yeah, that's definition . . . no—what's that, Rats? Defamation of character," Boxcar decided.

We reached the Ramada Inn, got our rooms, and headed down to the private dining room for the meal.

After lunch, when the guys had gone off for their power naps, Nykoluk took out some paper and started preparing the lineup.

"Let's see, we'll scratch Warren," he told André Beaulieu. "He could use another day's rest for his groin. Scratch Claude. We can use Hospodar with Beaton and EJ. That's some line, huh, though. We can use LaRose in Quebec, he does good there, they're a skating team. Jeez, look at this lineup! We got eight new guys from last year."

"They took four guys from us right away in the draft," André said.

Nykoluk went back to studying his sheet. "Watch Murdoch closely tonight." He sounded ominous. "He hasn't done much since he's been back from that injury. He's a hell of a player, when he wants to be."

I told Gresch. He was standing in the lobby after his nap, observing the teenyboppers with the cameras who were milling about waiting for Doogie. "They should draft those Buffalo girls." Gresch was allaying Boxcar's fears. "Put them in the front line, nobody would ever get past them." As soon as we boarded the bus, I told him.

"Nykoluk's told Beaulieu to keep an eye on Murder," I warned. "It sounded ominous."

Gresch took it in. "I'm not gonna tell him," he finally decided. "I'll get him going, though. I'll give him the puck on the power play all the time, so he can score."

Gresch tried. Murder didn't score, although he did have four shots on net in the first period. After that, zilch. But Espo, his linemate, was the number one star. He scored two goals, his 699th and 700th career NHL goals, and the Rangers walked away with the game, 6–3.

So, an hour later on the plane Espo was still ebullient. I settled into a seat between Espo and Gresch. The others had dispersed throughout the large passenger cabin. "Smile though your heart is breaking," Espo was croaking in a loud voice. Across the aisle the dejected Murdoch was trying to snooze. "I'll give you some good jokes." Espo pointed to my Sony. "I played with a guy so conceited that once on his birthday, he sent his mother a telegram of congratulations. You don't like that, huh?"

Gresch wasn't listening. He was in awe, staring at the nubile stewardess. "Phil," he said. "If I'm not doing anything tomorrow, remind me to get married. I didn't think Air Canada had stewardesses like that."

In front of us LaRose, Hospodar, and Hedberg were discussing Espo's milestone. "He scores seven hundred and they ask him when he's gonna retire." Boxcar shook his head.

"That's the big thing now." Phil leaned over. " 'When are you gonna quit?' Everybody keeps asking me."

"Is it really?" Anders laughed.

"My answer to them is I'm gonna play again next year for sure," Espo said. "Then after that if the club still wants me, I'll play. But I also say if I got traded now I'll quit tomorrow, I don't need it anymore. Besides, they've already put the money into the trust fund this year. Owwoohohoho, I love it," Espo squealed. "I'm a greedy son of a bitch, but whatever I go into, I'm gonna be more greedy. You can bet on it, boy. I'll work my ass off to make sure I'm the best at it."

Espo fell silent. "You know, of all the things I only regret one thing in my life," Espo began. "Not signing with Vancouver in the World Hockey League. I was gonna get the same deal Hull got. A million dollars in the bank, plus a five-year playing contract at three hundred thousand dollars per year, then another five-year contract to do anything at two hundred thousand dollars a year, and I said no to go back to Boston, and a month later I was traded. And the funny thing is Sinden offered me a no-trade clause. I said, 'No, I don't need it. If you don't want me, fine.' His exact words to me were 'You're my man. You saved my hockey life in Russia. You're my guy.'"

"He lied through his teeth," Gresch muttered.

"A month later I was traded." Phil shrugged.

The guys in front shook their heads and settled back in their seats. Espo told a few bad jokes, but Gresch was preoccupied with the stewardess.

As soon as we touched down, Mario was ebullient. He was home. "What a nice city dis is," he shouted, peering out of the window. Below us, a caravan of luggage carts had formed to unload the equipment. "Hey, look at all those French limos." Gresch pointed out the port window. "It's a parade for Mario."

But the trouble began when we exited the airport. There was no bus. It was after 1 A.M., a light snow was falling, no one was answering at the bus-rental office, and a lone cab waited outside, its engine belching.

"See you guys." Marois waved cavalierly and left with his entourage of relatives, who had braved the cold to greet their hometown hero. A few of the guys jumped into the sole cab, and it took off. From the back window Hospodar smiled beatifically and shot the bird at the standees.

"He's gonna get shaved again," Captain Dave cursed.

It was Carnaval time in Quebec City. There were ice castles and people flooding the streets, blowing horns and carrying on, drinking liquor out of long canisters to keep warm. So after the pregame meal, which according to Gresch was the "best on the circuit," Marois played host. He took me and Ed Giacomin, former Ranger All-Star and new goaltending coach, and EJ across the street from the hotel to check out the huge ice-castle sculpture.

All around, Quebecois were milling about, singing Carnaval songs and making merry. Marois led the way, his hands tucked into his jacket to avoid the chill.

"Hey, Mario, nobody's recognized you yet," Giacomin shouted above the din. "I'll run back and get your jersey."

Mario didn't know much about the history of Carnaval. But he did know how to beat the cold. It was a drink called a Caribou, a blend of wine and whiskey, and it packed a stronger punch than Fotiu. A couple of shots later, we drifted back to the hotel for the afternoon nap.

His first shift on the ice, Marois came on like a Caribou. He bumped with Nordique Goulet behind the net, and four straight right hands later, Goulet was sporting a bruised face and Mario was sitting for seven minutes. On his third shift he ran into his old teammate, Pierre Plante. Plante was one of the Rangers lost to the expansion draft last year. As they were lining up for a face-off, Marois told Plante that he couldn't make this year's Ranger team. After some shoving and slashing, Mario was banished again, this time for six minutes.

But Mario's histrionics didn't seem to inspire the Rangers. They played a generally sluggish game, and they were down

5–4 with four minutes left when Hedberg broke in all alone on the Nordique goalie. He deked to the left, pulled the puck onto his backhand, and aimed for the top shelf. Amazingly the puck flew over the vacant net.

Hedberg's miss was the prime topic of conversation on the subdued bus trip back to the hotel. "Nice if Anders bags that," Donnie Maloney said softly. Don Maloney was the one Ranger who always seemed to take every loss personally. He would bite his lower lip and shake his head in amazement and curse sporadically. He was young.

"Nine out of ten times he gets that in practice," Sarge shrugged.

"I would have bet my house on it," Murdoch said. They rode the rest of the way in silence.

• FEBRUARY 9

The Russians were back. They were back at the Garden, and they were dazzling the spectators with their incredible precision passwork and quick reflexes and fast skating game. By the time it was over it was 10–3. But it wasn't the Rangers who were victimized this time, it was the U.S. Olympic Hockey Team. This was their final tune-up before the Olympics at Lake Placid.

The Russians made them look silly. The U.S. tried to come out and play a hard-hitting, close-checking game and they did. For about three minutes. But the Russians' relentless attack and nimble puck control proved too much. The 11,241 spectators, who included Hedberg and Talafous, were impressed.

But there was something disconcerting about the victory for Viktor Tikhonov, the Soviet coach. He met with the media later in the Ranger press room. "The U.S. team has got a good future," the interpreter translated. "We showed what we could do and they didn't. We have the feeling that they held a lot in reserve."

Herb Brooks was next. He was the University of Minnesota coach who had spent the last six months, along with Craig Patrick, grandson of hockey great Lester Patrick, carefully assembling this U.S. team. This was the team that some felt had a shot at a medal in Lake Placid. But after this afternoon's display, no one was optimistic.

"Everybody looks like they're going to a wake," Brooks barked, shaking hands with familiar reporters. "I never knew New York people could look so grim." He reminded me of a cross between Don Cherry and Jerry Brown.

"Well," he sighed, thrusting his hands in his pockets, "it was a good lesson. The players learned a lot conceptually. The speed of their execution. We all respect the Russians. But I don't think I helped our team today." He lowered his voice, in confessional tones. "I think I hurt them by giving them too much of a conservative hockey game. I should have let them anticipate more, I should have turned them loose. I'm more to blame than the players. Take my players off the hook. But sometimes a good kicking is good for a quality athlete and a quality team. We won't be demoralized. We're not really worried about the Russians."

"Are you conceding the gold?" One newsman was startled.

Brooks smiled. "You have to be practical as well as idealistic."

"Were you holding anything back?" another person asked.

"No." Brooks laughed impishly.

Someone raised the issue of politics. Because of the rape of Afghanistan, there had been a movement to boycott this game. As it was, the Garden was more than half empty and security guards were everywhere.

Brooks hesitated. "Off the record? The Russians have never taken the body more. Maybe that had something to do with the political situation."

The media drifted out, but Brooks stayed around to field every last question. Finally, only one young attractive female reporter remained. "Are the Russians still taking oxygen?" she wondered.

An impish grin crossed Brooks' face, "I wish I knew you," he chuckled. "If I were back home, I'd say they were smoking good dope."

- FEBRUARY 10

Another ho-hum game. Quebec was in, and the Rangers won it 3–1 on Warren Miller's fifth goal. That made Miller feel a little better. He had just shelled out $200 for lizard cowboy boots.

But nothing seemed to make Ulf feel better. Or Beck—he still had the arm in a sling. Or Sulliman, for that matter. He took a pretty good check in the first period and he had to leave the game, spitting blood. So when the press met with Shero, it was like talking to a hospital administrator.

They asked about Beck and Sully, and then someone wondered if Ulf had returned from Sweden where he went to recuperate.

"I don't know if he got back yet." Fred adjusted his bifocals.

"Is he starting to skate this week?"

"I'm sure he'll be skating over there if he can't skate here," Shero said.

In the Ranger room Ulfie was standing around, dapper in an expensive suit. He was back. Someone had forgotten to let Fred know.

"I called Barbro the other day," I greeted him.

"You checking up on her, Rats?" Ulf smiled devilishly.

"Do any skating in Sweden?"

He shook his head. "No, I didn't. I'm feeling a little better."

"Will you be back for the play-offs?" By now a large crowd of reporters had formed around us.

"They can't say," Ulf said. "I'm going to practice tomorrow and tell Jimmy to take all the dust off my stuff."

"I imagine everyone in Sweden came up with home remedies," someone said.

Ulf smiled. "Yeah," he said brightly. "I had a lot of guys that wanted to cure my neck."

- FEBRUARY 14

Ron Duguay

One of the rising young stars in the National Hockey League whose aggressive, hard-working style has made him one of the most popular Rangers with the fans . . . Excellent at killing penalties and one of the fastest skaters on the team . . . Almost appears to be running on skates with his choppy style . . . Has fast, accurate shot that seems to explode on goalies . . . Enjoys tennis and baseball during off-season . . . Not married.

—New York Rangers Yearbook, *1979–1980*

The March *Interview* magazine hit the stands. And there on the cover was a rendering of Duguay. His cheek was resting on a hockey-stick blade, and his baby blues were beaming, and splattered across his curly goldilocks was the logo. He was smiling enigmatically, a chic Mona Lisa.

He had finally sat down to dinner with Andy Warhol and Catherine Guinness and writer Scott Cohen at some restaurant whose name he had forgotten (it was Quo Vadis). Also waiting for him at the table was a note, tucked in among the flowers. It was from Bianca Jagger saying she would like to meet him later. Martha Graham would be there and Halston too. Bianca's was the only name that rang a bell.

Herewith are the highlights of the encounter:

ANDY: You're one of the few hockey players who doesn't wear a hat. Is it really dangerous? Do people who don't have hats really get knocked out? Your nose is so beautiful, you can't wreck it.

SCOTT: Do you know any players who don't wear a cup?

DOOG: A guy'd be crazy to go out there without a cup. That's like risking everything.

SCOTT: How come after winning your first two fights during a game you never fought again?

DOOG: I'm not a fighter, I'm a lover.

ANDY: How come there aren't any black players?

DOOG: I don't think they get into playing hockey.

ANDY: But they roller-skate so well. Maybe they don't like the cold.

SCOTT: Have you been skating since you were two years old?

DOOG: Four years old.

ANDY: Those must have been little skates. They have five-year-old kids playing on hockey teams. Do they get their little noses broken?

DOOG: Yeah, but when you're five you don't even notice.

SCOTT: What was the first thing you bought when you signed?

DOOG: The first thing I did was go out shopping for a new car, and I found this beautiful white Cadillac Eldorado sitting in a showroom on Long Island. It had a white interior and a white exterior.

CATHERINE: Sounds like an uptown car.

DOOG: That's what they were saying. I went and bought that, and when I came back to pick it up, I went by this place in Long Beach where they were selling boats and there was this beautiful gold metallic speedboat, and the next thing I knew it was behind the Cadillac going back to Canada.

ANDY: Oren and Aretsky's our favorite restaurant. It's really butch.

CATHERINE: How often do you go there a week?

DOOG: I have to go at least three times a week because I never have anything at home.

CATHERINE: What do you have in your fridge at this moment?

DOOG: Probably just a bottle of ketchup, a jar of mustard, and maybe a little bit of cheese.

CATHERINE: What kinds of things do you collect?

DOOG: Phone numbers. I think I might start collecting cars.

ANDY: Just collect money. Don't own anything, just the place you want to live in.

(Dinner orders)

ANDY: How come sports stars still wear their hair long?

SCOTT: Tell him about your initiation.

ANDY: Did they make you get a haircut?

DOOG: They didn't make me get a haircut, they cut my hair. They have an initiation—I don't know how many years it's been going on—that whenever you come up and it's your first year, all the veterans on our team will tie the rookie down and shave him, from head to toe.

SCOTT: Pubic hairs and all?

DOOG: Pubic hairs and all.

ANDY: They tie you up naked?

Doog: They tie you up naked.

Scott: Who tied you up?

Doog: I don't know because I was blindfolded. It was after practice one day. I was just getting ready to go into the shower. Nick Fotiu grabbed me and when they're ten guys on you there's not much you can do. They put on shaving cream and use razors that aren't even sharp.

Andy: I've got to become a hockey player. You must have looked great. You'd be a raving beauty with short hair. You're a raving beauty now.

Catherine: John McEnroe showed me a picture of you with short hair and said you looked exactly like a young Bob Dylan.

Andy: Catherine, he does not look like Bob Dylan.

Catherine: Yes, he did. He looked just like Dylan did on his very first album cover.

Andy: Maybe his head looked like Dylan, but he doesn't look like Dylan.

Scott: Did you notice Dylan's fingers on that album?

Andy: They weren't his. How many commercials have you done?

Doog: Only one, Sasson Jeans.

Andy: Are you going to do a lot more?

Doog: Now that I've signed with Elite.

Andy: You're with Elite, how great. Do you want to model clothes?

Doog: I don't know what they have planned.

Catherine: Who gets paid the lowest on the Rangers?

Doog: I would say the lowest on our team would be about $70,000.

Scott: Claude LaRose doesn't get $70,000.

Doog: That's right. I would say he's $60,000. I would say the lowest paid player on our team would be $60,000.

Catherine: What would be the highest?

Doog: About $300,000.

SCOTT: The highest paid Rangers are Hedberg and Nilsson, right?

DOOG: Hedberg, Nilsson, and Phil Esposito. They're about the top three.

SCOTT: Why is your coach called "The Fog"?

DOOG: Because he just walks around and doesn't do much, just one-liners, and nothing seems to bother him.

ANDY: How does he tell you how to play?

DOOG: The only time he tells us what he wants done on the ice is before the game. He'll come in about four minutes before the game and tell us if we're to win, this is what we'll have to do and if you don't do it you won't win.

ANDY: So what time do you go to bed tonight?

DOOG: Oh, I would be in by twelve. The night before a game I should always be in bed by twelve.

ANDY: Can you have girls in your room?

DOOG: No girls.

SCOTT: Where would you go on a dream date?

DOOG: Probably to Oren and Aretsky's.

SCOTT: And then?

DOOG: Herlihy's.

SCOTT: In your heart of hearts, when you go into these bars do you feel you can pick any girl you want?

DOOG: Well, *I* know *they* know we come in here and the reason they come in here is to meet the hockey players, so if they're there to meet the hockey players, then they're probably willing to go home with them. So when I go to the bar, I just flash my Ranger ring.

SCOTT: Do you get the most girls on the team?

DOOG: I'd have to say Donny Murdoch.

SCOTT: What's more beautiful than a Canadian sunset?

DOOG: Eliminating the Islanders in the play-offs last year.

ANDY: A tequila sunrise. Let's go to Halston's.

So they went. And Doog schmoozed with Halston and that old woman, Martha Graham, whoever she was, and he met

Bianca and Jade Jagger. He spent most of his time there playing games with Jade.

• FEBRUARY 15

The sleek, black stretch limo purred its way through the side streets of Queens. I was sitting in the front seat with Joe, the driver. In the back Espo and Ulfie and Doogie and Gresch and Bubba were peering out the windows at the unfamiliar sights.

"Is this a rough section, Joe?" Bubba wondered.

"Nah," Joe said. "This is nice, this is Queens. This is where Archie Bunker lives."

The guys had spent all afternoon tanking up at a sponsor's luncheon, hosted by Howard Cosell, and then they drank some more at Espo's place, and now they were on their way to the annual Ranger Fan Club Dinner Dance. The one event each year where the fanatical fans get a chance to press the flesh with their heroes. You can imagine how excited this made the Rangers.

"Doogie can't wait to dance with those tight asses." Espo smiled. "I've never seen a reception like you get from those girls, Doog. They scream. I'm his agent now, Rats. I told Cosell and Werblin today."

They started talking about Ulfie's condition. Apparently, Liebler, the Ranger doctor, had just given Ulf word that he wasn't suffering from a slipped disk. That was good news.

"I'll be okay." Ulfie smiled. "All I need is a little more money."

We finally pulled up to the Cordon Bleu, a huge catering-reception hall, where 1,200 fans were waiting in anticipation. Including about thirty unsavory leather types outside. "Look at all the greasers," Bubba marveled. "We're gonna have a brawl in Queens."

They didn't. They stepped out of the limo and they were mobbed like movie stars and strange men in tuxedos ushered them in and they were sequestered in a few side rooms upstairs as the fans filled the multileveled banquet room. They were all here. Head, a girl who wears Espo's uniform and the Chief and the Charlie O's regulars and the ones that couldn't get into Herlihy's.

While they waited to be introduced by Halligan in numerical order, the Rangers and their wives and girl friends were milling about the side rooms and hanging out in the hall. Gresch was shit-faced and he was pulling guys' ties and patting Joanne Vickers's very pregnant stomach. Mario was also feeling no pain, and when Freddie strolled in with his wife, the defensemen went over and gave Shero a big hug. Fred looked embarrassed. Sarge, for his part, was upset. Nobody had laughed at his joke. "Can you believe it, Ratso? Nobody laughed. They asked me what I thought about acupuncture, and I said I've never seen a sick porcupine." He shook his head. "I guess no one got it."

Espo walked by and peeked into one of the side waiting rooms. They were bar-mitzvah garish. "Jeez, these remind me of massage parlors," he said. "This brings me back to my younger days."

And then they were summoned to line up, in numerical order, and they tried to remember their numbers, and they were introduced couple by couple, and the festivities began. Each table was graced with a Ranger and between courses they talked, and danced, and signed autographs, and posed for pictures. Mostly they posed for Polaroids. By the night's end they were seeing polka dots.

We finally made our way to the limo. By now it was me and Doogie and Murder. As we hit the street, a loud chorus of "Oh-la-la, Sasson" began. Doogie winced and jumped into the car. I rescued Murder from a last-minute cluster shot, and we were gone.

Almost. The two blond waifs caught Murdoch's eye. They couldn't have been more than sixteen years old. He stopped the car and rolled down the window. After a minute of negotiation, there were five of us in the back seat. They were from New Jersey. They were that young and they talked like this: "So youse guys are going for the Cup dis year?" was one girl's icebreaker. Doogie just shook his head in despair.

The limo stopped at Herlihy's. Before we went in, Murder had already flagged down a Checker cab and was loading the tiny-teenies into the back seat. He gave the driver forty dollars to take them home. Then he brushed off his jacket and entered his world.

- FEBRUARY 17

It was Hitch's homecoming. He was back in the Garden in blue. Toronto blue. And it was homecoming for Davie Farrish too. Farrish was Gresch's former defense partner and close buddy, and after being drafted by Quebec in the expansion draft last year, he had spent most of this season in the minors. But Toronto had obtained him recently and brought him up to the big club.

But around the Rangers all the talk was about Ulfie. They still didn't know what was wrong with him, and the latest word was that he was slated to take a myelogram, an exploratory operation in which they inject dye to determine if there is any disk impairment. They promised that he'd be recovered in a day from the operation, but Shero thought differently. He remembered that when he took the test, it took him two weeks before he could even walk. But that was thirty years ago.

The game didn't do much to make anyone feel any better. Except for Hitch and Farrish. Hickey picked up a rebound early in the first period and shuffled it into the vacant net, for his twenty-first goal of the season. Farrish played well throughout the game. By the time it was over, the Leafs had come out on top, 6–4. And the fickle fans, who had booed JD and the Rangers unmercifully all night, had come up with a new chant. It was catchy and easy to scream, and it had a certain charm and a crisp delivery. It was "OH-LA-LA, YOU SUCK."

At the buzzer the Rangers hurried off the ice and into their room. En route, Gresch slammed the puck down the ice, EJ cursed all the way down the corridor, and Mario broke his stick in two against the wall. They were not a happy bunch. I headed for the Leafs' dressing room.

"Hey, Ratso." It was Farrish. He had an ice pack attached to his elbow with an Ace bandage.

"Have you been up to Gresch's yet?" I wondered. "Did you see his new telescope?"

Farrish laughed. "He ain't fucking stargazing, is he? He's probably got it set up overlooking Doogie's apartment."

Farrish toweled himself off. "How is Ulfie anyway?"

"He's got to go for a myelogram," I said.

"Oh, is he?" Farrish shook his head. "That's a tough business. He's definitely out for the year. He may be history."

"That Orha played well in goal tonight." I changed the subject.

Farrish smiled. "He should be good. He practiced dodging bullets out of Czechoslovakia."

In the other room there was dead silence. JD and Espo were sitting at their adjoining stalls, looking morose.

JD slowly got up and walked to the shower. He turned on the hot water and stood under the spray for five minutes. Alone.

Gresch came over to me. "I'm not saying nothing. There's probably a good chance I might get traded."

"Get out of here," I scoffed.

"That's the way it's gonna be. I have a feeling, a gut feeling." He pulled on some corduroys. "Like these pants?"

"Calvin Klein." I read the label.

"I got seven pairs for nothing," Gresch boasted. "I never got nothing from Sasson."

Murdoch came into the room and flung his towel in disgust. "Right now, I hate hockey. I feel so shitty." He finished dressing and walked over to Doogie. "I gotta go to Charlie O's for a minute before we go to Oren's. I gotta meet a girl."

"Which girl?" Doog said.

"The one that sits across from the penalty box," Murder explained. "She said she'll be down there, she told me when I was skating around."

She was there all right, along with about a hundred other little puck bunnies who were all milling around ogling Pat Hickey. After a few beers Hitch went up to Cronies, his old haunt, for dinner with a few friends. Gresch and I met him there later.

"Tell me." Hitch had pulled me aside soon after our arrival. "Who traded me? Did Shero trade me?"

I related the time I asked Shero about the trade. Hitch was taking it all in eagerly. "I saw him before the game tonight," Hitch said. "It was weird. All he said to me was, 'How many homes do you own now?' Incredible line."

"What did you answer?"

"I told him, 'I have one in New York. Want to buy it?' " Hitch laughed.

"Imlach was asking me about you, Mud, and Doogie," Hickey told Gresch. There had been rumors circulating of a trade, a blockbuster involving Darryl Sittler, the Toronto captain, who was furious when his pal, Lanny MacDonald, had been dealt to Colorado for Hickey. But confirmation of negotiations coming from a Toronto player was too much for Gresch.

"What did you say?" Gresch was turning green. "Don't get me traded."

Hitch smiled. "Hey, I'm on the other side now. I want good guys to play with." He shrugged and polished off his beer. Greschner drowned his sorrow at the pinball machine.

• FEBRUARY 18

The first thing that Kinky did when we got to Bubba's apartment was to check out the shower. It had been a few days now, and Kinky's normally kinky moss had begun to resemble Rastafarian dreadlocks. Meanwhile, I made a bee-line for the refrigerator. There were a few cans of beer there and not much else. Just some ketchup and mustard.

"What's the matter, didn't any food come with the apartment?" I yelled. Bubba shrugged. He was wearing dungarees (not Sasson's) and a T-shirt that read "Fuck Me Like the Dirty Pig That I Am, Come All Over My Tits and Tell Me That You Love Me and Get the Fuck Out." It was a quiet Monday night at home and we were there to watch the Rangers play at Hartford on the tube. Bubba was there because his elbow was still sore.

I broke open some beers and unpacked the chicken and ribs we brought. Bubba settled onto the plush white L-shaped couch. It was a gorgeous couch, and it comple-mented the white shag rug very well. Everything else was elegant too. There were Warhol paintings and shrublike trees and a nice marble coffee table. Bubba of course had nothing to do with any of this. He had simply rented the place fur-nished from a friend of Richard Weisman's.

"Did you hear Cherry's playing Q at center now?" I asked Bubba.

"Probably. He had me at left wing for a few games." The defenseman shrugged.

Kinky came into the room from the bathroom, where he had finally taken a shower. "Hey, boy, that's a nice shower you've got there. Not like one of them hippy showers. But you don't use no B.O. bomb, Barry. Don't you want dates with young women?"

"What kind of guy is Cherry?" I asked.

"He's a good guy," Bubba related. "A player's coach."

I asked Barry to compare him to Shero. The big defenseman laughed. "Fuck, are you kidding? Cherry jumps up and down on the bench and tells you to fuck off and tells you you're a fucking asshole and a chickenshit prick."

"What does Shero do?" I asked.

Bubba shrugged. "Fuck, I never even heard him talk on the bench. I'm still wondering if that's really him. He looks like him, but for all I know, he might be coaching over in Russia somewhere."

• FEBRUARY 20

There were two topics uppermost in Fred Shero's mind after the Rangers easily beat Edmonton 4–1. The first was the injury to Ulfie. The results were back and they were negative. Yet, according to the reporters, he was still in pain. Shero suggested he may just have to live with it. After all, the coach himself had, as he put it, "a disk out and one that's crushed and I played for twenty years."

"Are you questioning his ability to play with pain?" one reporter asked.

"No, the thing is, who hasn't got back problems sooner or later?" Shero peered out from behind his bifocals. "You gotta live with it."

"Obviously he's afraid of jeopardizing his career next year," the newsman countered.

"*We* are afraid of jeopardizing his career," Shero snapped.

"If we said play, he'd play. There's others that wouldn't play."

"Are you coming closer to that point?"

"I wouldn't say that to any man," Shero said.

The second topic was intimately related to the first. It was the trade that the Rangers were pursuing. Of course, they were in the market because of Ulfie's injury. In the market for a center. Sittler was a center.

"We have one deal cooking where we'd have to give up quite a bit but it might be worth it," Fred said. "We got a couple of kids in New Haven that could fill in pretty good." This did not do much to allay Gresch and Doog and Murder's paranoia. "But," Fred went on later, "I would be apprehensive about making a big deal at this stage of the game. No matter if you think you got the best of the deal it could be upsetting. I'd sooner go for a little trade." He chuckled. "Two for one. I could make a big trade, but I think we'd get the worst of it." This seemed to take Gresch and Doogie off the hook . . . And left Murder twisting slowly in the wind.

But in the locker room all the trade talk seemed temporarily forgotten. It was Phil Esposito's thirty-eighth birthday, and to denote the occasion there were two rather large decorative cakes. One of which was smeared all over Espo's face, streaking it with red, white, and blue icing. The other one was in Bubba's hand and he was running naked through the locker room after Sarge. He cornered him near Gresch's stall, took aim, and hurled the sugary projectile. He missed. Blame it on the elbow.

In the midst of all this frivolity, Murdoch was bummed out. He had even scored a goal, a sizzling slap shot that nearly ripped the Edmonton goalie's glove off and continued into the far side of the net. But he was still morose about the trade rumors.

"It definitely bothers me," he was telling a small cluster of reporters in front of his stall. "You read it in the newspapers, your doorman hears about it, my mother hears. Everywhere I turn, instead of saying 'Hello' it's 'Are you getting traded?' Friends call and say, 'I hear you're going.'"

JD walked by, modestly holding a towel in front of him, headed for the shower. "You got your golf clubs out for LA?" he shouted.

"See what I mean?" Murdoch managed a smile. "There you go. I hope I stay here. I don't think there'd be any trade talk if I was scoring a lot of goals, though."

But it was harder for him to score, especially playing fourth-line wing. Dean Talafous, who had come back after spending much of the off-season flat on his back with a vertebra injury, had supplanted Murdoch on the Esposito line, and he had breathed new life into the trio. He was a wiry, cagey player, a born-again Christian in a sport rife with sinners, and his ability to go into the corners and dig out the puck neatly complemented Don Maloney's remarkable facility, and so now there were two of them to feed Espo, who would set up shop in the slot directly in front of the goalie.

Which left Murdoch out in the cold. "You're not gonna get traded," JD said as he returned from the shower. Espo and Gresch huddled nearby, waiting for Murdoch to finish with the press.

Espo had a present for Gresch. It was an authentic, so-help-him God, autographed photo of Gresch's favorite number ten, Bo Derek. Gresch seemed in ecstasy all the way to the elevators.

"If I find out this was a lie, I will personally cut your nose off," Gresch warned Phil. "It might take two or three days."

"Donna got it," Phil said. "If it was a lie, it would have been signed Gresch, that's what I call you. But Donna calls you Ron all the time."

The explanation seemed to mollify the defenseman, and he and Espo and Bubba headed uptown in Joe's limo. I joined JD and Kinky, who had been at the game, in Charlie O's.

"This might have been JD's best game," Kinky was declaiming to the goalie and his wife, "but the fans are like American driftwood. They ain't worth a shit."

"I screamed at them," Beaver admitted. "Any other game, there would have been a whole bunch of 'JD's."

"You know why women have pussies?" Kink asked. "'Cause if they didn't nobody'd talk to them." Everyone, especially Beaver, cracked up. "The point is, that's not a funny joke, Beaver's the only woman in America that thinks that's funny."

We finished our beers and haggled over where to go from Charlie O's. Kinky was pushing for Oren's, but JD was opting for the City Limits, a good ol' shit-kickin' country haunt down in the Village. We decided to divide up and meet later at City Limits.

So by the time Kinky and I and some friends hit City Limits somewhere around 2 A.M., the Ranger contingent was pretty well tanked. There were EJ and Sue, and JD and Beaver, and Frankie Beaton and his wife, and Pat Conacher, solo. And while everyone was up doing the Texas two-step, JD and I convened at a nearby table.

"See, Rats," the big goalie said, "you've been hanging out with the city guys too long. There's a big difference between the city guys and the country guys. Like this place, it's not plastic. We don't go for that shit. We're fun." JD looked out at the dance floor. "Look at Conacher. He's the best. That's the one rookie in two years that I wouldn't shave."

"There are real problems with the club," I said. "There's a real leadership vacuum. Maloney's just too young and immature. I'd rather see someone like Sarge as captain. He ain't a rah-rah type, but the guys seem to really like and respect him and I think the pressure would be good for him."

"You know who I'd make captain?" JD said. "Ulfie."

"Gresch is really bummed out. The fucking ignorant fans keep getting on him. And he's got a bum knee, he told me that yesterday, but does he get it checked out or rest it or tell the press? No." I shook my head.

"He's gotta forget about the fans," JD said.

"What about the draft picks? Dogshit," I fumed. "Keating's a total clown, and we really fucked up in the draft. They pick Sully first, he's a good guy, but why him? Because he was Donnie Maloney's teammate? What about Propp? He only scored about forty goals."

"You know the reason we didn't pick Propp?" JD said. "Because they got scouting reports that he drinks too much. Who gives a shit? It's what he does on the ice."

"There's just no leaders . . ." I reiterated.

JD downed his beer and cracked open a peanut. "I gotta be more assertive. Speak out more. I've been laid back all year, with the injury and everything. But Giacomin was talking to me the other day. He told me he thought I had real leadership qualities. He told me not to drink so much too because everybody'll stay at a place as long as I'm there." JD cracked another peanut. "So now I gotta find my own bars," he said.

• FEBRUARY 22

Amazing upset. Triumph for the Underdog. A Miracle on Ice. They were getting ready to trot out all the clichés and with good reason. As incredible as it may seem, the U.S. Olympic Team was in the process of beating the Soviets in a must game for the gold medal.

I was watching it at my friend Cusimano's house.

"Oh boy," Cusimano's voice bellowed across the living room, sending the frightened cats scurrying for shelter. "We got the Soviets on the pass. We got 'em by the balls. And we're crushing them by the Khyber Pass. What a metaphor."

There were a few minutes left in the game and the score was 4–3.

"They'll have to pull their goalie, what a humiliation," Cusimano exulted. "They've never done it before." The seconds wound down. There were fifty left, and the Americans were doing such a good forechecking job that the Russians couldn't even get an extra skater out on the ice. "They can't pull him, they don't know how," Cusimano was howling. "We're marching on Moscow. The fucking Russians can't stop the greatest Olympic victory in history. On the eve of World War Three, the Apocalypse, we're gonna win the fucking gold." The seconds were ticking off.

"You socialist cunts can't even pull your goddamn goalie." He was screaming at the screen now. "The bastards haven't had an original thought in their lives. Fuck Communism. Fuck Reds. Yea, Zen Buddhism. Brooks must have learned Zen from Freddie. Hockey's a great thing. The will and the act are so close in hockey. That's the ultimate power, the reason people dream of flying. If you print any of this shit, quote me. I'm on fire. I'm on fire." He leaped up to take a piss as the buzzer sounded and the U.S. team went wild. In Lake Placid they took to the streets.

The phone rang. It was Kinky. "Did you see that, Ratso?" He was ebullient. "That was worth ten thousand dollars a ticket. That made the Stanley Cup look like nerdball. That's more important than war, definitely. I can't see why the Ranger management can't learn from this. Did you hear what Brooks was shouting from the bench? 'Play your game, play your game.' That's a good lesson for life, boychick, Fred Fucking Shero should tell his guys that. Sonny Werblin would never know why we beat the Russians, he'll never know the spiritual side of hockey."

I agreed.

"By the way, we should call the film guys," Kinky urged.

"They should release 'Skating on Thin Ice' right now as a single. Listen, I gotta go. I've been talking to JD and Gresch. I'm gonna have to start napping more."

I had a compulsion to talk to a Ranger. But they were in Minnesota for a game tomorrow night. I called Joanne Vickers for the hotel's number.

JOANNE: I can't believe that. There was a rumor too that they would gas our management and sign Herb Brooks. Did you hear any rumors?

ME: None where Sarge's name was mentioned.

JOANNE: Yeah, Hickey's name wasn't mentioned either. I tried to call Steve last night, but all the guys were at Warren Miller's bar together. They didn't want to answer the phone. Steve gave me the third degree when I called. I said I just heard a rumor. Who is this Saganuck anyway? Is he a goon or a throw-in?

ME: Throw-in.

JOANNE: Steve heard that even Maloney might go. They don't understand Steve.

ME: What about the way they handled Gresch? He's bummed out most of the season and he's the best defenseman they got with Bubba.

JOANNE: Steve often said that Gresch doesn't get recognition. Especially that period when Steve wasn't dressing and we'd go right home and watch the game on TV, he'd say, "Fucking Gresch is great! He doesn't get recognition." I hope he doesn't get the same treatment from them.

ME: It's like Shero abdicated this year. He delegated all his authority to guys like Nykoluk and Keating who just can't cut it.

JOANNE: I never trusted Keating. He reminded me of a bald guy named Curly back in Des Moines. He owned an antique store and he'd pick up this little cat he had and he'd talk to the cat, answering your questions to the cat. I never trusted the guy. The other day after the game in Hartford, Steve came home and I said I can't believe all the different lines they had out. Is Shero hitting the panic button? Steve gives me that look and says, "Shero doesn't know the word panic."

ME: What does Steve think of Shero now?

JOANNE: He likes him. I don't think he understands him. He doesn't try to understand people, he tries to function under them. He's hardheaded that way. He plays his own game. It's funny, Steve doesn't believe that he functions best under pressure. He doesn't think it's a desirable trait. It creates ulcers when he gets down, but he doesn't believe that's the way he is. When Shero benches him, he gets defiant. He says things like "I want to play somewhere else where I'm wanted." But as a girl friend and now a wife, I understand what Shero does. I crumble under pressure, but Steve's good at it. When they brought Don Maloney up, they made him room with Steve. And he did well! If you're eating breakfast, breathing, eating, sleeping with a guy that's going for your job, it's like he might wake up in the middle of the night and stab you. But Steve responds to Fred. I told him to talk to him, but Steve says he doesn't have to talk, just perform.

ME: So how've you been otherwise?

JOANNE: Good. Except Steve is making me watch all these programs on TV about possessed children, and I'm having nightmares that I'm having Satan's baby. He thinks it's all funny.

• FEBRUARY 23

The trade-rumor mills were working overtime. While the Rangers were hiding out in Miller's bar in St. Paul, avoiding the phone, the papers back home were blaring the conjecture in banner headlines. It was brewing. Sittler, Palmateer, and Burroughs to New York for—are you ready?—JD, Gresch,

Doogie, and Murdoch. I called Murdoch, who was home in New York nursing a flu:

ME: I don't think it's true, but did you see the paper? If they do that, they're going to alienate a lot of people. I mean you're breaking up a team that went to the finals last year. You're tearing the heart out of the team. You, fucking Doogie, Gresch, JD . . .

MUD: If they traded all of us, there'd be 15,000 fourteen-year-olds jumping off the bridges. There'd be no fun on the team at all.

ME: It'd be horrible. Trade all my friends.

MUD: Gresch, me, Doog, JD. Jeez, that would be enough to make you get into football.

That night Halligan had to go on the WOR TV broadcast before the game started to allay the fears about the trade. Fifteen thousand fourteen-year-olds slept easier. And when Nykoluk told the team at a meeting before the game that there would be no big trade, Gresch and Doogie and the others slept easier too. Right through a 6–3 loss.

• FEBRUARY 24

The Americans won the gold and the Garden celebrated by serving champagne in the press room. And the Rangers beat the Islanders 8–2, with trade bait Greschner, Duguay, and JD playing superbly. Conspiracy theorist that I am, I was convinced that Shero had leaked the trade talk to motivate the players, since the rumors had gone public after Ulf's myelogram results had been negative. If it was purposeful, it worked marvelously. The Rangers were flying, hitting, passing crisply, completely overwhelming a listless Islander team. And taunting them too.

That came with less than a minute to play. It was 8–2

already, but EJ and Gary Howatt, the Islanders' combative wing, scrapped along the boards. Bubba forced his way in and whacked Howatt in the head. Then Gordie Lane, the Islander defenseman, tried to get in. A few feet away Gresch was taunting him unmercifully. "You suck, Lane," Gresch said, laughing. Sutter, who had cheap-shotted Hickey in preseason, injuring his eye, pointed to his orb. "I'll give you another one of these," he sputtered. Gresch laughed in his face. Which prompted Lane to throw his glove at Gresch's nose. By the time everyone was untangled, Howatt, Johnstone, Beck, and Lane were out of the game.

But in the confusion they sent Beck out the wrong door. He exited at the Eighth Avenue end and he was walking down the corridor toward the Ranger dressing room when Howatt began his charge. Bukka, who had sensed trouble, ran back to the room along with some security guards. Just as he got to the threshold, Bubba heard Howatt and spun around. "Fuck you, you cocksucker." He lunged toward the small Islander. Bukka and the cops held him back and just managed to slam the iron door, right in Howatt's enraged face. Murdoch, who was watching from the sidelines, still struck by flu, banged on the door. "Fuck you, Howatt," he roared with delight. In the stands the fans were still screaming for blood. Except for one little enclave of fourteen-year-old Doogie-ites who were standing in their seats, surrounded by a sea of bloodthirsty suits, chanting "NO MORE FIGHTS, NO MORE FIGHTS."

They got their wish that night. They played out the last minute, and Bubba led the team back into the dressing room chanting "CHILI, CHILI." But later, at Charlie O's, the talk was still of the would-be trade.

"I got drunk Friday night and left town," Beaver said. "When I saw that Sonny mentioned it in the paper, I got worried. JD said he would quit if he got traded."

"They all say that," Sue Johnstone scoffed.

"Yeah, but JD played two games in a row and the second was against Toronto," Beaver said. "That's when I got worried."

"You thought they were showcasing him, eh?" Sue asked.

"Pieface called me two A.M. after the Atlanta game," Larry Rauch, JD's agent, said. "Leslie said that Nicky couldn't finish eating dinner after he heard that JD was gonna get traded. So Nicky called me two A.M. and said, 'Is it true about the JD trade?' I told him, 'No.' He said, 'Good. I would never want to come back to New York then.' I said, 'Who asked you to?'"

• FEBRUARY 25

Sasson struck again. This time it was a Heart Fund benefit at the Electric Circus. A fashion show featuring Espo and Doog and Anders and Maloney, the French Jeans Connection. Fifty dollars a crack. A few hundred fans showed up. But no Rangers.

It was a bizarre night. Each Ranger and his wife/girl friend were to model an outfit, dancing (or a reasonable facsimile thereof) to a heavy disco beat. Then they'd run downstairs to the dressing room and change into another outfit, and come back on the ramp and do it again.

It quickly became apparent that in order to do this sort of thing, they had to get shit-faced. So all afternoon during rehearsal, the group freely availed themselves of the free bar set up downstairs. The alcohol seemed to put things in perspective.

"I'm so fucked up everything's coming at me," Bukka was ranting in the tiny dressing room as the guys prepared for their initial outfits.

Esposito pulled on his Sasson suit. Smart company, into

diversification. "Holy shit, do I look big." He fretted at the mirror image.

"Hey, Orca," Maloney said, laughing, "go back in the water."

Anders was pulling on his jeans. "Hey, Ratso, with these jeans I can get into any bar in the Village, eh?" He shook his head. "What am I doing here? I'm a hockey player, aren't I?"

Meanwhile, Doogie was still in his underwear. Brief blue bikini shorts. "I ought to go out like this." He was pulling down on his underpants. "Modeling Sasson shorts. Holy fuck, would that fuck everyone up. Put a big Sasson emblem on my dick. Oh-la-la . . ."

They all got dressed and made it as far as the dressing-room door. There they were attacked by the licensers. They were loud and obnoxious. Garment center people, the ones that make the schlock suits Sasson subcontracted for.

"Dave, Ron." Mr. Subcontractor's wife mugged them at the door. She was shoving a little minicassette tape recorder in their faces. "I want you to say hello to my little Jeff here." She played the tape, and a small, subcontractor's son's voice wafted out asking for autographs.

"Say hello, Ron." She clicked the recorder on.

"Jeff, I heard your message, thank you very much," Doogie improvised. "Too bad we're meeting over a cassette."

"Is he something?" Mrs. Subcontractor was in ecstasy. "Ron, someday you're gonna be in the movies. My son is going to go crazy. He'll sell these tomorrow in third grade. Anders." She was reaching out now. "Come and say hello to my son."

They finally made their way upstairs. The crowd was feverish now, and WNEW disc jockey Bob Fitzsimmons was handling the introductions. With a slight sardonic twist.

"Are you ready to see the Rangers?" He hyped the crowd. "With all their little tushies here? Okay, this guy is second all-time in goals, he admits to being thirty-eight, and he shows his little tushie on TV. Don't be afraid to come out, c'mon, Phil." Espo and Donna boogied out and the crowd went wild. They went wilder when Anders and then Doogie made their appearances.

"Show 'em the side ventilation," Fitzsimmons told Doogie. "I've never seen a guy so shy. That's how they dance in Canada, folks. We did that about twenty years ago."

Maloney was waiting in the wings. "Moon 'em," I whispered, "just like in training camp."

"Dave's the youngest captain," the DJ announced as Maloney went into his peacock routine. "The way things are going you may be a corporal next season," Fitzsimmons snickered.

Mercifully, it was soon over. And downstairs Espo thanked all the guys. Werblin was bantering with Mario Marois, who was the only Ranger to attend. He showed up as soon as it was all over.

In the dressing room Espo and Bukka commiserated, "Who stole my sweat shirt?" Phil scoured the room. "And where are the extra jeans they gave us?"

"Anders took them," Bukka reported.

"He only makes about a half a million dollars a year. Nice turnout from the guys, huh?"

Espo sighed. "That's all right, don't say anything, Joey, my day will come. Mario was the only guy that came down, huh? He's on my list. He's a good kid," the superstar said and carefully folded his crisp new jeans.

• FEBRUARY 27

I was leaving Charlie O's after the Rangers beat LA 5–4 when I saw a cluster of young fans.

"Ratso," one of them called out. "Marcus told us that Murder's gone."

"What's going on?" another pleaded.

"Is he gone?" the third, a doe-eyed blonde, worried. "What's he gonna do? He won't be able to go to Oren's. No more Herlihy's." She shook her head sadly.

• FEBRUARY 28

They wanted fans for the film. Real dyed-in-the-wool Ranger fans. I got them Head Esposito. Esposito wasn't her real name, but she was using it semiofficially in honor of number 77. That's what it said on her buzzer downstairs. Of course, Head wasn't her real name either, but she didn't get dubbed that, as Beaver had suspected, by the guys. No, Head had no real contact with the Rangers. She was simply an Esposito fanatic. She wore his uniform to every game. She collected his broken sticks. She had every promotional poster he had ever done, hanging on her walls like icons. When she played hockey herself, in goal, she used his brand sticks.

So, by extension, she was a Ranger fan. Along with her number 77 uniform top, she wore Ranger caps. Ranger bracelets, Ranger earrings, Ranger tiepins, and the rest of the outfit was color-coordinated, Ranger red, white, and blue. She was thirty-three years old, worked as a messenger in Manhattan, and lived in Brooklyn.

She made the film. Martin, the cameraman, was screwing in a stronger bulb in her bedroom when we discovered the depth of her attraction to Esposito. "The year he got seventy-six goals he saved my life," Head said matter-of-factly as she arranged some memorabilia on the bed for the shoot.

"Saved your life?" I repeated.

"Yeah, I was ready to bump myself off again for the third

time, and he and Vince Lombardi sort of provided the one-two punch that I needed," she said as she brushed her long, dirty-blond hair out of her eyes. "Lombardi got me going with all his good sayings and it just seemed that nobody appreciated what Phil was doing and I felt that he needed somebody to be close to him, so I figured why not get close to him? Without him, I know I would have bumped my-self off."

"Were you depressed?" I asked.

"I was on the way to suicide a third time. I tried pills the first time and I slashed my wrists the second. Well, you see, the first fifteen years of my life I had been used as a medical guinea pig, and it's taken this time even now to be able to be halfway emotionally set. It does affect your mind." Head was relating all this with, as the psychiatrist would say, very little affect. "I was sick when I was young and they didn't know why, so they decided to use drugs that altered my sexual makeup, and that hurts. It was cortisone and it gave me sec-ondary sex characteristics of a man, and I had a kidney prob-lem and throat problems for the first twenty years and that does tend to depress someone, especially when I was nine-teen and I wanted to go into nursing and they said, 'No, not until you get your knee fixed up,' and I got it fixed and it broke down seven years later. Now I only have thirty per-cent use of it and I had to give up the career I wanted."

"How do you play hockey?" Martin marveled.

"Three braces," Head said. "I wear one most of the time, then I put two more on. I'm a goaltender, not a good one, but in my next life I'm gonna be fantastic. I got it all arranged and if I don't come back, then the Lord is gonna be deeply, deeply in trouble."

"You didn't meet Phil when he saved your life?" I said.

"No, no." Head drew the words out. "It was only until last year that I've been able to say 'hello.' He's had me that scheezed. I wrote him a letter, it must have been the second year that I started going to the games. I said he's got to know that somebody likes him, so I wrote him a letter, how well he read it I don't know. I think he must have thought it was a joke."

"As a Ranger?"

"No, a Bruin," she corrected. "That's why I got Ranger tickets to see him when he came in."

"You rooted for the Bruins?" I asked.

Head shook her head. "No. I used to root for the Rangers and Bruins, but if either would win by one goal, I would want Phil to score the winning goal. If anybody else got it, I didn't like it."

"You must have been in seventh heaven when he got traded," I said.

"No, I was mad at both sides," she remembered. "I was mad at the Rangers for suggesting it and I was mad at the Bruins for taking them up on it. I was upset for quite a while. What was I gonna do with my three Bruin uniforms? It hurt me worse than it did him. I had one to clean the house, one to wear in the house, and one to wear to games. I've got that folded up, I've never put it on since." She smiled.

She picked up a pair of skates, the same brand Phil uses. "Would you believe I put these on to go to bed the first week I had them? Only during the play-offs, though, I get scheezy."

"You wore them to bed?" I repeated.

Head laughed. "You think that Phil's superstitious, you haven't seen anything yet. Why do you think I wear certain things on certain days to the games? But Phil, if he doesn't see me in that seat by the bench, he gets paranoid. I'm a good-luck charm, but I'm not gonna be there tomorrow. I wrote him a note, though. He gets bent out of shape if he doesn't know. If I'm not there, he feels it's the worst omen in the world."

Head then showed Martin all her old Espo sticks. "Do I have enough stuff?" She smiled and tugged at the turtleneck underneath her uniform. The same turtleneck Phil wears. "Did he tell you why he wears these turtlenecks?" she asked. "He had a sore throat up in Toronto, so the manager gave him a turtleneck to wear for his throat and he got the hat trick that night. For a while after he was traded he didn't wear it and it used to just drive me nuts."

"I thought it was because Donna gave him a big cross that he wears," I said.

"Isn't she gorgeous?" Head smiled. "I love her. She has done so much for him, I'm just forever grateful."

Finally, we were set up and the camera rolled.

I was scanning the room and my eye caught a big altar. A candle was burning. Behind it was a bookshelf full of books, some of them religious.

After Martin finished, I lingered in the room.

"Wasn't your faith in Jesus enough to keep you from killing yourself?" I wondered.

"I didn't think that before," Head said.

"It's interesting. When you talk about Lombardi or Phil, it's almost like you're talking about Jesus," I said. "You say things like when they came into your life."

Head smiled. "Lombardi was religious also, but he used the Bible to tell his players how they should be."

"Do you see Phil as Christ?" I asked.

"One step removed." She laughed. "No, I don't worship him like people who go to Jim Jones or Billy Graham as if they are Christ. I know Phil isn't and I know Lombardi wasn't, but by example they lived and they came when I needed it at the time. There's some stupid reason God wants me, because he wouldn't have had Lombardi come along. Plus I also suffer from severe migraine headaches. Pain every day of my life and when they get bad, I may joke about wanting to have a shotgun, but I don't mean it." Head was

244 ■

smiling enigmatically as I headed for the door. "Don't forget to stand up for us common fans," she implored me, squeezing my hand good-bye.

• MARCH 2

The Bruins were back again and this became an occasion for the thoughtful hockey media to reflect once more on the "violent" nature of the game. And they did, all the locker-room liberals and bleeding-heart beatmen penning their predictable columns. But now it wasn't only the game that was to be condemned, it was the fans too.

Again nobody said anything about the refereeing.

But the myth of hockey violence dies hard. And tonight NBC was about to wallow in the myth. So they sent Betty Rollins to the game.

They invaded my box, four strong. There was Betty, properly stunning in a bright yellow sweater, and her female producer, a young bespectacled go-getter, and a two-man camera crew. Rollins, who rode to national fame on the strength of her mastectomy, the book describing it, and the TV dramatization starring Mary Tyler Moore, was there on assignment from John Chancellor's nightly news program. She was there to get inside the psychology of people who love to see violent games. She was there to wax eloquent on the needs of a culture that would celebrate violent sports. She had come to bury hockey, not to praise it. It was her first hockey game. I tried to set her straight.

"I don't want to hear that, don't tell me it's not a violent game." She was setting up a chair in the box, while below us the teams were going through warm-ups. Betty had a folder full of clips, the liberal-press line on hockey violence, and she was doing her homework. She was such a good little student that before the warm-ups were over, she had already drafted her on-camera lead. I peeked over her shoulder and read off her yellow legal pad:

Of all sports fans, hockey fans are probably the most violent and it's no coincidence that the game itself, the way it's played, is violent.

It was almost a self-fulfilling prophecy. She had about five fans ready to tear the crew apart because the camera was sticking way out of the box, blocking their view. When they made her lower it, she sulked and curled up on the floor of the box.

"You better watch out for the puck." I smiled sweetly as the players lined up for the opening face.

"You mean the ball can come up here?" She was aghast.

"Are you kidding?" I warned. "You know how many people lose their eyes?" She ran over and warned the others.

Then the game started, and she curled up again and went over her clips. She missed one of the best hockey games in memory, a spectacular exhibition of skating and good, clean hitting and masterful passing. The Rangers drew first blood forty-four seconds into the game when Talafous pounced on a weird bound off the boards and shoveled it past the startled Bruin goalie. Then five minutes later, Hedberg, using Tkaczuk as a decoy, wristed his thirtieth past Gilbert. Rollins went on reading her "Ice Wars" article.

Marcus distracted her, though. He was over to the box, visiting me, and she immediately picked on his first blood-curdling "BUBBA" chant. She ordered the camerman to turn the camera around. Marcus was ready.

"Let's go, JD," Marcus yelled. "This is the big time, huh? NBC. Let's go, Carol." He was like a banshee.

"Hit someone for a change. C'mon, EJ, hit someone."

His face was turning beet red. "You want me to jump up like a maniac?" Marcus asked.

"Mellow out," I instructed, but Marcus was out of control.

"MURDOCH," he screamed. "Hit 'em, hit 'em. Let's go, Spoon."

In the second period, Betty got what she seemed to have come for. O'Reilly mugged EJ, plowing his elbow deep into the Ranger's face. Eddie came right back and cross-checked the Bruin across the back. They both tumbled, tangled up, to the ice. But Betty was too preoccupied with putting on her makeup to notice. It was nearing the end of the period and she was about to do her intro.

"Why don't you set up behind me and I'll sort of lean over the rail here?" she suggested, and the producer snapped to it. The on-camera personality snuggled up to the rail and turned back to the camera. Then they turned the flood-lights on.

They nearly blinded Esposito. It seems that ol' Betty had chosen to do her shtick exactly when the players were lined up right below us for a face-off. Esposito pulled back from the circle and pointed his stick right at us. The linesman looked up and pointed, yelling at the cameraman to cut the lights. A few cops started running over. Betty sat on her perch, blithely unaware of what was happening. As soon as the period was over, Sonny himself rushed over.

"Which one did that? he asked me. I nodded toward Rollins.

"I'm sorry but . . . " she began, but Sonny cut her off.

"You should have criminal charges filed against you." Sonny was wagging his finger. "Do you realize you were blinding the players and they couldn't see?"

"I wasn't," Betty said lamely.

"Who held the floodlight?" Werblin roared.

"One of our lighting men." She was cool.

"Whoever it is," Werblin retorted. "You talk about riots and trouble here. You could have someone killed."

"Well, I'm sorry," she said as Sonny stormed off. She turned to me. "Who is that?"

I told her. "I don't know who he is," she said. "I have no idea who Sonny Werblin is."

"He's only the biggest impresario in sports," I replied.

"Then what's Mike Burke?" she asked.

"He works under Sonny," I said.

"Oh," Betty shrugged. "It's nice to be chewed out by the boss."

She behaved herself the rest of the game. Huddled on the floor of the box, looking at the *Times* magazine section. Investigative electronic journalism at its best. "It's nice down here," she chirped. "I can't see a thing."

She thought it was nice till some boisterous fans started throwing things. Paper cups, and then a few lumps of soggy pretzel. Betty looked around nervously. "They could be aiming at the band," I said. "So, what do you think of hockey?" I asked cheerfully.

"What do I think of this?" She gestured contemptuously. "All sports . . . I find it's not a world that I like. It's not my thing, that's why they wanted me to do this." Objective electronic journalism at its best. "I don't like it, I don't like groups of more than ten people to start with."

"This is like the first time I went up to the South Bronx," she told me later. "You have to know the territory."

The Rangers held on and won 2–1, and in the locker room after, Doogie interviewed me. "What did you think of the *Interview* mag thing?" he asked as soon as I came over. "Wasn't that the fucking worst?"

"Yeah, but that's their style," I said.

"What about the picture? Did it do me justice?" he worried.

"Of course not," I grunted.

"Sometimes it takes a while for me to express myself," Doog said. "You think the answers were okay? Do you think I sounded dumb?"

"No, you can't expect to look good with that setup. The

whole format is ridiculous." I consoled him.

"Yeah, dumb questions, eh?" he agreed. "When I read it, I wasn't happy with it. I thought the pictures were so good, if we had a decent interview I could be proud of myself."

Larry Brooks came over. Brooks was the columnist for the *Post*, a writer whose passionate attachment to the Islanders and their general manager, Bill Torrey, made him sound like an Islander management consultant. His coverage of the Rangers often read as if it were designed to foment dissension by trying to turn players against each other. But this time he had come to apologize. His last column was in praise of Ron Greschner. He had praised Greschner by suggesting that you could find five Duguays before you'd find another Greschner. This didn't sit too well with the sensitive wing.

"I don't have anything against you," Brooks told Doogie. "Maybe I should have said two and a half instead of five. You're playing really well."

"Thanks." Doogie was polite. "When you're having a tough time, things like that don't help."

"I don't have anything against you, " Brooks repeated lamely and then drifted away.

"If he doesn't have anything against me, then why put it in?" Doogie whispered to me. "He's got nothing against me, then he puts me down."

Sarge came by and handed me a cigar. Joanne had given birth the other day, two months prematurely, and the baby boy, James Vincent, all of three pounds and change, was now in intensive care.

"Everything okay?" Tim Moriarty, the *Newsday* man, asked.

"He's coming along good," Sarge said. "And Joanne's okay. The baby had a few anxious moments there. He's stronger the last couple of days. He's starting to motor."

"I was going to put it in my column as a note," Moriarty explained. "She's at North Shore?"

"Yeah, but don't put that in there," Sarge warned. "A couple of crackpots called already. They said, 'Why did you have such a small baby? Steve's such a big hockey player.'"

• MARCH 3

The latest manifestation of hockey chic took place tonight at the Roxy Roller Rink. They don't play roller hockey at the Roxy. It's a big silver-domed room, fueled by rock 'n' roll money and Studio 54 sensibility. A place to don skates and listen to disco music and stargaze. If you're lucky, you might see Mick or Andy or Brooke. If you're unlucky, you get to roll around and around in circles, slowly burning calories.

But tonight at the Roxy you could cop real stars. The U.S. Olympic Hockey Team in all its golden glory. The Roxy was one step on a whirlwind New York postvictory celebratory spin that included a nice green Volkswagen commercial.

They marched in wearing their familiar red, white, and blue parkas. The latest names, Morrow and Wells and Harrington and Eruzione. And Herb Brooks. Brooks faded to the sidelines and watched his charges. The young stars milled around and took a few publicity shots, and after a while they got into the swing of things, pulling on roller skates and going around and around.

Naturally the roller bunnies followed suit. "Jesus, did you see that?" Brooks nudged me as we watched from the stands. He pointed to Cheryl Rixon, Penthouse Pet of the Year, who was skating around scantily clad. "Some of these skaters are quite good," the coach assessed.

"Where the hell did that broad go?" Brooks had an eye peeled for the Pet. She rolled around this time with an escort. Harrington and Wells had lassoed her, and each had an arm. "They got her." Brooks elbowed me. "Two of my guys got her." He beamed like a proud father.

Around midnight they introduced the guys. By this time Doog and Gresch and Murder and Bubba had shown up, out of professional courtesy. And Andy and Catherine had followed in their wake.

They finished the intros and the guys skated around with some models provided for the occasion, and by one o'clock the place had emptied a bit. So now it was the Rangers' turn. They had to coax Gresch, but soon there was Bubba, immense in a Chocolate Haagen-Dazs Ice Cream T-shirt, and Doog in his royal-purple Oren and Aretsky warm-up jacket, and Mud, likewise, skating backward and boogieing and being pursued by a photographer on wheels.

Andy and Catherine were on wood now, and Andy grabbed Doog's hand. They went around a few times, *pas de deux*. But tomorrow was practice, so soon they filtered off and got changed. Andy and Catherine were at the door to bid adieu.

"You gotta get Gresch hooked up with Catherine," Warhol pleaded with me as the defenseman headed out. "I don't know what it is, but our timing's always off with these hockey players. You gotta help us. Ratso, get us both dates with the Rangers."

"Which one do you prefer?" I asked Andy.

"Anyone for me." He smiled. "Catherine wants Gresch, but our timing seems to be off."

I told him I'd do what I could. "We gotta go ditch our dates." Andy winked and grabbed Catherine. "They're Mafia."

- MARCH 4

Doogie was already getting fallout from the *Interview* piece. The little girls at the Garden were all holding up the cover whenever he skated into their corners. And Steven

Spielberg saw it too. He liked it so much he called and set up supper with the winger to discuss his next film. A twenty-two-million-dollar job, with the shooting starting in June. Just about when the last of the ice disappears.

• MARCH 5

They beat Buffalo tonight 4–2, and that made it five wins in a row, and suddenly this team was jelling. Gresch was paired with Beck, and as a result he found he had the space to execute his deft stickhandling. Doogie had come alive and tonight he got his twenty-first goal. Bothwell was worked in as a sixth defenseman, and he was playing well enough that Fred allowed, "We don't worry about him when he's out there anymore. That's a good sign." Espo kept rolling, picking up his twenty-ninth, the insurance goal. And Davie Silk, the Rangers' Olympian, made his NHL debut and wound up plus one. Everybody seemed happy but Murdoch. He still sat.

He wasn't the only one upset. I was at a table with Gresch and Dave Maloney and his fiancée, Vicki Frost. Vicki was an attractive girl from Greenwich, Connecticut, who had met Dave in the practice-rink parking lot during the play-offs last year. After a rough first double date, where a friend of Dave's spilled beer all over her dress, the two had become inseparable. And midway through the season, they had announced their engagement. Which did not sit too well with the Charlie O's groupies.

"Sometimes I wonder what I'm getting myself into," Vicki confessed after Gresch and Dave went to the bathroom. "It's like marrying a physician, his time isn't his own. People hold him up and exalt him. And then there are the sickos. You should see the things they wrote in the ladies' room here, in one of the stalls. I was tempted to write a reply."

"Want to go to Oren's to get a bite?" Dave asked.

"We got that meat at home," Vicki said, then turned to me. "He only goes out with the boys."

"Oh, Vick." Maloney's face turned red.

As soon as they left, to go home and cook their meat, I moved into action. Henry sent a bouncer to blockade the ladies' room. I sent Rachel in to hurry the occupants. And then, in the purest interests of investigative journalism, I checked out the first stall on the left.

To find the message, you had to be sitting. I plopped down onto the seat. Then you had to peel off the torn wallpaper. There, written on the white plaster underneath, was the missive:

> The future MRS. DAVE MALONEY (and I'm referring to Vicki Frost) is just using 21 year old baby charm to use DM. She's trying hard to get him *wrapped around her finger* but it won't work if Dave is *smart* and I know he is. Even if he doesn't show it all the time he does have a lot of BRAINS and unlike Vicki he's MATURE. The Maloney Brothers are #1.

Next to this, two replies had been scribbled. One read: "Come June, see if you still think so." The other read: "Why are we here on earth? To live shallow lives or to live with wholesomeness and to better ourselves from the inside out?"

• MARCH 9

Montreal snapped the streak last night, but tonight the Rangers were back to their newfound winning ways, beating a fleet young Minnesota team 4–2. And for the first time in his career, Dave Maloney scored the hat trick.

Afterward, Shero seemed almost jovial. "If anyone told

you weeks ago that you'd get twelve out of the last fourteen points . . . " someone said.

Shero took a drag off his cigarette. He was dapper, almost Cherryesque in a pinstriped suit tonight. "I don't know, we're bound to beat somebody. We weren't beating anybody for a while. Why shouldn't we beat somebody?"

"Did you say anything after the first period?" The standard imaginative queries began.

"I don't speak to them between periods, Mike does," Fred explained. "I tell him what to say and . . . " He was drowned out by the laughter.

Again the questions were about Murdoch and his recently expressed desire to be traded. After dancing around the subject, Freddie was intercepted on his way out by Walt McPeek of the *Newark Star-Ledger*. "Is Murdoch's problem off the ice or is it not checking, not playing tough? Is it a disciplinary sort of thing?"

Shero stopped and cocked a cold eye at the reporter. "I'll tell you as long as you don't put it in the papers." McPeek was amenable. "Okay, don't put it in the papers. It's off the ice. There's nothing wrong with him. He scored eighty goals for me. I gotta love him, all right?"

In the locker room everyone surrounded Maloney. I waited for the crowd to thin out, chatting with Greschner. "To do this book, who did you talk to, Rats?" Gresch said. I told him the mechanics. "Halligan didn't tell anybody else. He didn't tell any brass."

"How do you know?" Something was up.

" 'Cause we had a meeting on the ice today, at practice. Nykoluk said he didn't know from a management point of view that you were supposed to go on that trip. He thought you were assigned by Werblin."

"Assigned to do what?"

"To cover us for your book."

I was baffled. "Management knew about it from the start."

"I don't care." Gresch shrugged. "I'm just telling you what they said."

I walked over to Esposito. "What did Nykoluk say today?"

"I can't tell you what he said, Rats"—Phil was drying between his toes—"because I don't listen to him when he talks. But from what I understand it was something about being careful, he thought you were employed by Sonny to write a book and you're not. Some fucking thing like that. Ask the honk, Gresch was telling me about it."

"He sometimes gets it confused," I said.

"I don't listen to Nykoluk when he talks," Phil said. "I go in the back. 'Cause I don't know what the fuck he says sometimes and I don't give a fuck what he says too. How do you like that for apples?"

I finally got the lowdown from Silk, the new boy in town. "He told us to be careful what we said around you." Silkie smiled ingenously. "He said that Ratso could bury us in the book."

- MARCH 10

Tonight was the annual Lester Patrick Awards dinner, and this afternoon there was the obligatory press conference and John Ziegler, NHL president, was behind the podium giving the obligatory upbeat report on the state of the game. To his left sat Herb Brooks, Bobby Clarke, Flyer owner Ed Snider, and Shero. They were all to be honored tonight.

After it was over, Rejean Shero roamed around getting autographs, and GM's conclaved in corners with agents. Most of the Rangers hightailed it to the Plaza bar. Outside it started pouring.

Silkie was standing by the bar with some friends, talking to some girls.

"If you can't cab it, you can all pitch a tent on my bed." He dangled his Plaza key. Doogie came over to wish him luck. Tomorrow was the trading deadline and it was also the day the Rangers would decide on Silk's fate: the Big Apple or the Crabapple. The girls lingered, then left.

"I didn't want them anyway," Silk shrugged. "They had some chops on them."

"I had tears in my eyes during that film on the Olympics," Doogie told Silk.

"I was pumped up too," the Olympian admitted. He reached in his pocket and handed me and Duguay little plastic Team USA pins. "I'm thinking about having an earring made out of one for the summertime."

McClanahan, another Olympian, came over, and he and Silk were talking when Baker, another teammate, walked in with Ruby from Charlie O's. The Americans' jaws dropped as they eyed Ruby.

"I'm getting cocky," Silk said. "I hope they don't tell me that I'm going to New Haven tomorrow."

McClanahan turned to the bar. "Let's get some beers for the wake. You'll like New Haven."

"How do you like that?" Silkie professed amazement. "My own teammate stabbing me."

"I can"—McClanahan was eyeing Ruby—"with my boner."

"Semiboner." Silk laughed. "If I stay past noon tomorrow, I get a New York Rangers emblem tattooed on my forehead. Okay, girls, here I am."

Frank Brown, the AP writer, came by and picked up Silkie's large plaque, admiring it. "You can't get past the metal detectors with that," Brown said.

"So what?" Silk shrugged. "They don't have metal detectors in Greyhound stations." He laughed ironically and went back to his conversation with his agent. They were talking about the poster Silk wanted marketed, the poster of him in the Ranger jersey, wearing the gold medal.

• MARCH 11

Two people cried today. Silkie, for all his bravado of the night before, broke down in tears when he got the word after practice that he was being sent to New Haven for seasoning. He went back to the Plaza and got his stuff together and packed to leave.

So did Murdoch. He got the word shortly after noon, the trading deadline. Nykoluk came out on the ice and called him over, and JD and Bubba and the others who were at the optional practice knew that was that. Murdoch did too, but he just walked numbly into Freddie's office, and Shero told him to have a seat.

"I don't know if this is good news or bad news, but we traded you to Edmonton," Shero said. In return, the Rangers got a tough journeyman forward, Cam Connor, and a future draft choice.

In many ways it was a very strange transaction. After sitting him out for so long and depressing his market value, they had finally let him go for next to nothing. The second-guessers would have a field day.

But right now Murdoch seemed to take it well. He got up and thanked Shero for everything, and then he left the office and hugged Joey Bucchino, and then the guys lined up and shook his hand and said their good-byes.

It wasn't until that evening, when he had some friends drive him to the airport, that reality hit home. He was flying back to Canada, back home, leaving New York, and the realization of that made him cry like a baby.

- MARCH 12

Reality was intruding everywhere these days. It had even drifted out to Denver, Colorado, and punctured Q's Rocky Mountain high. The Colorado Rockies were in town to play the Rangers, led by their acerbic coach, Mr. Cherry. And their fleet defenseman, Mike McEwen, was nowhere to be found.

The story behind his absence was extremely bizarre. It seems that the other night in Colorado, in a game against the Black Hawks, Q was on the ice and refused to come off. Each time the defenseman would skate by the bench, Cherry would call him for a change, but each time McEwen would pretend not to hear. He stayed on the ice for two and a half minutes, and Chicago scored what turned out to be the winning goal.

So, when he finally came back and sat down on the bench, Cherry went wild. He grabbed Q and shook him like a rag doll. "Don't ever try to show me up like that again," Cherry fumed. McEwen told him to fuck off. That night he left the team and went home to Toronto.

In the Ranger room after they beat Colorado, the story was Cam Connor. He didn't score in the first game, but they didn't get him to score. He did hit and hit hard, and he wound up tangling with Rockie defenseman Ramage in the third period and getting an additional ten-minute misconduct tacked on to his fighting penalty. And the fans loved every penalty minute of it.

After the press filtered out, I volunteered to steer Connor to Charlie O's. I was waiting for him, chatting with Esposito, when he walked over.

"You guys want to see the Stanley Cup ring from last

year?" He flashed a diamond. "You must have a couple of those, eh, Phil?"

Esposito smiled. "If we ever win a cup for that guy Werblin . . ."

"He'd give us a ring, eh?" Connor interrupted.

"We'd have to have two fucking hands to carry it," Espo said.

"All right." Connor was psyched. "Let's win it."

"That's all I want to do," Espo allowed. "And then I can say I quit and I can go up in a television booth and call everyone assholes. Whoweewoeweee."

- MARCH 13

Marcus called. He was depressed.

"My job with the Rangers doesn't look so good, Ratso," he moaned, "because of my escapade with NBC the other night, screaming for the camera. Krumpe was watching and he didn't like it. But what can I do?" Marcus fretted. "I'm still a fan!"

- MARCH 16

Poor Connor. He was getting it already from the Garden fans and this was only his second game. After he fanned on one shot, someone in the reds yelled, "Connor, you're a bum. Bring back Murdoch. He's better on drugs." They were also beginning to get on Captain Dave.

I got a litany between periods from Sid. Sid is a lawyer from Queens who sits behind the net in the reds and who spent the better part of the season getting on Captain Dave. Whenever Maloney made a mistake, up shot Sid, hands cupped, lungs bleating. Maloney was aware of Sid and asked me to investigate. So we convened in the hall, by the concession stand.

"You could say I'm not pleased with Maloney's performance," the counsel began. "Last year, I thought he was a very good defenseman. He obviously has the ability to play, but I don't think he plays the way he's supposed to. He gets out of position, he makes a lot of stupid mistakes. Look, I'm not a slave to numbers, but there are certain things statistics tell you. Number one, he leads the league in two-minute penalties. That's hooking and tripping. If he's playing his position properly and laying back at the blue line, you don't take those penalties. Two, he doesn't use the body enough. One week I was yelling at him that he ought to donate his body to science since he wasn't using it in hockey.

"Maybe it's my imagination, but he's been here for five years now and he had been getting progressively better and better, and I don't know if it's psychological or what, but as soon as his brother Don got here, I think it affected his defensive game. His brother Don is fabulous, works like mad, grinds all the time. I think Davey forgets to do that sometimes. He also takes a lot of stupid penalties by losing his temper. After a call, instead of just going off the ice, he argues. A captain of a team should realize another two minutes can really hurt the team. I don't think he's mature enough to be captain. He's a hothead. He's gonna get in trouble someday because of his temper."

It didn't take a half hour for Maloney to fulfill Sid's prophecy. There were less than five minutes to go in a laugher when it happened. Maloney had the puck and he tried to clear the zone, but St. Louis's defenseman, LaPointe, stole the pass at the blue line and wound up and shot a bullet past Davidson. Five to two, Rangers, now with 3:59 left. Big Deal.

It was to Maloney. He was so pissed about his giveaway that he skated back toward the net and slammed his stick across the crossbar. So he thought.

The next thing anybody knew, JD was down like he was shot. He was writhing on the ice in pain. Behind the bench Shero thought that Maloney had hit his own goalie in the head with his stick. It looked to me like the defenseman had missed the crossbar entirely and whacked Davidson square on the leg.

Like that famous New York sportscaster says, "Let's go to the videotape." That's exactly what Gordon and Chadwick did up in the Ranger broadcasting booth:

GORDON: Davidson is down.

CHADWICK: Davidson is hurt.

GORDON: He made a move for the shot and the next thing you know he is down. He put his hand on the back of his left leg, where the hamstring is. Oh, is he in pain. They called a stretcher. JD had a knee operation, but it does not appear to be his knee. We're too far away to diagnose. Oh, what a shame, what a shame for his season.

CHADWICK: He's trying to get up. He may have been hit by one of the Ranger sticks. Let's take a second look at the play. There's Dave Maloney, number 26.

(Slow motion shot of Maloney's stick clearing crossbar and hitting square on Davidson's Achilles heel.)

GORDON: Oh, no. Oh my Lord.

CHADWICK: It was Dave Maloney hitting him. Uh-oh.

GORDON: Talk about a terrible thing. Dave Maloney is disconsolate on the side. Everyone was around him, holding him. I think he's crying. Oh, what a tough thing to happen. Look at this. Oh Lord. Let's see it one more time. See if we can get a better look at it.

(Replay of stick creaming Davidson.)

CHADWICK: There's Dave Maloney wearing 26.

GORDON: I thought it was around the Achilles tendon. Wouldn't that break your heart. All the way and something like that to happen. Maybe it's only a bruise.

It didn't look that way. JD finally was escorted off the ice, looking like a lumbering wounded bear. And, as soon as the final buzzer went off, Maloney was the first Ranger off and into the dressing room. Later, when the press filed in, there was no sign of either one.

JD made the first appearance. He hobbled into the room with only a towel around his waist. They surrounded his stall immediately. "It's a little stiff." He eased himself down. "I got all numb there. At first, I thought something was broken, but it's just in the Achilles tendon area. It'll be all right. David's still on my Christmas card list."

Everyone laughed. "You'd do anything for attention, John," Marv Albert, the NBC broadcaster, said.

JD grinned cautiously. "Things were going along pretty well until I saw the stretcher. I said, 'No, no, that's it, the end.' It's a little stiff, but it'll be all right, for sure. It felt at first like an electric shock. I've broken bones before and I thought at first that I had broken the ankle and it went all numb on me and I didn't know what the hell to do, but the pain subsided and the feeling came back to the ankle. It's just one of those things, it'll be a joke in the dressing room tomorrow morning, I'm sure."

"Did you realize that it was Dave Maloney that did it to you?" Albert asked.

"Yeah, I realized it was Dave Maloney because he kept on yelling at me to get up," JD said sardonically. "And I said, 'I'm trying, I'm trying.' I feel sorry for him. It was just one of those little accidents that happen and it's nothing serious, thank goodness, and we'll get ready for tomorrow."

262 ■

"He looked like he had a tear in his eye on the ice," someone noted.

"Oh, he's such a sensitive guy and such an emotional intense person on the ice," JD said. "He's there every day whether it's a practice or gamewise. Every shift he works hard. He was disappointed that we had given up a goal that late in the game and he was on for a goal against. It's just something, a reaction that happens, it's not something serious. I understand it coming from such an intense young gentleman as Dave Maloney."

"What did you really tell him?" Marv prodded.

"I haven't told him yet," JD laughed. "I'll tell him tomorrow morning."

"What are you gonna do the next time a goal is scored, run?" someone suggested.

Meanwhile, Maloney was in the shower, with his brother. I walked over to the shower room.

"You better stay in there," I warned. Maloney frowned and went back to the players' lounge. Minutes later, he stuck his head in the room, saw all the press surrounding Davidson, and flashed in, grabbed his clothes from his stall, and hightailed it back to the off-limits lounge. But his brother, Donnie, was around.

"Dave feels better?" one reporter wondered.

"Yeah, he came in right after the game and I guess he checked out JD and he was in good spirits, so it's just an unfortunate accident. It's ironic, these things sometimes happen."

"I guess it'll just become a joke in a couple of days." One scribe parroted JD.

"Well, I personally don't think it's too funny," Don Maloney said sharply. "Some of the guys made comments, but it's just nothing to joke about really . . ."

The reporters left. Don leaned over to me. "He feels like a piece of shit, eh? I would too."

"JD handled it great," I said.

"I couldn't believe it." Donnie shook his head. "It was pretty ugly."

But it didn't seem to have much of an impact on the other guys. Gresch was walking around, inviting guys to have showers with him, and Bubba was getting dressed to rush up to Oren's for dinner, and Sarge stopped by to tell me his latest joke. The one about the Polish parachute that opens on impact.

Cam Connor seemed unconcerned too. He discreetly called me over to Bubba's stall and then pointed at the small bucket that each player used as a spittoon. "Between you and I, take a look at that," he said. I gingerly pulled out a letter. It read:

Dear Mr. Beck,

Hi, how are you? I have only one question to ask you. When the hell are you going to give me your jock? It would give me such happiness to have it hanging over my bed. I could dream about your balls every night and about how good they probably taste. Every time I lick the seal on an envelope I think about licking your asshole. When you told me that my letters could be better, I felt like saying—FUCK YOU! And I meant that literally. This libido that I have for you is driving me crazy. When I see you throwing your body at other players, I just wish that you would throw it at me. Just think of the things I would do with it! I would even lick you clean after you go to the bathroom. I hope that you get a big "head" after you read my letters (and I don't mean the kind Duguay has). Stay just the way you are because you make me cream!

Pervertedly yours,
Susan R

264 ▪

P. S. Now the only thing I've come to trust is an orgasmic rush of lust!

• MARCH 19

The Rangers did it again. This time they fired Eddie Giacomin, the goaltending coach and former Ranger hero who, everyone agreed, had done such a great job with the multitude of goalies the Rangers possessed. Well, not exactly fired. It seems that he was working without a contract, just a verbal agreement. Which didn't mean much around the Garden these days. All the players seemed upset about Eddie leaving. The consensus was that he had a good glove hand, but he got beat in the corners.

• MARCH 23

In retrospect, as soon as Maloney's stick came down and chop-chopped Davidson's vulnerable tendon, that was the beginning of the end of the Rangers. It was certainly a fitting metaphor for the interpersonal relations on this team. And it showed up on the ice too.

They lost two on the road to Edmonton and Winnipeg, both less than powerhouses. And tonight they were simply outclassed by Montreal 6–1. Afterward no one was happy.

Even Dave Maloney and his fiancée were fighting. Well, not fighting but disagreeing. Maloney was defending a column by Brooks. The journalist, after the Davidson incident, argued that the captain should grow up. Maloney agreed. "I deserved it," he said, sipping a beer. "I've got to learn how to control myself."

Vicki to the defense. "Yeah, but the press is after you.

They don't like you. They put up Doogie, he can't do no wrong. JD can't do no wrong." She turned to me. "At least David shows some intensity out there. He cares. Sometimes you wonder whether Beck is just going through the motions."

There was one bright spot tonight. A new Polish joke was making the rounds. Why does Poland have no hockey team? Because they all drowned in spring training.

• MARCH 26

The hockey writers had a luncheon today, and they gave the good guys cooperation award to Anders Hedberg, who then spent a half hour after the lunch was over demonstrating why he won the award. But the occasion was really an excuse for the press corps to get together and gossip about the team. The hottest item circulating was Esposito's line about his new line. "Connor and Talafous," Espo reportedly moaned. "Next they'll put me out with the stick boys." "Real team man," Larry Brooks spat.

• MARCH 29

They finally won one tonight, a 4–3 squeaker over St. Louis that featured spectacular goaltending from JD. The win boosted the Rangers' record to six games over .500. They were in third place in the Patrick Division, two points ahead of Atlanta. But what's the difference? Everyone knows that the regular season in hockey is just an exhibition season anyway, eh?

• MARCH 31

A strange game tonight. After two periods the Rangers trailed Detroit 5–2, and Beaver was consistent with the hordes in her evaluation. "He's brutal," she said of hubby. "It's time for Baker." But then the Rangers stormed back and scored five times in the third. Donnie Maloney got three of them, giving him twenty-five for the year, including the game winner, a fluke flip shot that hit a chip in the ice and bounced crazily over Rogie Vachon's shoulder.

Afterward Shero seemed strangely pleased for such a shoddy game. "You think this was Connor's best game?" someone asked.

"I thought he was the reason for one goal," Shero said. "I said to Mike he's got to get a break somewhere."

"While one goal was being scored, he was punching the hell out of somebody," someone else noticed.

"Well, that's what we want." Shero laughed. "Put that in the paper."

"How about Donnie Maloney? He belittles himself as a scorer. Do you consider him a goalscorer?"

Shero mused. "No, I don't think so. A goalscorer wouldn't play the way he does. He wouldn't go in the corners that often. Goalscorers say the hell with you, let someone else go in the corners. Right?" He chuckled.

"Doesn't sound like you're too disappointed he's not a goalscorer," someone followed up.

"Maybe the reason he's scoring now is because of Talafous," Shero guessed. "He's going into the corner, whereas Murdoch wouldn't. He's controlling the puck and fighting for the puck and getting a beating."

"Murdoch used to go in, but he very seldom came out with the puck," McPeek declared.

"Yeah, he'd go in late." Freddie chuckled. "Where you're sure you're not going to come out with it."

"Fred, you're not supposed to be that honest," McPeek gasped.

"Don't put those things down," Fred said. "I mean . . ." He shrugged.

"I write slow." McPeek laughed.

Shero wasn't the only one remembering Murdoch tonight. After the game in Charlie O's, one of the guys came over to the table where I was sitting with Audrey and Irene Nicen. Audrey and Irene worked for Sasson and were responsible for coming up with the idea of using hockey players to sell jeans. And in the course of their work, they met and became friendly with Don Murdoch.

"I saw Donnie Thursday," Audrey reported. "He was in to pick up his clothes. It was so depressing."

"I've got a picture of Mud on the wall as a tribute," Irene said.

"Do you have some vials of cocaine up there too?" the eavesdropping Ranger said sardonically. He got up and left Irene shaking with rage.

• APRIL 2

The Rangers gave out their annual awards before tonight's game, but it didn't help. Anders Hedberg was voted the team's most valuable player by the media, and Donnie Maloney won the players' player award, a team vote. And Phil Esposito got the Ranger Fan Club's Frank Boucher trophy —voted most popular Ranger on and off the ice.

Davidson got nothing but trouble.

He gave up four goals in the first period, and they listened to Beaver's plea of the other night. They brought in Baker to start the second. Beaver meanwhile was depressed.

"I don't know what's wrong with John," she fretted. "He should have had three of those goals. Except that he's bored and he has diarrhea."

After the game Davidson looked exhausted.

He was sitting and talking about the fans, who had once again turned on him tonight. "How many people in the world can you trust?" JD spoke softly. "How many can you genuinely trust? Your own friends and I trust my friends. As far as the rest of the world goes, most people in this world are two-faced as a whole. That's just a fact of life. All I'm trying to say is the guys in the dressing room have to keep the faith amongst themselves because you have to keep that or else you may as well just jump off a sinking ship and say good-bye."

"Doesn't it become almost a humorous thing?" one radio man asked. "Like the other night you were down and they were booing, then you went ahead and they started chanting 'JD, JD.' Aren't you tempted to just say they're jerks?"

"It's not very humorous whatsoever. It becomes disheartening 'cause you work your ass off for so long, and then all of a sudden, bang, you have a bad period or a bad little area and the people just . . ." He trailed off.

After a while they let him be and Davidson dressed quickly. I drifted over. "I know this much, Ratso, I'm sick of these fucking fans here. I almost said it to the press but I didn't. Fuck it. They're a bunch of stiffs, they're crazy. They can go fuck themselves." He sat down.

"You see, Rats, you say it's the greatest place in the world to live." JD seemed softer than usual. "Sure it is. You meet people. If you can afford to meet them, and that's true."

"It's also the toughest city in the world to live in too," I added.

"I live in other places. Most people here say it's the greatest place in the world, but they've never been out of fucking Manhattan, Ratso. Hey, there's more to life than being shit on, I'm telling you."

"That's true, but don't take it so personal," I tried. "It doesn't matter who's in there. Iran has something to do with it. The whole economic situation. You have nothing to do with it. You're not playing for those people, the ones that boo."

"I know," the big goalie whispered.

"You're playing for the people that care about you," I finished.

"I'm fed up." JD picked up his coat. "I'm fucking fed up, though."

He passed Gresch, who was coming back from his shower. Last, as usual. "Jesus, we got beat tonight and they didn't even boo me once." Gresch feigned shock.

"Hey, Rats." It was Espo. "When is your book coming out? You gonna give us a copy?"

I walked over with Gresch. "Sure." I was saccharine. "I'll give free copies to all my friends."

"I guess I'll have to buy a copy—is that what you're telling me?" Espo said.

"It means he's only giving me one," Gresch said.

"I got a couple of friends." I shrugged.

Greschner leaned over and touched Esposito's trophy, which was resting on the stall next to him.

"This hurts, this hurts." Gresch smiled.

"It hurts them," Espo snickered. "Does it ever hurt the fucking management? 'Cause they can't fucking stop that one. Does that bug them?" He had an impish smile as he picked up his trophy and walked out of the room to Joe and the waiting limo.

• APRIL 3

I was on the phone with Cusimano.

"It's all motivation, that's Shero's forte anyway," I was explaining. "And look what he's doing now. He knows that this team is rife with dissension. He knows everything, that remote fog shit is just an act. Just a way to catalyze things, by allowing people to act in the vacuum he creates and prove themselves for good or bad. But so far what the vacuum has produced is an incredible power struggle between Nykoluk and Keating. They both want Freddie's job so bad it hurts. And Maloney is palsy-walsy with Nykoluk and Vadnais to the exclusion of the other players. And the city guys think Nykoluk is too provincial. He doesn't understand their outside interests.

"So what does Shero do to remedy this going into the play-offs? He gets everyone pissed at him, man. He unites them by fucking with their ice time and their lines, and they come together by virtue of their shared anxieties and frustrations about Shero. He sacrifices himself for the team. Heavy."

"I hope you're right," Cusimano said. "But he's such a weirdo. Well, the proof is in the pudding."

- APRIL 4

The shit began to hit the fan. After the other night's disastrous loss to the Flames, some of the Rangers began openly criticizing their coach, accusing him of being remote and uncommunicative for the record, and accusing him of drinking too much, off the record. Lawrie Mifflin bannered the charges in a backpage spread in today's *News*: RANGERS VOICE DOUBTS ABOUT SHERO'S COACHING. She cited their on-the-record concerns.

"It's tough to have confidence in a guy when you never see him," one Ranger told her. "When he never talks to you, never comes on the ice at practice."

"He doesn't even come and talk to us between periods anymore," another complained. "Mike does."

This was nothing new. But the Rangers were in disarray and Shero was handy. So was Mifflin. She conveniently broke the story the morning that Werblin decided to go out to practice and raise hell. You couldn't have orchestrated the media blitz better if Sarah Caldwell was on the ice.

So Sonny did his Sonny act. He took Shero aside after sweeping in with Jennings and Krumpe. Then he addressed the entire coaching staff and the players in unison. Then the press, who had been alerted, grilled Werblin.

What did he tell Shero?

"To get his act together," Werblin grunted.

What did he tell the players?

"To get their act together."

Did he chew out everyone?

"Oh no," Sonny purred. "I just talked to the team, couldn't have been for more than two minutes. It was a bit of a pep talk. The team is not polarized, but I talked about unity, let them know they're not alone. I think it's good for a team to know somebody above the coach and general manager is concerned, interested." Sonny and the brass seemed very interested indeed.

That was the impression Bubba got. We were having dinner at Oren's, talking with Marc from Studio about Sonny's visit and the controversy over Freddie and the upcoming play-offs. Beck had been an enigma since he had come to New York from the Rockies. On the one hand, he had shown what a presence he possessed on the ice, how dominant a force he could be. When he wanted to. But on the other hand, of late Bubba had seemed to be holding back. There were those who whispered that he had his parachute on.

But injuries had played a factor. It was ironic that this massive specimen of human rock, this man-mountain, had since his arrival played with all sorts of physical maladies. His groin pull constantly bothered him, and his elbow forced him to the sidelines, and he played for weeks with a nagging flu that made him resemble a zombie. It was clear that the Rangers still had not seen a healthy Beck playing up to his potential.

But tonight, sitting in the back room, gnawing on a steak, Bubba looked healthy. And hungry.

"You go to practice today?" I asked.

"Yeah, at nine-thirty. We had to go watch fucking films of the Atlanta game," Bubba grunted. Only the defensemen had to watch."

I brought up Sonny's media blitz.

"Some of these reporters are the worst, I can't believe it," Bubba said. "Two-faced bastards. And they love the dirt. Someday I'll go in there and tell them we got a couple of guys that are quitting tomorrow and one guy's planning on running away with another girl. One guy killed his baby boy today. They love to write about dirt. The next play-off game, if we lose, Gresch and I are gonna start a makeup fight when the reporters come in. They'll take pictures of it and put it in the papers the next day, 'Battle Inside Dressing Room.' "

Bubba laughed. "Christ, you should have been at practice today. Everybody was there, Werblin, Jennings, Keating, all the reporters. Sonny told us how the guys were getting on Shero and we should try and look at ourselves, you know, the same old bullshit. I know it's once you start losing you start blaming everyone else but yourselves. The best line I ever heard was when I was playing in Denver, we had a four-on-four situation and Mike Christie had his man in front of the net and they scored a goal and he came back to the bench. Cherry says, 'What happened there, Mike?' Mike says, 'Well, I had my man.' And Cherry says, 'What are you, a fucking Mountie?' Cherry's too much. He has this bulldog, Blue, that he loves and takes everywhere. One of the first games we played in Pittsburgh, they had a big sign that said 'Kill Ole Blue.' They hated the dog and when Cherry came on the ice, they all started barking. So after the first period we were losing 3–0, Cherry comes in and he was giving us shit. He says, 'Goddamn you bunch of fucking assholes. Goddamn Blue is out there dying for you guys and you don't do a goddamn thing.' Cherry's a players' coach, he wants everything for his players. He was negotiating my contract for me there."

Bubba laughed. "How about the other day? Sonny comes in and looks to me and Espo and says, 'Who the fuck is André?' We told him he's one of the new assistant coaches. He says, 'I don't even know who the fucking guy is and I find out we got a new assistant coach and he's been coaching for a month?'"

"The other night Bubba was cruising and nobody would go near him, and then Hamel nails him and later, Bubba gets a chance and creams Hamel back into the boards and the crowd goes wild," I remembered. "Later I saw Bubba, and I said, 'Great check,' and he says, 'Fuck, I thought I was dead. I wanted to lay down on the ice.'"

Bubba frowned. "When I hit him, I knocked the wind out of myself. So I'm on the ice and I can't breathe and I don't want to go off 'cause I don't want all these guys going 'Hey, you're hurt,' so I'm going 'Argrgrhg, I can't breathe.' Trying to suck up air through my nose anyway. So I stayed on for about twenty seconds and I said, 'I gotta get off, I'm gonna pass out.' I was wobbling around. I got on the bench, I almost fainted. In that game too I socked myself. I went down to take a slap shot and I went out with my elbow and hit myself right in the balls. I couldn't even walk. That was a good one. Christ."

"That's almost as embarrassing as Maloney hitting JD." I laughed. "You should have heard Gordon and Chadwick trying to explain it."

"Gordon's the good one." Bubba shook his head. "It doesn't matter how bad you're playing. I've seen games where I've played the worst I've ever played and he wanted to give me a star. I play horseshit and he says, 'Beck played a fine game tonight.' "

Just then, two girls who have hovered around the table, making continual trips to the bathroom as a cover, finally summoned up their courage. "Hi," one said. "I couldn't take it anymore. We were waiting twenty minutes for you to come out."

"How you all doing?" Bubba was amiable.

"Fine, you remember us?" the other gushed.

"I remember you being outside practice one day," Beck said.

"They chased us out. We snuck in through the locker room," the first one explained.

"I'm just going home." Bubba smiled. "I got a game tomorrow."

"That's right, you should have been in bed by now," one giggled.

"Take her up on it," I hissed.

"If I'm home by one I'm okay," Bubba explained.

"Yeah, but alone?" the second one cooed. "We're gonna check to make sure."

"Oh no." Bubba held his head. "Not another bed check?"

"Doug's in the hospital," one of them said. "We saw him this afternoon." Sulliman, the number-one draft pick, had run into a board and needed knee surgery.

"How is he?" Bubba asked.

"He was all drugged out," one girl said.

"Drugged out? Lucky bugger." Bubba laughed.

The girls remained standing and they told their stories. One was from the Bronx, one from Jersey, both computer operators, both Bubba fans. Both had been sitting up front, waiting, staring at the door, unaware we were in the back eating.

"Are you gonna fight Howatt tomorrow?" one wondered.

"He'd eat Howatt for breakfast," I spat.

"I'm not into that violence stuff, I don't like that." Bubba frowned. "I'm into body checking."

"You body check the best," one cooed.

That was enough for Bubba. We paid the bill and rushed out and grabbed a cab and went back to Beck's apartment. Without the Bubbettes.

"Check these out." Beck showed me some sketches of sleek-looking cars. "My friend and I are opening up a business in color Ferraris. They give me three to five thousand to put one in shows now. I got it in fourteen shows this summer."

Beck put on a record and popped open some beer. "I'm into cars, yeah. Fast cars, fast horses, fast whiskey, and fast women," he drawled.

He sat down and started talking about the mental dimension to hockey. "It's a real mental game, no doubt about it. If you had to play eighty games on just physical and no emotional ability, you'd be fucked. You couldn't do it. You'd be too tired. Hell, we go from place to place like Colorado, Winnipeg. We're not prepared for the game like we would be in Montreal or Boston. Christ, I know I'm not."

"Shero always talks about wanting the puck," I said.

"Any sport is eighty-five percent mental," Bubba said. "It's not that much physical. I've been tired, but I can still play if I'm emotionally ready for the game. I can go out and play with one hour sleep if I'm emotionally ready."

"You've been getting rapped lately in the press. They're saying you don't dominate a game like you should."

Beck smiled ironically. "I'm waiting for the play-offs. Right now we are so bored. With so much shit that's going on. Fuck. All we want to do right now if we could we'd go down to Martinique or Florida or anywhere hot for a week, just to get away from everything."

"I remember watching you against the Russians and you

almost singlehandedly mauled them . . ." I thought back to the Challenge Cup where Werblin first saw Beck play and knew that one day he'd have him in a Ranger uniform.

"Those type of games you play on emotion. Play-offs. I like that, but right now sixteen teams make the play-offs. When I talked to Reggie Jackson and he tells me, 'Sixteen games make the play-offs? What the hell are you busting your ass for eighty whole games? You can get hurt or something.' Christ, those guys play 162 games a year. No way you can get up for all those. I can't. Lot of times you get out there and say you want to do your best but hell, your mind just doesn't do it and when your mind don't want to, it doesn't matter what shape you're in."

"Come the play-offs, I keep telling people that you'll be a dominant force, that nobody'll go near you."

Beck shook his head. "Lot of times it's no good me even being out there. Shit, I'm just standing out there. Nobody's around me. The puck hardly even comes near me sometimes. I say to myself what the fuck am I doing out here?"

"But in the play-offs . . ." I began.

"That's a whole different game. The only way we'll lose in the play-offs is if we beat ourselves. We can beat any team we want to. But if we play stupid, do things we shouldn't do, make too many mistakes, make ourselves tired, get caught up ice, you beat yourselves. If we get in a tight game, no way we're gonna lose. We'll either get beat by three or four goals or not get beat at all. There's only one thing we gotta have and that's JD plays the way he can, nobody's gonna beat us."

"What was with him the last few games?"

"He's tired," Beck said.

"I can't believe Gresch tells me the other day that he's playing hurt most of the year. His kneecap feels fucked up. He doesn't tell anybody, the fans get on him . . ."

"That's the way those fans are," Bubba said. "One minute they cheer, next minute they boo. In Colorado they didn't know if you were doing something wrong. If you lose the puck and a guy gets a breakaway and scores, they'd go 'What's going on?' "

"They loved you there," I said.

"I was a popular player. Christ, we didn't have too many guys there. I was the only one they could really write about. Everyone else was married and I was driving around in a Ferrari. I was twenty-one . . ."

"Beating the shit out of guys." I laughed. "I remember the preseason game last year against Vancouver where you beat the shit out of the whole team. You went wild."

"I was in a rough mood," Barry remembered. "My girl friend and I had a spat that day, so I was in a bad mood. I fought about three guys. They couldn't stop me, I had to stop myself. It finally got to the point where I said, 'What kind of animal am I?' I felt like I was in a circus. I was upset, I never get like that. Usually it takes somebody to get me mad before I'll do anything and get crazy like that. But I went a little bananas. Christ, there was blood all over the place. I was punching some guy in the head and another guy would lip off and I would give him a backhand." Barry shook his head.

"What's it like on the ice for you? I know when I play the weirdest little things can tick me off."

"Sometimes a guy can spear you and punch you in the back of the head and you'll think nothing of it," Beck said. "And then a guy'll come by and give you a tap on the shin pads, and Christ, you'll have the gloves off and have an arm around the throat. You just get a little weird sometimes, it's part of being a player."

"Do you feel like the ultimate enforcer?"

"Nah," he shrugged. "I think most of the smaller guys look up to a bigger guy to do that. If I was a small guy, I'd want to make sure if I get into any trouble I had somebody."

"Gresch tells me you skate over and threaten to take guys' eyes out," I said.

"That's just part of intimidation. We need Gresch on the ice, he's a great hockey player. They don't give him enough credit, though. He's really good with the puck and he's better when guys aren't running the shit out of him. Christ, if you get run every time you get the puck, the first thing you do is give the puck away all the time, so I try to give him a little more room to maneuver in and make sure nobody takes any cheap shots at him."

"So you really do that shit, curse them out?"

"Oh yeah, you don't really have to say anything. Just let a guy know that if you're gonna run him you may as well run me too. Or anybody else on the ice. We don't play enough together, me and Gresch. They play us and then they don't play us and then they do and then they don't. They will in the play-offs."

"All season long they fucked with Gresch's head, told him to change his style, but I think it was all Shero's strategy. Like what he did with Sarge. Now they're motivated. There's a real psych job there."

"The only thing is nobody knows that." Bubba frowned. "We just wish he would tell us about that. He doesn't tell us anything. It's like Freddie's keeping something from us he doesn't want us to know. It'd be interesting to see what happens in the play-offs because I don't know what the fuck is going on."

"I think that's the way he wants it." I shrugged.

"I think it is too, but I don't know that. Christ, we got guys behind the bench now yelling, 'Hey, Shero, are you allowed to talk? Can you move your lips?' He never says anything. When he does talk, he doesn't talk to you, he talks to you as a group, like the defense. I don't know why he doesn't come in between periods and talk to us."

"He tells Mike what to say and sends him in." I smiled.

"Why doesn't he come?" Bubba almost seemed hurt. "I know that's the way he wants things run but . . ." Bubba paused. "I don't even think his wife knows him, for crying out loud. His kids don't even know they got a dad."

"I'm not impressed by Nykoluk or Keating," I said. "They're no brain surgeons. I really respect Fred, though. All that talk about his drinking, I don't care . . ."

Bubba cut me off. "I don't care what he does off the ice. I don't care if he drinks ten six-packs a day as long as when it comes time for the game he knows what the hell is going on. But we'll just have to wait and see in the play-offs. I don't know what's going on now and I don't think anyone else does."

"My analysis is that the team's been divided since day one this year," I said.

"Animosity," Beck agreed.

"That wasn't there last year, to the same extent. Lot of it had to do with the outside interests, the commercials. But if you guys don't play well, there won't be any of that stuff. Hockey comes first, without that Gresch would be back in Goodsoil running a Buick dealership . . ."

"And I'd be working for him." Bubba laughed.

"What does Nykoluk say to you guys?" I asked.

"Oh Christ," Beck said with disgust, "don't even ask me. He's two-faced. I hate people like that. He wants Freddie's job so bad, he's trying to get Freddie out of there so bad. Granted he knows quite a bit about the game."

"I think he's gone," I guessed. "Besides, he's never impressed me. He just says mundane things, things people want to hear."

"That's right, he always says what he thinks the reporter wants to hear, good things all the time."

"Keating's just as bad." I frowned.

"He's just there because he's a good friend of Fred's, that's all," Barry said. "Hell, if we lose out early in the play-offs, you wait till you see the papers. What Lawrie Mifflin'll write. She knows everything. What's going on with the players, what players don't like what other players, what's going on with the coaching."

"How does she know?"

"She just knows," Beck stressed. "She's a hell of a reporter. She gets right in there, the little bitch. I tell her too. I say, 'You little bitch, you're right in there.' She says when you're small, you gotta do that. She knows what guys are assholes."

"She knows that?" I was surprised.

"She knows all that." Bubba laughed. "She knows that Freddie has a six-pack before practice. She knows all the little dirt. And she told Phil, 'I want to know the right story before I write anything because if you guys lose out in the play-offs, I'm gonna write it.' She wants to get all the facts straight because she hates Maloney. She told us, sitting on the bus once. She knows everything. The stuff she says to us is just like talking to one of the guys."

"Who's her source?" I asked.

"Probably Espo," Barry guessed. "She even had Werblin phone her up and Werblin said, 'What's going on here with my players and coaches?' That's how bad it was, honest to God."

Bubba got up to get more beers. When he came back we swapped Fog stories. I told him about the marble tabletops Fred used for ashtrays and the unique way Fred hangs up his jacket.

"How about Christmas Eve? What did he do, fall over a shoe and break his ribs? How do you do that? That's what they said. He was so hammered, I can see him getting out of the car and falling into the garbage can and waking up all the neighbors."

"How much has he talked to you?" I asked.

"I maybe talked to him twice," Bubba recollected. "And

that wouldn't be for more than twenty seconds. One time he told a joke and the other time I think he asked me for a beer. I don't even know him."

"Did you feel a lot of pressure on you after the trade?"

"No, it didn't bother me at all," Beck said. "When I played juniors, I got traded for five guys too. I know I can do good and I know I'll do good, so it doesn't bother me. There's no pressure on me."

"You don't feel the fans expect maybe too much?"

"They should expect something from me. Christ, I was traded for five guys. They'd be stupid not to expect something from me, but I know the way I can play."

"Have you played up to your expectations yet?"

"No, not yet." The big guy shook his head slowly. "I've just been cruising along, getting used to everything. It doesn't bother me a bit. Hell, I haven't put out the way I know I can. Not because I haven't wanted to. Sometimes I just don't get into it. There's too much going on around me. This is a bad place to play hockey. There's so much going on."

"How do you combat that for the play-offs?" I asked.

"You get in the play-offs. That's when you start playing for money. Money for the other guys, not only for yourself. You make your money over the season. The play-offs you can play thirty more games and get twenty-five thousand dollars for it. That's almost half a season. But each round you go further, you're making more money for the guys that make less over the year. That's when you start caring a hell of a lot more. When you start doing the little things you didn't do before, like diving to block a slap shot."

"Does intimidation play a big factor?" I wondered. "Sometimes I see you sort of go into automatic pilot and start cruising for guys. Someone said you look like a shark in water."

Bubba smiled. "I put it on cruise control and cruise, and if any trouble happens I jump in there. Some guys can be intimidated, some guys can't. When a guy gives clean body checks,

I think that's all right. I want to give him one back, but that stuff doesn't bother me. It gets me in the game more when a guy hits me 'cause then I start thinking, 'All right, I want to get into it.' If someone goes out there and leaves me alone all the time, I feel lost. 'Hey, someone come over and hit me or something. I'm out here, c'mon.' I love playing against the bigger teams. Atlanta. I like to hit Plett, Houston, and I want them to hit me. It gets me in the game."

"But very few guys'll go near you."

"That's why I want to put in the paper, 'Hey, will someone please hit me? Don't you guys want to hit me for a while? Not too hard, not too much.'"

"What do you think of the New York night life scene?"

Bubba scowled. "We got bars like that in Denver. Guys pick up chicks. There are groupies out in Denver too. It's boring."

"Does it affect the way you view women after a while?"

"It makes you feel like a slut . . ." He laughed. "I feel like a slut when I go into those bars where women throw themselves at you. And it's great."

"Be serious." I chastised him. "Would you want to settle down with any of those women?"

"No, of course not. Absolutely not."

"What's your dream girl?" I felt like *Interview* magazine.

"I have a dream girl. The girl I got out now in Colorado. The one you met."

"Really. Gee, I'm sorry I called her a hog." Beck got bigger before my eyes.

"Nasty. She's my dream girl. I'll settle down with her eventually. I'm only twenty-two."

"People forget that. You look older. Your hair is even intimidating." I admired his moss.

"I've been through a lot. I've been in jail, I've been in a lot of shit with the cops."

I perked up. "What for?"

"I had a whole lot of assault charges against me in Van- couver. Breaking and entering. Hell, I was a bad dude. I remember the cops got a hold of me once. They pulled me over for speeding and no registration, no nothing, and in the back of my car I had TV's, stereos, tape decks, cameras, all hot stuff. I was fighting cops to get away. I beat up a couple of them. I didn't want to get caught."

"How'd you get involved in shit like that?"

Bubba smiled. "That's what I did. There was no reason. It wasn't like an attention-getter or anything. I wasn't bored or nothing. I just did it."

"You hung out with the wrong people," I guessed.

"No, I was the bad people." Bubba laughed. "That's what everyone else's parents were saying, 'Quit hanging around with that Beck kid.' "

"You hated your parents." I turned social worker.

"No." He shook his massive head. "There was nothing like that at all. It wasn't like my parents used to beat me up or anything."

"What did they do?"

"My father's serving fifteen to twenty and my mother's a madam in a whorehouse," Bubba straightfaced. "Seriously, my mum's a saleslady in a department store and my dad's an engineer-inspector. Middle-class family. I have two older brothers, one's a jeweler, the other's in computers. I should have been a librarian or something. I first moved away from home when I was fifteen to play hockey. It was only fifteen miles from home, but I had to live there to play, and when I was traded from there to New Westminster I was able to stay home and play. But I never went to school or nothing."

"Why?" It still didn't compute.

" 'Cause I didn't want to," Beck boomed. "Hell, I was an easy rider. I was a rebel without a cause. That's what I wanted to do and I didn't want anyone telling me what to do. I wouldn't take orders."

"You were big enough not to," I observed, respectfully.

"I was never really big. I was always short and fat till last year. I was five foot seven inches last year. But I was always fighting, fighting all the time. I loved to fight. I always wanted to be a boxer. I still think about walking down Forty-second Street and going into a gym and boxing. One day I'm gonna do it. Say I'm looking for extra money and spar a few rounds."

"What do you like about punching somebody out?"

Beck frowned. "I don't like to beat anybody up. There was a time when I used to, when I loved to hurt somebody, punch someone in the head. I got a kick out of it. I was a juvenile delinquent." He smiled impishly.

"You wouldn't get a kick out of beating on someone who was messing with you, even if you're two goals up and two minutes to go?"

"Then I'd go over and say, 'Hey, fuck off,' and bang him one. Do I get satisfaction out of it? It doesn't make me feel good."

"It's incredible how you've channeled your degenerate antisocial tendencies into a successful career," I laughed.

"I changed overnight, I think." Bubba was serious. "Hell, I was ready to be thrown in the can for a long time. I was really in trouble. And I got a lot of help. My junior coach helped out quite a bit. He knew the Supreme Justice of all BC, which really helped. If it was anybody else, I'd still be in jail."

"You were a star too," I reminded him.

"Not right away. I was just another guy when that happened," Beck said. "I was a crook. I used to go into parking lots, jack a guy's tires up, and take 'em off. I'd break into people's homes with my buddy. We were both pretty bad apples. We've been in some brawls. Brawls in bars, stabbing guys with beer glasses, breaking glasses and stabbing 'em. This finger here . . ." The defenseman proffered one index finger. "I still have no feeling in this one. I got cut with a beer glass. I was an ornery young punk."

"You really settled down. You're a pacifist now," I marveled.

"I became a reborn Christian."

"Fuck you," I snapped.

"I had to change, Rats." Bubba got serious. "Or else I'd still be a laborer back in Vancouver . . ."

"What did your parents think of all this?" I asked.

"Oh Christ." Bubba shook his head. "They couldn't understand what was the matter with me. My other two brothers were great kids. They didn't know what to do. My mum would cry all the time. They never took me to a shrink, but they would sit down and talk to me and I would go, 'Yah, I'll never do it again.' Christ, next day do it right again. Then my dad would take off the old belt and give me one of these here." He mimicked a whupping.

"I was into enough shit so I decided to get serious. I didn't play hockey really until my last year in juniors. Then I went to Colorado and I did good. I scored twenty-two goals my first year, and that was the first time I was really away from home and it was great. Lots of girls, and all of a sudden I was dating all these great-looking broads and having a great time."

"But it couldn't be the same as here," I said.

Bubba shook his head. "Not here, if I would have been a football player, though."

"You could have been," I interrupted. "Why'd you pick hockey?"

"Make more money," Beck said. "I wouldn't have been able to last as long as a linebacker. They only last about four years. Hockey you can last into your thirties. I was always a better football player."

"It had nothing to do with the love of the game?"

"No, I always loved football more than I did hockey," Barry admitted.

"You still do?"

He grimaced. "Hum, that's a tough question. I don't know. I love football. I don't hit like other hockey players. I use my upper body, like in football. I bull people the same way I did in football. I like playing hockey, but I don't love it the way I love playing football."

"Why?" I prodded.

" 'Cause in football you could hurt somebody," Bubba said.

• APRIL 5

Gresch played today, despite a death threat. He got a call last night, and the caller left a message on his machine. Something to the effect that he would stab him as he left the Islander ice tomorrow afternoon. Then the caller called back and amended the message: he would shoot him. But there was a game to play and Gresch played. He just didn't linger when the buzzer sounded.

It was a good game. The first decent effort in weeks. As bad as they were against Atlanta, they were that good against the Islanders. They lost 2–1 but it was a moral victory, as they say.

Maybe it had something to do with the new walkie-talkie system that Shero had installed. André Beaulieu was behind the bench with the headphones and Nykoluk sat up in the press box, transmitting. Shero, behind the bench, wanted no part of it. André would talk directly to the players.

But for the first time all year, Freddie talked to the players, between periods. Everyone seemed happy to see him.

"What he say?" I asked Bubba afterward.

"He just told us we were playing good," Beck said. "Who should start the period and just to keep going."

"Was it nice to see him?" I smiled.

"Fucking right," Bubba grunted.

Doogie grunted too. He grunted on the way out when he was surrounded in the Islander corridor by at least fifty little Islander fans who were waiting patiently for their heroes.

Doogie wasn't one of them. As he walked out, they broke into song! It went: "Oh-la-la Baboon."

• APRIL 6

Another good night, the last night of the regular season. The Rangers bussed down to Philly and walked out on top, 8–3. And Greschner, who took off like wildfire after teaming up with Beck, scored two goals, giving him twenty-one for the season. Only three Ranger defensemen had done that before.

So it was a happy bus that rolled back to the Apple. And it was a crowded equipment van that rolled along in its wake.

Joe Murphy was driving and Jimmy Young, the longtime trainer, was in front, munching on a Wendy's burger. Stretched out over the bags in the back was Danny, a stick boy. I sat up front on the hump.

Danny was talking about the *News* article the day Sonny went to practice. "How was it that the brass was out there eight in the morning?" he asked, chewing on some fried chicken. "You think they fucking read the paper and said let's get a limo and go out to practice? No way. They set that up with Mifflin. She just doesn't get up and decide to write that article. I've heard those quotes for months. It wasn't written after the bad loss to Atlanta, it was written the next day."

"But that *News* story seemed misleading," I said. "I don't think Fred's job is in jeopardy."

"I think it's more serious than you think, Ratso," Danny said. "This team has feelers going up to the brass. A lot of guys have dinner with Werblin and Krumpe and mouth to them."

"Well, if they had any brains they'd know how Freddie operates," I decided. We drove in silence.

"You know, Mario was the only guy that showed up at Phil's charity thing," I said.

"I've never seen a guy changed like Mario," Danny said. "He's a star now. He used to be a fucking Donnie Maloney."

"He can't be sent down now he's got a one-way contract," Jimmy said.

"Yeah, and Vad took him under his wing. Told him not to get himself hurt, just to cool it down," Danny said.

"I wonder why." I laughed. "I bet Vad would love to take every young defenseman under his wing and cool them out. What about Bubba? I think he'll be a terror in the play-offs."

"I hope so," Danny said. "He's fucking mellowed out. When he first came here you never saw a more ferocious guy. Now he's Mr. New York. He don't want to get a bruise on his face."

"He's picking his spots," I said. "He told me. Wait until the play-offs."

"Good, then he's not stupid," Danny decided. "I don't think he is, but you know what happens to these guys. They fucking float through the year. Then when they have to put it out, it's not there anymore. He's just not the same guy he was when he came here. Then he was hitting everything in sight."

I grabbed a box of chicken.

"You know, the first press conference Freddie ever gave when he came to New York he said, 'I have to get rid of ten guys,'" Danny remembered. "Look around, he got rid of them. Hitch is gone, Q is gone, Luc is gone, Farrish is gone, Murdoch is gone, the goalies are gone. Look at Hitch, all the talent in the world and he refused to play Freddie's System. No hard feelings, but he's gone. And now look at the team they got. It's tough as hell. Bubba, Connor, Mario, Ciggy, Vad. They can all handle themselves."

"Take the stick away from Vad, forget it," Jimmy said.

"And other teams can't run us anyway," I said. "Look at the power play. You throw out either the Swedes or the Espo line, and at the point you got Bubba and Gresch. Nobody wants to take penalties against us."

"Nobody ever did." Jimmy laughed. "Remember the Cherry sisters at the old Garden? These two old ladies used to sit behind the visitors' penalty box and every time someone would get a penalty, they'd stick the visiting guy with their hatpins. The cops didn't stop them, they thought it was funny. You should see their backs at the end of the night. Those broads would just reach in through the screen or under the screen and jab 'em with their needles."

Everyone laughed and Murphy asked for some chicken, and then he gunned the van toward Manhattan.

• APRIL 8

You knew today was special. JD got his favorite dessert, pineapple, and Ciggy was glowing with excess energy after he got home from practice, despite an elbow that he could barely lift over his shoulder. Never mind about the mangled thumb. And Ulfie was feeling it too. The normally mild-mannered Swede stopped to snap at his kids, who were running around the house. Why was this night different from all other nights?

This was the first round of the playoffs. Best of five. What the eighty-game exhibition season had been pointing to all these months. Only five of the twenty-one teams got the early vacations, and the rest were now beginning the elimination process that would enable one to take temporary custody of the Cup.

The Rangers drew the Flames. Now, this did not bode so well for the Rangers, since they were 0–3–1 versus Atlanta this year, and Atlanta was 7–0–2 in their last nine outings to New York. But come play-off time, you can throw the stats out the window.

Start with the last regular season meeting between these two teams. That night, Shero was throwing out the kitchen sink and frustrating his players into a 7–3 loss. But tonight, from the opening face-off, Shero was a master behind the bench.

He used three lines for the most part and he rotated them every thirty seconds or so, and the net result was an incredibly fast-skating, breathtaking game. The Flames drew first blood in the second period when Don Lever jammed home the puck after Davidson had made two sprawling saves while the Rangers were shorthanded. Guess who was in the penalty box? Sid the lawyer's favorite player, two minutes for tripping.

But the Rangers tied it up eight minutes into the third period. Greschner got the puck off a face-off deep in Atlanta's end and sent a floater up to the Atlanta goalie, Dan Bouchard. Only the puck never reached Bouchard. It hit someone in front and bounced to the right of the net, where Vickers pounced on it and backhanded it into the vacant net. The place went wild.

They kept up a torrid pace for the next twelve minutes, but nobody scored, which meant—overtime. And it meant using every edge you can get because the first puck in wins.

Which was why Marcus was screaming at Bouchard as they lined up for the face-off. He was sitting down in the red seats, two rows from Dom, and the combo was deadly. "Bouchard, you stink," Marcus bellowed. "Gimme a rock," he told me. "I'll knock Bouchard out."

"You stink," Dom was screaming through the crack in the boards. "Hey, Russell, everywhere you go you lose. Houston, you're a bum. Choke, choke, choke." He grabbed his Adam's apple and snarled.

Then the play started and it was lightning swift. Pekka Rautakallio, the Atlanta defenseman, slammed the puck into the Ranger end, but Greschner picked it up off the carom and charged. Just before he hit the red line, he snaked a pass to Vickers, who slapped a shot on net. Bouchard kicked it out, but in the confusion, Russell, the Flames' other defenseman, fell and slid into his goalie. The puck went straight out to Greschner, who immediately backhanded it to Vickers, who was in his familiar perch to the left of the net. Sarge directed it over the hapless goalie, and that was that.

They mugged Vickers on the ice, and then as the gleeful Rangers walked to their room, they were mugged again. Keating was beside himself, and he was bear-hugging each player, slapping their backs, screaming at the top of his lungs, kissing Sarge. Shero walked by, cool as a Canadian cucumber.

In the locker room there was bedlam. Everyone mobbed Sarge, who explained the goal patiently time after time. Werblin was floating around with a smile frozen to his face. Someone asked him if it's nice to win in overtime. "It's nice to win anytime," he barked. "Overtime, othertime, even with the lights out."

JD came over. "What do you think, Rats? Did we send the people home happy?" He smiled and walked out.

Soon the city guys were ready, and they pulled Bubba away from the X-rated *Midnight Interlude* on the cable TV and headed for Joe's limo. Joe was outside with a mile-wide grin on his face.

Phil and Gresch and Doogie and Bubba piled into the back of the car. I rode shotgun with Joe. We slowly pulled out and cruised down Thirty-third Street. Outside of Charlie O's Sonny was getting into his own limo.

"Shit, we should have rolled down the window and screamed out to Sonny," Espo moaned. "Fuck me. I'd have loved to have done that."

"Sonny loves that," Gresch said.

"First stop, the Bubba," Espo yelled up to Joe. Joe made his way up Eighth Avenue. Outside the tinted windows was Forty-second Street in all its sleazy splendor.

"There's my man in the street," Bubba pointed. "See the dude there with the shoes? He's got foxy ladies. Foxy ladies."

"Fucking Mickey almost broke my fucking back," Gresch said. "What was he doing there? I'm gonna slap his harelip."

"He grabbed me by the waist and my stick was right in front of me and it hit him in the chin." Doogie laughed. "He kissed Sarge."

"If he kisses me, I'll drop him," Gresch said. "Right in the fucking harelip." Gresch started doing a rah-rah Keating imitation.

"Did he give you one of those tonight?" Espo asked.

"He did before the game," Gresch said. "He comes in and goes, 'Ronnie boy, let's go, Ronnie boy,' fucking Ronnie boy."

"Surround his eyebrows with punches." Espo laughed. "That's Murder's line. The first time I heard that we were flying back from Los Angeles and the captain comes on and starts talking and Murder is sitting next to me, on the rag, and he says, 'If that fucking captain don't shut up, I'm gonna go up to that cockpit and surround his mouth with punches.' Fuck, was that funny."

"I wish we could play LA," Gresch said.

"It's nice out there now," Doog sighed.

Joe let Bubba out at his apartment and then headed toward Espo's place. "Nykoluk was worried that the guys won't go to bed, I can't believe it," he said. "André Beaulieu told me. Us guys in the city."

"I went to bed Sunday night, the fucking guys in West-chester went to the fucking Mug and Ale. I'm gonna stay up tonight, fuck that shit. Who won the game tonight? Who scored from Westchester?" Gresch spat.

"Ulfie got a point," I noted.

"All right, they got a point." Gresch shrugged.

"I can't believe we got to drive all the way out there tomorrow morning to practice," Doogie moaned.

"Hey, I agree," Espo said. "Even JD said there shouldn't be any ice. I said to Mickey, just make the guys that didn't play tonight go. Tell the other fucking guys to sleep in."

"I'll get tired tomorrow night for sure now," Gresch predicted.

"I can't sleep now till three," Doogie said. "I should sleep tomorrow till twelve, get up, get a bite to eat, then just relax. You don't have to go back to bed then, but, no, they just want to make us fucking aggravated by getting in the car and driving out to Westchester. Oh fuck. They're so fucking stupid."

"Don't go, Phil," Gresch counseled. "Fuck 'em."

"You're not thinking of going." Doog was amazed.

"I was," Espo admitted.

"Fucking Walter got a day off," Gresch said. "There's a big difference between thirty-five goals and a dozen. I had a fucking horseshit year, they tell me, and I got twenty-one. Everybody else had a good year, they got a dozen. Maloney got a dozen."

Espo departed and the limo snaked uptown. Doogie and Gresch stretched out. "If we do anything on the ice that's fucked up, Mike gives us the dirty look," Doogie said. "Today Vad and Davey and Ulfie fucked up, he laughed it off. They were all laughing."

"I couldn't believe Keating." I laughed.

"His job's on the line," Duguay said.

"They all are," Gresch added. "I'd just like to win tomorrow so there's no problem. I skated hard the last three games. My hands are sore. They don't care. Mike doesn't give a fuck if my hands are sore or not."

"Does he know?" I asked.

"Yeah, he knows," Gresch said. "I showed him yesterday."

Doog got out at Jim McMullen's for dinner. Gresch and I headed up to Oren's.

"I missed a lot of goals tonight," Gresch complained.

"I liked that experimental power play with you in the middle point," I said.

"Some teams have been checking us in that style. We work it by ourselves a lot. Me and Phil did it. Phil's the guy that gets the power play going. Without him you might as well forget it."

"Ulf and Anders got to start playing hockey," I said. "I'm glad their line got two goals tonight. They really want to win."

"Everybody wants to win," Gresch stressed. "But I give them credit for going into the fucking corners. For their size they work their balls off."

We got out and walked into Oren's. Everyone from the doorman in was jubilant. Kenny Aretsky gave Gresch a bear hug and he pulled us to a table in the back. All eyes followed us. A champagne bottle appeared out of nowhere. Gresch drank beer.

"Ratso was right," Gresch was telling Aretsky. "He told me months ago that come the play-offs you and Bubba are Number one." Gresch patted me on the back. "All right, buddy."

He pulled at his pants. "Did we get ice time," he gushed. "I lost seven pounds during the game."

Aretsky called the waiter and ordered some more beers, and Gresch began right in on filling out his waistline.

- APRIL 9

You know it's the play-offs when a $600,000-a-year man dives in front of slap shots to smother the puck. Ulfie did that tonight and the rest of the guys played just as inspired and the Rangers won again, this time easily, 5–1.

But there was a cost. Tkaczuk, who didn't dive at a slap shot, had one hit him square on the ankle, and he wound up hobbling out on crutches and getting X-rays at Lenox Hill Hospital. Connor also was injured. He broke his hand, on a Flame's head.

- APRIL 10

Getaway day. We flew down to Atlanta, where we were booked at the Hyatt Regency, a colossus of a hotel which features see-through elevators that whiz up and down a pole in the middle of the lobby, and terraced floors that overlook that same massive tree-strewn central area.

After checking in, the press met by the elevators. They were planning tomorrow's activities.

"Parton'll find a way to get free tennis courts," a Jersey reporter said.

"He always has an angle," Walt McPeek agreed.

"Except for his stories," Naughton said of his *Times* colleague.

- APRIL 11

Someone leaped to his death this morning at the hotel. Because of the unique architecture of the place, that meant he climbed over the balcony latticework and hurtled fifteen or twenty floors and splattered right smack in the center of the beautiful lobby. On the way down, the suicide hit a tree, which decapitated him. His head rolled to a stop just short of the Eastern Airlines reservation desk, leaving the lady on duty a little disquieted. There was lots of blood and entrails all over the place, and it took a clean-up crew an hour and a half to mop the mash up. "It could have have been more dramatic," Wayne Thomas observed. "He could have hit the coffee shop roof." There was no truth to the rumor that immediately after the incident the Flames took a head count.

But then again, this was a crucial game for them. Perhaps the last ever in Atlanta. The rumor had it that a Calgary combine had made an enormous offer for the team, and there was truth to this one. Enough truth to prompt the banner headline that was neatly clipped out of the Atlanta paper and Scotch-taped to the Ranger dressing room at practice this afternoon:

FLETCHER TO FLAMES—
YOU'RE FIVE PERIODS AWAY FROM CALGARY

Apparently their GM had told them that after the first period the other night in the Garden when the Rangers had taken a 4–0 lead. So now they were three periods away.

I was reading the clip after practice when Espo walked in from the ice. "That's fucking bullshit." He ripped the clip off the door. "You don't want that in your book."

Inside the room the guys dressed quickly. It was a gorgeous spring day, and most of them wanted to get in a little noonday shopping before their power naps.

"What time is the game tonight?" Don Maloney asked.

"What time can you make it?" Gresch said. "We'll work it around you."

On the bus ride back to the hotel, Gresch and Bubba sat up front, looking out the window and ogling the Southern belles on their lunch break. But half a block from the hotel, a car stalled in front of us, and the bus ground to a halt. After waiting for a few restless minutes and a nice bit of maneuvering, the driver managed to squeeze past the offender.

But not before Markham was able to lean out his window and deposit a rather large globule of thick, ropelike sputum on the stalled car's windshield. Thomas leaned back in his seat, shaking his head. "I didn't see that," he moaned.

Then we were back and Vad and Sarge led the charge to a nearby boutique, where they scoured the place for golf shirts and matching pants. Boxcar tagged along, peering curiously at the garments.

A few hours later after the naps, the bus was waiting in front of the hotel. Walter walked out with Sarge, limping noticeably.

"You're limping on the wrong foot," Doogie said.

"God loves you, Walter." Mario laughed. "You're healed. Deano prayed for him." After a while the bus left for the game, half full. The other guys had left early to walk off their pregame jitters.

With good reason. The Omni wasn't packed, but there were enough raucous yelping fans, urged on by a cheerleader/organist with rather huge breasts, to intimidate any visiting opponents. And having Madill as a referee didn't help. Especially when he threw Markham out late in the first period for being the third man into a fight. With Tkaczuk and Markham out, the Rangers were hurting at center.

The Flames exploited it in the second period. It was 1–1 as the period began, but they soon sucked the Rangers into playing a wide-open, end-to-end undisciplined game. And three minutes in, it paid off when Ken Houston beat JD to the post with a forty-five-foot slap shot from the boards.

The Rangers came right back to tie it, though, when Hedberg tipped in a Beck point shot. But then it was all Atlanta. They threw everyone up and took the body every chance and Vail put in two consecutive goals and it was 4–2. And the Rangers were forced to play Atlanta's game. Even Tala-fous, the Rangers' mild-mannered wing, wound up fighting with Bob MacMillan late in the period.

Up in the press box, McPeek typed out his lead between periods. "It was a very nasty hockey game," he started. "How nasty? It was so nasty that a born-again Christian ended up exchanging punches with a former Lady Byng Trophy winner."

"How about 'thanks to an agent of Satan, Madill,'" I suggested.

I went down by the Flames' net to view the last period. At the glass Walter and Markham were watching the action.

There were four and a half minutes left, with the Rangers still down 4–2, when Bill Clement, for no apparent reason, mugged Esposito, who had set up shop in front of the crease. They tumbled to the ice and when they were separated, Espo was livid. They were screaminng at each other all the way to the penalty box.

"What the hell did you do that for?" Espo asked.

"I don't care," Clement screamed. "I'll kill to stay here. I got a house and a family. I'll kill to stay here."

Espo stood up in the box and screamed back, "Fuck you, they're gonna trade you anyway. Get off the fucking pulpit. Freddie told us about you. He traded you because you couldn't play anywhere but home."

It worked. Clement picked up another two minutes for unsportsmanlike conduct when he tried to go back at Espo-sito. But the Rangers came up blank on the power play. Only a post off a screamer from Bubba.

"You mother sucker whore." Walter hit the glass. Time was running out.

"Doogie's not in this game," Markham said.

"He's in space," Walter agreed.

There was a minute and a half left when Dave Maloney

got called for holding. Markham hit the glass in disgust. "Can you believe that? The guy has the puck in his hand and we get called for holding. Good call, you jerk," he yelled.

The buzzer sounded and the players filed into the dressing room. Quietly. The reporters knotted around Espo's folding chair.

"It's just that the inconsistency in the refereeing is a big problem," he said slowly. "If there's another guy refereeing tonight, they're in the penalty box all night. We have ten or twelve power plays, right?"

I walked over to Anders, who was nude, perusing the stat sheet.

"They should have had two pages for the penalties," I said.

Hedberg frowned. He pointed to the listing of the three stars. "They got it wrong. That ref was the fucking first star of the game tonight." Then he tore the sheet up and sat down and pulled his socks on.

• APRIL 12

A rainy Saturday morning. The Rangers went through a light skate at practice and then divided up into regional teams and had a shoot-out. Team USA won.

After the practice they were talking about clothes in the dressing room. Vadnais was sitting on his chair, carefully wiping between his toes, kidding Greschner about his sartorial habits.

"I got twelve pairs of socks," Gresch protested. "One pair for each month."

"See, it's 'cause of guys like that that you get athlete's foot." Boxcar consoled Vadnais.

"Don't stick up for me." The defenseman had a big cigar dangling out of his mouth.

Bukka came by and collected the used towels. Vadnais had at least four scattered around him. "Look at this, another towel." Bukka shook his head.

"Sure, blame Vad," Vadnais said. "Blame Vad."

"You walking back?" Maloney asked his partner.

"If it's not raining, me and Ulf are going to get some Lacoste sweaters. I'm gonna buy a black one. I need a black one badly," Vadnais said.

"Is there a sale on?" Talafous overheard.

"No sir, no sir," Vadnais snapped. "So you can't come, Deano. Hey, Ratso, I don't give a fuck what you write in your book but you better write I'm the best fucking dresser around this fucking team. Look at these fucking jerks wearing jeans and fucking corduroys and every fucking piece of shit. Dat's bullshit." He scowled and waved a hand toward Greschner. "Look at those fucking pleats. They look like 1942 pants."

"There's thread on your pants there, Vad." Dave Maloney pointed out helpfully.

Vadnais quickly picked it off. "I noticed dat, don't you worry about dat."

The bus finally rolled back, and Ulf and Vad got off early to go shopping. But most of the other guys went back to eat and snooze.

After lunch I tried to nap but I was too nervous. So was Bukka and we met in the lobby for some tea. "There's a big brawl on top," Bukka confided. "Mickey, Mike, and Fred are feuding. Mickey wants the guys to get some time off, he thinks they work hard enough in the games. But Mike says he's running the show. Freddie's backing him up so far." Joey stopped to sip his tea. "I wrote something on the blackboard today, 'We got the horses. Let's win the race.'"

We finished the tea and walked back out into the lobby. Nykoluk was sitting on a couch reading *The Book of Insults*.

"You know why Mike can't sleep?" Joey whispered. "He's gone in a week if we lose this round."

In the locker room Bukka tried to psych Beck for the game. "Bubba, they're pushing our boys around," Joey said. "It's up to you to stop it." Bubba frowned.

"Here." Joe proffered his hand, and Beck squeezed it till it almost broke. Then he went out for warm-ups. When he came back he had a problem with his gloves. He asked Joey to fix them.

"What for?" Bucchino smiled. "You won't be wearing them tonight."

But the Rangers didn't need any fisticuffs from Beck tonight. They came out storming. On their first shift Vickers made a nice move around Plett and passed the puck over to Hedberg, who wristed a quick shot past Bouchard. Four minutes later the Rangers took advantage of an Atlanta penalty when Talafous outhustled a Flames defenseman and picked up Beck's rebound off the boards and shot it past the startled Bouchard. Two goals in three shots. Thirty-four seconds later even Boxcar got in on the act. Conacher, who had been brought up from New Haven to fill in for Walter, rushed the puck into the Flames' zone and dropped it to Doog, who made a marvelous cross-ice pass to Hospodar, who was hanging to the left of Bouchard. Boxcar tapped the pass in and it was 3–0. They held on and Davidson played superbly, kicking out thirty shots, and the Rangers eliminated Atlanta, 5–2.

They mobbed JD at the final buzzer, and then they rushed off into the dressing room. Espo put a protective glove over his head and gave his stick to a kid as he ran in.

Inside the room everyone seemed happy but low-key. Except for Hospodar. He had a mile-wide grin, and he was relishing the attention bestowed on him by the gaggle of reporters that surrounded him.

"I did lousy in the shoot-out this morning," Boxcar explained. "So I told the guys, 'I suppose you'll be laughing at me when I score the game winner tonight.' They all got a chuckle out of it. So tonight during warm-up I skated over to Warren, my roomie, and I said through the hole in the glass, 'Hey, Warren, would I be a star on Broadway if I scored the game winner?' And then the first shift I'm out, I scored. Holy shit, I couldn't believe it. Then with a minute forty-five left, Charlie told me I could have the winner. So when Sarge went down and blocked a shot, which he never does, I was just cheering. Boy, my first NHL goal."

Gresch walked over to me. "They never got into our end once to really force us," he said. "Dean and Donnie, they were unreal. They came back, everybody. Doogie, he was all over the ice. It was easy out there for us."

"What did you say to Bouchard after Bubba scored the last goal?" I wondered.

"I told him he was brutal." Gresch smiled. "He is brutal. He mouthed off, he deserved to lose."

The room was unbearably hot, so I walked outside for some air. The arena was emptying now, and they were beginning to take the ice out, for the last time ever here, in all likelihood. Freddie and Keating were out in the corridor sitting on a table.

"Ratso, how are you? What's your problem?" Keating had a demonic smile on his face. Earlier he had told me that I wouldn't be able to fly back with the team on the charter, that no press were allowed. After I told him I had learned that Brooks and Mifflin were given clearance, he mumbled something about their being "hardship cases." Another lie bites the dust.

"If we win the Stanley Cup, it'll help your book quite a bit, eh?" He was all sunshine. Freddie looked distracted.

"Speaking of books, here's that book I promised you,

Fred." I gave him *Games Zen Masters Play*, the book I bought him that afternoon. Shero shyly took it, without making eye contact.

"I figured you might be able to get some good blackboard quotes from it," I said.

"Some players never even look at the board." Fred shrugged. Mickey laughed a bit too loud.

"But if I said there was a party tonight somewhere, they'd be there already, they're there waiting." Fred chuckled ironically.

"The other night I was talking to a friend, trying to develop an argument that hockey's really a Zen sport, that you can't really think too much . . ." I began.

"I read a beautiful book on golf," Freddie interrupted. "I forget the name. I don't know who gave it to me. It was the most amazing book I've ever read on positive thinking and how to will the ball into the cup. The guy was from Scotland or Ireland, whatever, and it applies to every sport."

"Give some examples," Keating turned student.

"It's the same thing," Fred said. "The other day I said to myself, 'Beck,' he didn't see Hedberg at all, so I said to myself, 'Left, please, left,' and sure enough he throws the puck left, which he normally never does. He didn't see him and Anders touches it in midair and it went in. I was saying, 'Please, left, it'll go in for sure.' You have to pray a little bit." Fred chuckled.

Back in the room a reporter asked Doogie, "Want to play Philly next?"

Doogie grimaced. "Who the fuck wants to play Philly?"

"Buffalo?"

"Sure, we can beat Buffalo," Doog said.

"You can beat Philly too," I said.

"I know." Ron pulled on his sports jacket. "But who wants fucking scars all over their body?" he said and headed for the bus.

The bus to the charter. I couldn't go on the charter, so I went back to the hotel and wound up having drinks with Sonny and his wife, Krumpe and his wife, and Jim Judelson and his wife, the latter being the Gulf and Western executive and the boss of all bosses as far as the Rangers were concerned. Sonny was very interested in why I couldn't fly with the team.

But I was very interested in getting smashed, so later, Naughton and McPeek and Malcolm Moran, another *Times* stringer and I went out drinking. I spent most of the night defending Shero and his unique motivational style. McPeek and Naughton spent most of the time telling me that Shero was a drunk who didn't need to motivate class athletes like the Swedes. I didn't buy the Shero story, but they assured me that it was true. After all, that's what Ulfie had told them, way back in November.

- APRIL 16

It was 1 P.M. and I was wiping sleep out of my eyes, looking for some razors in the motel's newsstand, when the Rangers trooped in. There were Ulfie and Anders and Sarge, and Sulliman on crutches after a knee operation, and Connor with his hand in a cast.

Tonight they opened against Philly and by the newspaper accounts of Philly coach Quinn's comments, it was going to be a bloodbath. Gordon and Chadwick were in the lobby huddled over the blaring headlines.

"It sounds like a scared hockey team," Chadwick said.

"I'm glad our guys have too much class to mouth off like that," Gordon agreed. Mifflin came by and, spotting Freddie sitting alone in the coffee shop, she rushed in to ask him about Quinn's warmongering. A few seconds later she came out with a quizzical look on her face.

"What did he say?" I asked.

"Fred said Quinn can say what he wants. He's a beautiful person." She shrugged and pointed to her head.

A few hours later after the naps, some of the players filtered into the coffee shop. At the next counter a few rabid Flyer fans were loudly cussing the impending series, oblivious to the Rangers on their left.

"I wonder where the Rangers are staying," one said.

"That Madison Square Garden is the worst building in the league." The fat one's voice boomed over the restaurant. Marois looked up from his paper. "Those fans are the worst bunch of ignoramuses, morons, ignorant human beings. I feel sorry for a team that's got to play the Rangers. The ice stinks. Look at what happened to Dale Rolfe, fell in a hole, Brad Park. The Rangers don't play hockey there, they only send that idiot, Hospodar, out to start trouble. And that sissy, Vadnais, that stickman. We're gonna wipe out this New Amsterdam team."

His friend nodded and looked at the paper.

"Shero knows only one style of hockey, goon style. Look at the improvement of Nicky Fotiu once he got off the Rangers. The Rangers finished off where they left last year, a couple of bums."

Ciggy and Wayne looked over at the fat kid who was getting himself worked up.

"The Boston fans are nice compared to the Ranger loonies," he continued. "They put up that ten-foot glass to keep the loonies away from the players. Rowdies isn't the word. You should hear those chants they got there. In unison. IN UNISON." He shook his head.

The players finished their rich desserts and rode over to the Spectrum. The ride was the most fun they'd have all evening.

From the opening face-off the Flyers swarmed. They were all over the blueshirts anytime one of them had the puck.

Kenny Linesman, the little antagonist, was buzzing around, flaying the Swedes with his stick and taking runs at Davidson without any retaliation. Paul Holmgren, the massive winger on that line, was bumping everything in sight, and Mel Bridgman was all over Espo, jabbing, jabbing. But Davidson was remarkable. He managed to kick back eighteen shots in the first period alone. The only one that eluded him was a Rick MacLeish wrist shot from a weird angle at 4:49.

So when the Rangers tied it up at 3:47 of the last period, on a goalmouth scramble, it looked like the momentum might change. But two minutes later Greschner took a shot from the point that hit a Flyer defenseman square on the blade, and the puck rebounded out to Linesman, who broke. He passed it to Holmgren on the right wing, who was ridden out of the play by Beck but managed to squeeze a pass across the crease. Behn Wilson, the big Flyer defenseman, shook off Greschner and directed the puck past Davidson. That was that, Flyers 2, Rangers 1.

Afterward Freddie felt that his team didn't play physical enough. Bubba was less eloquent. "Fuck, we played horseshit." He was sitting in his stall, wiping his face with a towel. "We were horseshit and they only beat us by one goal. They won't beat us. Fuck, nobody played good."

Nobody except JD, who was brilliant in turning back forty shots. He was sitting morosely, with an ice bag on his arm where Linesman had speared him. Doog and Bukka and I watched the big goalie.

"That Linesman's a fucking little smart ass, eh? He was insulting me before every face-off, but when the ref took off I looked at him and said, 'What the fuck are you saying? Pretty cocky, aren't you?' I just laughed at him," Doogie said.

"Someone should have taken a run at that prick," I said. "He caused a lot of trouble out there."

"Definitely, that was a problem," Bukka agreed. "He went by the bench, he said, 'Freddie, one down and three to go.'"

"No shit." Doog looked disgusted.

We drifted over to Espo, who was talking with Mifflin. He was toweling off after his shower.

"Pat Quinn said the line match-ups were speed versus speed, Linesman versus the Swedes, determination versus determination, Tkaczuk versus Clarke, and you and Bridgman, muscle versus muscle," Mifflin said, smiling.

"Pat should know, he played against me long enough, ha!" Espo laughed. "Listen, muscle doesn't have to be shoulder, you know. You can be strong without having bulging muscles."

"Espo's a big man," Bukka interjected, "with a beautiful head too. He looks like John Travolta, 1920's."

Espo grimaced. "I got the flashes," he warned.

"I'm out of here." Bukka scrambled away. "Everytime I'm near him he gets the flashes."

"I'm getting flashes," Espo sang and scratched his leg.

"Have you got the gunk?" Mifflin asked. The gunk was a mysterious skin rash that was unique to hockey. Some players suffered so much from it that they were unable to play.

"Lawrie, so bad," Espo moaned. "I have Donna putting on Vitamin E every night. Putting it all over my body." Everyone laughed.

"You gotta watch for the kachkis around here," Espo warned. "It's not as dirty in this place as in Atlanta or Pittsburgh, though."

"Take care, Phil, fifteen minutes till the big buffet at the motel. I'll see you there." Mifflin walked out.

"I'll see you, Lawrie." Phil waved as she left. "I'll come up there, give you the scoop, kid, the fucking mouth-to-mouth scoop. I'll put some good sauce on her throat." Doogie and the trainers cracked up.

"I'm embarrassed." Phil looked at me. "I got to say, I should have put the towel over my balls, but she doesn't give a fuck. Amazing too. I know why I get flashes. I mean it's unbelievable the way she talks to Bubba. Bubba's like this and she's like this." Esposito pointed out their relative heights. Everyone laughed.

"Larry Sacharuk used to play with himself and get a hard-on before the broads came in, and he'd go, 'C'mon, babies.' Ha ha ha ha."

"What a fucking nut." Doogie shook his mane.

We rode back with Bukka to the hotel. Halligan had set up two buffets, one for the players and one for the press. I chose the bar. After a while I was heading for some cold cuts when I ran into Talafous. He had fractured a rib during the game after he got smashed in a corner, and he was still walking somewhat unsteadily.

"It's pretty sore, Ratso." He held his side. "I think we started playing better, though, and they lost their drive. It's gonna be talent versus talent now and not emotion. You always figure the first period they're up, the crowd, they had rest, but now it's the same as last year. They have to win on talent. You could see near the end there they couldn't keep up with us, we have more talent. I hope that's what happens. We need guys like Gresch and Ulf controlling the play."

Just then JD came by with an armful of beer, trailed by Bubba and Gresch. We all got on the elevator.

"Push penthouse," Bubba ordered. "Rats gets all the broads down here. He knows them all."

"Deano, they give you any pain-killer?" Gresch wondered.

"The doc gave me quite a few," the soft-spoken wing said.

"You'd feel a lot better with a shot of heroin." Bubba elbowed Gresch. Gresch hit him back and then they broke into a few "TOGA" chants, and then they got off at the penthouse to drink their beer and get some sleep for tomorrow.

• APRIL 17

More of the same. A light skate and then nap, and now it was 5:00 and the guys were back in the coffee shop, eating their desserts for the extra sugar rush: Ciggy was eating pie a la mode and Mario had a sundae.

In the lobby Esposito had come down and was besieged by small kids for autographs. Two of them held out hockey bubble-gum cards for Phil to sign.

"I won't sign cards," Espo announced. "Please understand. One, I signed last night and we lost, I'm superstitious, and two, those jerks who made the cards do it without permission."

The bus left and I rode over to the Spectrum with Hugh Delano from the *Post*. In the press room he greeted an old friend who covers the Flyers. "How's Freddie's drinking problem?" the Flyer journalist asked. "When he was here, I was the only one who would drive him home after Saturday games. Pelletier wouldn't and he lived on the next block. I remember one time we were driving back after the Flyers got beat 9–1 by Montreal and Freddie was sitting in the front of the car with a can of beer and he kept saying, 'Dornie's legs went just like that. You never know, Savard, Robinson, maybe next year this time their legs may go.'" The Philly scribe shook his head condescendingly.

A few hours later all the Rangers were shaking their heads. The Flyers came out flying again and, Talafous to the contrary, outplayed the Rangers in every department. They gave the Swedes no room to freewheel, they forechecked Greschner effectively, and despite another great game from Davidson, they won easy, 4–1.

Afterward Hedberg was disconsolate. "Are you surprised

that they can frustrate you and Ulf so much?" Naughton asked.

"Surprised? No!" Anders said slowly. "I'm disappointed in myself. In our performance. I think our line, as well as the rest of the lines, we have to skate and really skate, create things, force them to make mistakes so they throw the puck wrong or hit someone when they try to pass. By creating those mistakes, that's when we get the breaks and we haven't got them so far."

The dressing room was dead still, and Keating was walking around looking like he had lost a brother. Everyone was dressing quickly, partly to get on the bus back to New York, partly to avoid answering questions and dwelling on the defeat.

I was getting a ride back to the city from a photographer, Danny, who was covering the series for the Flyers.

For the next hour and a half on the Turnpike, we talked about the Rangers' plight.

"They're playing much too cautiously," the photographer pronounced as he gunned his Lincoln down the Turnpike. "Every face-off, Linesman puts the butt end of his stick into Ulfie's chest. Ulfie says he's trying to do it back, give him a fucking shot in the puss. Don't even go for the puck. Tkaczuk did that once to Sanderson, he put the stick right in his face. And Beck is some disappointment. They're playing like they're so tense."

"They miss Talafous," I said. "He's the reason they traded Murdoch, and now he's out and Espo seems lost."

"Beck has to intimidate some people," Danny said. "He always shoots the puck the same way around the boards, wide of the guy coming to forecheck. He's got to take a couple of shots right at people. It'll open up like the Red Sea. Maloney is ridiculous. How can you be captain out of the penalty box? Imbecilic penalties. Last night he took two pen-

alties in a row. He doesn't understand when you hook somebody, hook them by the waist or by the leg. You hook them
on the shoulder, everyone in the whole building can see it."

"There's just this whole esprit de corps that's missing," I
moaned. "They had it last year and now it's totally gone."

"You've seen that all season. They certainly had the horses
to have a better season, but there's too many chiefs and not
enough Indians on this team," Danny decided. "Too many
egos. They have a lot of young, immature guys on the team,
and Shero's personal problems don't help the team. They
need leadership."

"But Freddie's style has always been to create a context
that leaders can emerge out of, like Clarkie in Philly. I think
he was trying to do the same thing with Maloney here. Only
Maloney's not Clarke," I said.

"If you're gonna be coach, be coach, period," Danny said.
"Between us, you and I know that Freddie has a drinking
problem. Players go up to him in Westchester, I don't know
if you're aware of this, in practice, and he's in the back there
drinking beer every day half fucking smashed. They go to
where the equipment is, and in the gloves and the skates
there're empty beer cans. Now you have to have some
respect for your coach. They have respect for his intelligence, no question, but some of the things he does adds to
the bickering."

"Like what?" I still wasn't buying the drinking problem
explanation. It seemed too easy.

"Some of the changes he makes," Danny said. "Maybe he's
dumb like a fox but these kids are naïve. He never tells them
he's sending them down. He fucked up the Soetaert-Thomas
thing. That can have an effect; one effect it can have is
people know there's no security, they have to bust their ass
to make it. Okay, but then you got Gulf and Western here
pumping these guys up and making them into celebrities and

312 ▪

stars, and on the other hand, they don't know what the coach is doing."

"They got two games to figure it out," I said glumly, and we pulled off to get something to eat.

• APRIL 18

It was Friday night, a night off before the series resumes at the Garden, and Bubba and Gresch and I were sitting in a theater on Eighty-sixth Street watching *Apocalypse Now*. This was my idea. I was trying to convince Bubba that Linesman and his cohorts were gooks.

But by the time Martin Sheen finally stumbled upon Brando's bizarre encampment, I was beginning to see a lot of Shero in the Kurtz character.

"Have you ever considered any real freedoms?" Brando mumbled to Sheen, sitting like a Buddha in the dark. "Freedom from the opinions of others, freedom from the opinions of yourself?"

"That's Fred." I nudged Bubba.

"Why do they want to put down my command?" Brando asked.

"They told me you had gone totally insane," Sheen said. "Your methods were unsound."

"Are my methods unsound?" Brando asked enigmatically.

"I don't see any methods at all, sir," Sheen replied.

"I expected someone like you," Brando smiled. "You're not an assassin. You're an errand boy sent by grocery clerks to collect a bill."

"This guy is fucked up," Bubba grunted.

"Hey, Bubba," Gresch said. "I see a lot of him in you."

And then the deed was done, said Sheen was chop-chopping away, and all you heard was "the Horror, the Horror" and Jim Morrison moaning "The End." We got up and walked over to Cronies for a bite to eat. In a daze.

Outside Cronies some kids recognized the defensemen. "Hey, it's Gresch and Bubba," one screamed. "Go get 'em, win one tomorrow." Another slapped Bubba's back.

He didn't feel a thing. "I'm still fucked up from that movie," he groaned. "You wouldn't catch me going up that river. I would have bailed out a long time ago. Whoa. That was whoa material." He picked up the menu and tried to concentrate.

"Jesus, am I fucked up." He rubbed his eyes. "My brains are hurting. I'm going to go home and look at the walls. I'm gonna check my closets before I to go to sleep."

• APRIL 19

The next morning over eggs at the Mansion, where the city guys met to drive out to practice, Bubba was still thinking about the movie. I was still making the case for Linesman as VC.

At the rink Joey had written a message on the blackboard: "No matter what, don't let others take your talent from you. Protect what is yours." Mickey Keating had scribbled an addendum: "Use your talent fully." But the message seemed to be lost on Captain Dave. He was talking to a few of the guys about summer vacation and going to Florida.

They went through a light skate, typical for day-of-game practice, and then Gresch and Doogie and his friend, Butch, and I went back to the city and had lunch at Alda's, an Italian restaurant on Eighty-sixth Street. Pasta, good for energy.

"Someone ought to spear Linesman in the face." Butch buttered some bread.

"You do it, Gresch," Doogie decided.

"You do it, Doog." Gresch smiled.

"I'll do it if you hold Holmgren," Duguay said.

"I'll hold Leach," Greschner said.

I started talking about the fight at the Islander-Bruin game the other night, a bench-clearing, drag-out brawl.

"I got that on tape," Gresch said. "They showed all the fights the other night on the news."

"Did you see my fight?" Doogie wondered. "When I fought, what's his name? Busniak?"

"Yeah, they showed you tapping him on the head like the guy on *Benny Hill.* Tip-tip-tapping him, on the top of the head. This is a sick game," Gresch said.

"Yeah," Doog agreed. "I fought that guy. What for? We're playing animals, I figured I might as well get it over with. I picked up my stick after and I was thinking there was no reason for it, what we have to do. It's crazy."

"So I heard the great motivator, Maloney, was talking about summertime already," I said.

Doogie cracked up. "The great motivator. You should see him during games against like Minnesota and those teams. He's standing up on the bench yelling at the guys. When we play Philly, he's quiet, sits on the bench, never says a word." Doogie snickered.

"If we only had Nicky back," Gresch said dreamily. "He'd get us going."

They didn't have Nicky, though. But they had Head, and she was sitting in her familiar seat behind the visitors' bench during warm-ups, wearing her Espo uniform. And she had a secret weapon.

"I believe in whammies," she said matter-of-factly. "We destroyed Roosevelt Weeks, he broke his ankle."

"Try Linesman," I suggested.

Head motioned me toward her and whispered in my ear. "I want Pat Quinn's body so bad I'm going crazy." This information took me aback. "I want Clarke too," she confessed. "But I'll have to wait till I'm dead and I'll be a ghost and on the face-offs I'll tie his skates together. I had a night-mare the other night, I dreamed I married Hoyda and I woke up in a cold sweat. Well, all we can do is hope and pray. But I wish they'd keep their grubby mitts off Phil."

"They should put Hospodar on his line," I said.

"I want him too." Head's eyes lit up. "But if I can't have Quinn's body, I want Joe Kadlec, the PR man for the Flyers. He's gorgeous."

To our left some early arrivals were practicing their "FLYERS SUCK" chants.

It wasn't long before they got to use them. I was sitting in my little press box, along with Frank Beaton and Davie Silk, who had driven up from the Hav to see this important game And as soon as the Flyers took the ice, the "SUCK" chants cascaded down on their heads.

It didn't do much to help the Rangers' cause, though. Eight minutes into the game, big Bob Dailey, the Flyer defenseman, intercepted a Ranger pass and broke toward the Rangers' net. At the blue line he wound up and fired a slap shot that somehow eluded Davidson. It was 1–0. What was worse, it was a shorthanded goal.

The Rangers tried to regroup, but they never could get anything sustained going, especially on their power-play opportunities. By the third period it was still 1–0, but it didn't look good. "Looks like the Sarge is out for a short skate," Silkie said after Vickers had committed a grievous giveaway with a man advantage.

There was dead silence after Barber battered in a center-ing feed from Mel Bridgman a few minutes later. But then five minutes after that, when Beck lost the puck to Holmgren and MacLeish circled the Ranger net and stuffed, the booing began. Followed by a mass exodus.

At first they drowned out the boos by chanting "JD." It was a moving tribute and a class gesture. "He's the only one out there making a fucking effort," Beaton said. "New Haven would have put on a better fucking show tonight."

But then every time Beck went near the puck, the boos rolled down in waves. Bubba's baptism. He looked crushed on the way into the dressing room. Shero didn't exactly look jovial either.

"It seems we're trying but we're not accomplishing that much," Shero said. A cigarette burned unheeded in his right hand. "We're not getting in for the second effort. We got to fight our way in and get it. I don't know if it's a lack of intensity or not. It's just concentration. You gotta think, 'I gotta go, I gotta go.'" He hunched over and acted out the forwards' dilemma. "As soon as the man shoots the puck in, you gotta say 'I gotta arrive, I gotta arrive.' You have to *will* yourself so you're gonna arrive there. If you don't, you're gonna be late."

"Why are they getting there late?" someone asked.

"Ask them," Freddie shot back. "I don't know. You tell them and you tell them."

In the room nobody seemed to know. Except Bubba. He knew that the booing was not pleasant. He sat in his stall, a towel flung across his lap, naked except for his socks and cowboy boots. He was staring at a hole in the carpet, facing the music.

"At least I know what the fans want from me anyways," he mumbled. "It's pretty obvious. They want me to fight, so I guess I'll go out and do that." Everyone around him scribbled away. "I always thought I was more valuable on the ice, but maybe I'm not. I don't know."

Krumpe made his way through the reporters and leaned over and squeezed Barry's hand. Beck kept examining the floor.

"You gotta give them a little credit, they're playing pretty good hockey. We're not making excuses, we're trying," he stammered, "but there are obvious reasons I guess why they're booing me."

Bucchino came over. "Tell them to go fuck themselves," he shouted. "That's exactly right. He's God on the Cross, huh? He's supposed to do it all? We got twenty other guys."

The reporters ignored the outburst. "Obvious reasons?" One picked up the thread.

"The reason is they want me to fight, that's why," Barry explained, sipping a cup of milk.

"Don't take this question in an antagonistic way," the reporter continued. "But why don't you fight?"

"Well, the thing is I've always been told that I can do a better job on the ice than off it. But obviously we haven't been winning, so I'll have to do things differently. It hasn't been a case where . . ." He paused, trying to collect his thoughts. "Ah, shit, I don't know . . ." he trailed off.

"The booing seemed to rattle you, you became nervous," the interrogation continued.

"Yeah, it rattled me. Christ, I was upset about it, but I'll just turn it around tomorrow night, that's all. It bothers you, no professional athlete wants to be booed. It hurts your pride and I've got more pride than that, and the only thing I can do is go out and do something that they'll cheer, that's all."

"It takes a hell of a lot of courage to do what you're doing." The interrogator extended his hand. "I admire you." Bubba halfheartedly grabbed it, and the pack of reporters dissolved. I sat down next to him as he sipped his milk.

"First of all, it wasn't everybody booing, just a few duos," I said.

"I'll go out tomorrow and get in three fights, out of the game . . ."

"Fuck that," I interrupted. "Fuck them."

"That's what I'm gonna do," Bubba mumbled. "That's what they fucking want."

I looked down on the floor. There was a green piece of paper and I picked it up. Another fan letter from Susan R—:

Dear Mr. Beck (Whopper),
I really feel bad that you lost the first two games of this series, but I know you'll beat their balls off this time. Knock somebody's jock off just for me. Tell the rest of the team I said to screw the Flyers sideways. As for me, you can screw me anyway, anyhow, and anywhere you like. I would love for you to split me with heavenly pain. I think of you as a tidal wave, with a crest rising to its peak, crashing down, wetting the sand. Until you fuck me, I will remain . . .

Pervertedly yours,
Susan R————

By the time I finished reading, Bubba was up and slowly walking toward the showers. At the back of the room, JD, Espo, and Mifflin watched his progress.

"He's gonna be a major force for a long time," JD said.

"You know what," Espo interjected. "Gresch put it best. They're playing like we did last year."

"They sure want it," JD agreed. "I'll tell you that. But nobody knows how dedicated Bubba is. He works every day. Everybody's been booed here. Vad has, I have, Park got it bad for years. Eddie Giacomin got it. It's a part of growing up, I guess. He's going to be a superstar, that's my opinion."

"That's mine too," Espo agreed. "And I've seen a lot of them."

Downstairs I joined Beaton and Silk, who were sitting in Charlie O's with some friends from New Haven. One of them was Dave Snopek, a burly winger who in his rookie year had scored thirty-five goals for the Nighthawks.

Except for the regulars, the dining room was dead. Sonny's long table in the front of the room was ominously empty.

Marcus scurried over. "Ratso," he moaned. "They're booing Bubba. They're booing him 'cause he isn't scoring. Is that his fault? I still love him, tell him that."

We drank some beers and Silkie told some Hav stories, and after awhile Donnie Maloney came by, on his way out. He said hello to Silkie and Beater and then left.

"Bye-bye, Don," Snopek said, from the corner.

"He didn't see you," Beater said.

"Fuck me," Silkie scoffed. "He saw left wing, thirty-five goals, rookie of the year. That's what he saw." Silkie laughed. "It's good we didn't go into the locker room. We would have been like the ghosts of Christmas future." I pointed to Sonny's vacant table. "Looks like the Last Supper, eh?"

"That's tomorrow." Silkie smiled.

• APRIL 20 AFTERNOON

I was reading the big Oh-la-la Duguay feature in the *New York Sunday News Magazine* section when Cusimano called.

"They got to get rid of Shero." He was fuming. "Number one—the guy shows no evidence of significant player development—Gresch, Beck, Mario, Maloney, Duguay, nothing. They need coaching, they don't seem to be getting it. Number two, player acquisitions. The worst. Drafting Sulliman in first round, what an error! I have no sense that the Rangers have an efficient scouting system.

"Third and most important. Shero doesn't deal with his players. What he does do, according to you, Sloman, is use clones to do it. He doesn't want to relinquish control, so he uses guys who are basically incompetent, stupid, have little to offer, in short, are weak men, in puppet roles. People put in that position are inevitably going to earn contempt from the players. But Shero will always be forced to use people like that, that's his personality flaw. Look, Shero was washed up when he came to the Rangers. His technique had dissipated in Philly, he was on the way down. He's a loser. The perception of him being a drunk by his players is a bad sign.

"One other thing, the strategy of throwing the puck is a losing strategy. It's giving the other team the initiative, saying that they're going to beat themselves. I don't want to watch this team anymore. Shero's team. I find them boring. They're off balance, disorganized, they play like they hate each other. Who sent Maloney to the hospital yesterday? One of his own players?"

I waited patiently for the tirade to subside. "What should the Rangers do?"

"Bring back Q," Cusimano bellowed.

- APRIL 20 EVENING

Lost in all the booing the other night were the two tremendous checks Beck threw that decimated Linesman and Watson, the Flyer defensemen. They both were out indefinitely. So was Ranger defenseman Dave Maloney who Cusimano thought was a victim of fragging.

Without Linesman the Rangers were able to move, and without Watson they were able to penetrate and get some rebounds around the net, and they took advantage five minutes into the game when Doogie picked up a second rebound on his backhand and shoveled the puck in. Doogie duplicated that feat twice more, once in each period, and Esposito added a goal in the second period, a nice tip-in of a Vadnais slap shot, and the Rangers went on to win, 4–2. Finally.

Afterward Davidson talked about character. "I was real proud of Bubba 'cause he fought the challenge and came back real well. Hockey players have so much goddamn pride, they'll run through walls to try and achieve things," Davidson said. "We could have been partying right now, we could be playing golf tomorrow instead of going to Philly where it's gonna be a real battle. But we're proud. We didn't lie down and roll over and say that's it."

Pride. That was the key word tonight. Bubba and Ulfie and Anders and the others stood around and talked to the press. Doogie posed proudly with three hat-trick pucks. Perseverance. They weren't dead yet. They would just play period by period now. They were cohesive at last, a team that had found itself.

Duguay was the last to shower. He came out dripping into the now empty locker room. Only Jimmy Young was there, tidying up.

"There he is," Jimmy shouted. "Mr. Fuck, you should have had four."

"Five," Doogie said.

Duguay looked at his stall. There were two pucks by his toiletries. "Hey, there should be three pucks, there's one missing."

"This is your press people," Young said.

"Oh well." Doogie shrugged and left to dry his hair. "Just take one of these and say it was my hat-trick puck."

Jimmy grabbed a puck and started bouncing it off the floor. "You want to make it a hat-trick goal; it's got to have scuff marks on it." He was flinging it around the room now. "The one that's in the Penn Plaza Club for the ten thousand Ranger goal, fuck, I made that one too. Doogie wants this one abused a bit."

I walked around to the sinks.

"Fuck, I came here tonight, I was so fucking down and tired. I never even read that article," Doogie said. "I just thought, oh fuck, they're gonna be all over me, the fans. Oh-la-la Duguay, you know. Lucky for me. And everything was touch and go there for a while with my girl friend back home. All these things were happening to me. But what hit it off again was that article they had on me in the *National Star* because I talked a lot about her. It was all about her, so she thought it was really nice. She was thinking that I'm trying to make myself look like a playboy and fucking everybody. She was ready to gas me." Doogie looked doe-eyed.

"Notice I wasn't wearing the 'C' tonight?" Doogie said as he put his clothes on. "Vad was the captain. Whose idea do you think that was, eh? I've been getting too much fucking publicity. Nykoluk must have read the fucking paper tonight, eh?" Doogie shook his head. "Mike's got no class. He's been in the farm leagues all his fucking life and that's his mentality. He can't see doing anything else but getting up in the morning and going to play hockey. A fucking hockey bum."

Doogie got up and walked back to the sink to brush his hair. "Isn't it great not to have Maloney here?" he asked rhetorically. "Fucking Maloney just yaps and yaps and screams 'Let's go,' and it was so quiet, so nice tonight. You wouldn't have believed it. He's the worst thing to this team. That's why I felt so different tonight. I felt I could walk around the room, do whatever I want. I don't have to watch what I say, so he'd give me one of those looks." A scowl of condescension crossed Doog's face. It was a good imitation. "It was loose, I was just joking around."

"The whole team looked loose on the ice for the first time," I observed.

"I don't like being in the same fucking dressing room as him," Doogie said. He finished primping and we walked outside and hailed a cab. "Things are going so good for me right now that there are some companies who are seriously talking about using me as their new face, you know, a couple of commercials a year like Joe Namath or Farrah Fawcett," Doogie said as we speeded up Eighth Avenue.

"Nykoluk'll love that." I laughed.

"He's fucking minor league," Doog said. "He's got his mind on one thing and that's the way he thinks. Just like Maloney.

Maloney thinks one way and everybody's got to be like that. They're a good pair. And for me to be talking about these guys like this. I have a fucking hatred for these people. They're on my own team and here I am talking like this and I don't care who I say it to. I'll say it to anybody that asks me. That's what they've done to me and I haven't done anything to them."

"You should be telling this to people like Werblin and Krumpe," I suggested.

"Fuck, you think I haven't?" Doogie smiled slyly. "Whoa, I fucking fill Krumpe in like you wouldn't believe. How about Phil? Think Phil didn't bury those fucking guys? They shit on Phil, they laugh at him, they make fun of him. That's fucking Phil Esposito! And they're making fun of him! He's a big man. They should be having him psyched to play this fucking game. They should be using him."

"What's Shero's role in all this?" I asked.

"I don't know," Doogie said. "I really respect him. I like the way he treats me 'cause he uses me a lot."

"I hear Nykoluk's gone anyway after the series," I said.

"Believe me, they're on to fucking Maloney and Nykoluk like you wouldn't believe," Doogie said. "Vad too. 'Cause Phil was telling them from day one what they're like, and I sat down with Krumpe and his wife and told them everything I know. I told him, 'Jack, if it weren't for NYC I'd go up to you right now and ask to be traded', I'm so fed up. Fuck, you wouldn't believe how nice it was in the dressing room tonight. Night and day. Night and day. You get so fed up listening to him scream and rah-rah stuff."

"I noticed Davey does that on the road, all that high school shit," I said.

"That's the way they are, fucking playground." Doogie shook his head. "Tonight when Krumpe talked to me I should have told him how nice it was in the room tonight.

Just keep burying the fucker. 'Cause I'll tell you, Maloney buried fucking Murdoch. He wouldn't try to help him. He fucking buried him first."

We got out at Oren's. There were two girls hovering near the door and one of them approached us, but Doogie was ushered in by the doorman before she could make contact. Our table was waiting in the rear.

"You were sensational tonight, though, all over the ice. I couldn't believe how much ice you were covering," I said.

Doog ordered some beer, then peered around the room. There were at least twenty girls scattered at various tables who were giving him the ol' fisheye. "It's funny. Tonight I felt terrible and I fucking skated like a madman. I thought I was gonna have a heart attack. I told Butch I didn't know how I was gonna play in tonight's game. I felt like doing a bennie or something, that's how bad I felt."

"I saw Butch during the game. He told me you bet him five dollars that you would lose tonight," I remembered.

Doogie smiled sheepishly. "I told Butch before the game that I hope they scored after each goal I got, so we'd lose but I'd score. I was so depressed. But you shoulda seen Bubba before the game in the dressing room. He looked like he wanted to kill someone. He wasn't talking, he was glowering at the floor."

We talked some more and ate and drank some, and watched as Reggie Jackson came in, and we looked at the models. Then we got up to leave. The doorman stopped us on the way out. "There's some pigs outside." He pointed through the glass. It was the same two girls. "They've been waiting for you to come for over an hour and a half."

Doogie just shrugged and we walked out and they gingerly approached him and he signed an autograph and posed for a Polaroid, and then we went to Herlihy's to meet Murdoch, who was in town visiting his old cronies.

Out on the ice, big Bob Dailey was taking slap shot after slap shot at an empty net. The Rangers had just finished their morning practice, and the Flyers were about to begin theirs and their big defenseman was working his injured shoulder back in shape.

I was sitting with Bukka. "Everybody wants to win but it comes down to the mental now," the trainer explained. He waved at Behn Wilson as he skated by. "They can't think of the nice weather and the sun. Bubba's really sore on his left side, he's got to block that out. They got to forget that the golf courses open tomorrow. They can do it. They're hyper. If Freddie only came in tonight being spastic, yelling. I'm the only one yelling and they told me tonight to be quiet." He shook his head in bewilderment.

"A couple of our guys got the fear in them," he confided, and then he headed to the dressing room.

Talafous walked out. He was sidelined with the rib, but he still came to practice to lend support. "Barry's gotta come out and run them from the start. No one's challenging him, not even Holmgren. If he runs some guys right now, the Swedes'll be flying all night."

He tried. He tried on the first shift of the game, and it was Holmgren he had lined up against the boards, and as he started barreling toward the big wing, his skate hit a rut on the ice and he could actually feel that sickening sensation of muscle tearing internally. The groin again. His Achilles groin, the same one that had bothered him his first two months as a Ranger.

Nobody in the stands knew it, of course, because Bubba was your basic stoic. He finished out that shift, and he didn't miss a shift all night, even though they frantically bandaged him up between each period, adding tape as the pull tore further and further into his abdomen. But on the ice Bubba didn't look hurt, he looked ineffective, just like all his teammates.

The Flyers drew first blood with less than a minute to go in the first period. Bridgman raced Bubba for the puck to Davidson's right and, while the two scrapped, it lay at their feet. Greschner, aware of Beck's injury, skated over to help out his friend, leaving Al Hill alone in front of the net. Bridgman shoveled the puck over and Hill beat JD easily.

Philadelphia scored again in the second when Esposito lost a face-off in the Ranger end and Behn Wilson slapped a bullet past Davidson in off the post. The Rangers then seemed to wake up, but when Holmgren shot one in off Maloney, making it 3–0, their fate was sealed. Duguay's lone goal in the third period saved them from a shutout.

At the buzzer the teams went through the ritualistic handshakes, and the Rangers slowly trudged back to their room. Shero looked drawn as he met the press on a makeshift stage set up in the press room.

He talked about injuries and the Flyers not taking stupid penalties, and he complimented Clarke. The Rangers, he felt, tried hard. The Flyers shut off their game.

"You think this team was at all successful this year?" someone asked. Shero slowly shook his head. "No, not really."

"Did you get the kind of on-ice leadership that you might have needed from some of your older players?" Naughton asked.

"Well, I think you can't ask any more of Vad and Maloney, guys like that," Fred said. "They're leading all year and they're good guys and good hockey players."

"I'm not talking about anyone who wears a 'C.' I'm talking about the other guys who have been around a while," Naughton clarified.

"I think they're all trying," Shero said.

Someone asked about priorities.

"I wouldn't worry about goaltending, we got five goalies really," Shero said. "I think we got to get a few more abrasive people. A few more guys who like to fool around with the opposition. We don't have that physical a team. I know that. We got by Atlanta because they weren't that physical."

"Did you sense the same motivation was there?" I asked.

Freddie shrugged. "Yeah, what's the difference? They're trying."

"Well, maybe the whole Cinderella thing last year . . ."

"That's bullshit," Shero snapped. "They're pros. If you see somebody out there not trying, tell me so I'll know."

He headed back for the room. Inside, a handful of reporters were talking to JD, Espo, and the Swedes. Werblin and Krumpe were standing around trying to look chipper. But Werblin was having a hard time hiding his hurt. He hated to lose, anywhere, at anything.

"I thought we were alive," he was telling a small cluster of the press from New York. "The team had capability but we came up empty, it happens." He shrugged.

"What do you do now, meet with Fred, Mickey, Mike . . .?" someone wondered.

"Now I go back and worry about the Diplomats next Sunday and try to straighten out a few things at the Garden that aren't exactly right. Take complaints."

"Going into this, did you and Fred discuss what he was afraid of happening and what he needed to try to go over the top?" A veteran reporter from the *Times* finally got the tortured question out.

Werblin gave him a look of incredulity. "Discuss anything with Fred? Are you kidding? You haven't been around for a while." Then he laughed.

In the trainers' room, Keating and Nykoluk and Shero were sitting around listlessly. But back in the main room, there was a strange lack of emotion. It was as if the Rangers had left their game and their emotions somewhere else. The only one near tears was Don Maloney.

And Bubba. He was alone in the shower. He was standing under the hot water, one hand holding the wall for support, the other holding a can of Mountain Dew. His midsection was wrapped in yards and yards of Ace bandages, supporting his ravaged groin. He looked like a warrior of antiquity.

He stood there for a while, motionless, then he crushed the can and threw it into the garbage and slowly lurched back to his stall. Frankenstein's monster. He eased himself onto the seat.

"What happened?" I asked softly.

"My skate caught and I went into the corner with Holmgren. It just caught. I just kept skating on, and it just kept ripping," he managed to say between paroxysms of pain. He pointed near his intestine. "It's up to here now." He grimaced.

Bukka came over. "Want me to tie it? Want to come home with me?" he asked solicitously.

Bubba was trying to put his underwear on, with great difficulty. Joey and I steadied him. "That's good, I got it . . ." he gasped. "Couple of fucking beers . . . Where's the doc?" He almost collapsed. We lowered him to his seat.

"Tell him to give me some pain-killer," Bubba said. Bukka scurried away. Mifflin walked over. Bubba was struggling to get his pants on.

"I just caught my skate." Bubba repeated the story for her. "I couldn't skate. We wanted to go out and hit everyone hard. When I sat down on the bench, it hurt even more."

"Does it hurt now?" Mifflin asked.

Beck's features were etched in pain. "Yeah, it hurts," he grunted. "I got to go." He slowly pulled himself up and limped out to the bus.

Over in the middle of the room, McPeek was talking to Ulfie.

"Everyone recognized the game is turning back to speed and your coach talks only about getting tougher guys." The journalist shook his head.

Ulfie shrugged. "I don't know, 'cause he got rid of Nicky, one of the toughest guys in the league, the beginning of the season. So it's kind of hard to say the reverse at the end of the season."

I walked over to Captain Dave. He was sitting in his underwear.

"I'm a chapter short," I said.

"Two chapters," he corrected. "Fuck, fuck." There was a hollow ring to his protestations. "We didn't have the bodies either. Walter's on one leg, they were running the shit out of Ulfie." He shrugged.

"You traded away a hundred and five goals too," I reminded him.

"I know, that's obvious," he snapped. "So what? Like, I mean that's not for me to say. It's a fact. I got to go and comb my hair." He vanished.

Ulfie and Anders remained, answering questions in their underwear, Anders especially digging deep for explanations to the Flyers' mastery. Then they got dressed and darted outside to the bus.

I rode shotgun on the equipment van again. It was a quiet ride back. Except for Jimmy Young's long recitation of Rangers who needed surgery in the off-season, we rode in silence. Murphy made good time and he pulled the van into the Garden, past a sleeping guard. It was after 2 A.M.

He inched the van up the widening ramp and then pulled it around a curve and through an archway, and suddenly we were smack in the middle of the empty arena. All around us, scores of workmen had already taken up the ice and were working on the boards. Murph drove right up to what was the center ice, and then he backed the van slowly toward the dressing room. He and Jimmy unloaded the bags and dragged them into the dressing room.

All the stalls were bare except for a spare pair of skates below and a shiny white helmet perched on top. Duguay's Cheryl Tiegs montage was the only adornment.

I was admiring Peter Beard's elephants when Boxcar and Conacher walked in. They had stopped up to pack some sticks for the New Haven games. The farm team was still in contention, and they were flying out tomorrow to rejoin their old teammates and play in yet another series.

"In a way it's kind of a letdown," Hospodar explained. He leaned down on a stick, testing its flexibility.

"Letdown? You still got a chance to win the Calder Cup." I tried to be enthusiastic.

"That's good and tomorrow I'll be back in the groove but now . . ." he trailed off.

"Want to go to Herlihy's with us?" Conacher asked. "The guys are gonna have a fucking all-nighter. I can go for that."

They picked up a few dozen sticks and we went down to the car. EJ, Miller, and Connor were waiting in the car. We pulled out and started up Eighth Avenue. Outside, the working girls looked lonelier than ever.

"You seem subdued, Ratso," Connor said. "Your eyes look fucked up. You're quiet."

"I'm thinking of the last two chapters," I said from the back seat.

"After tonight we'll give you something to put in there," he said cheerily.

"What do you think, Ratso?" Hospodar said. "I'm sorry your book had to come to this conclusion. But we'll be the Calder Cup champs. If we lose out to the fucking Mariners, I'll bust my fucking balls."

"Fucking Stanley Cup to the Calder Cup," Conacher muttered.

"You think Herlihy's is crowded?" Hospodar wondered.

"Sure," I guessed. "Last fucking shot at the Rangers this year."

We drove past Columbus Circle. "Yell at the Gulf and Western building, if you want to." Hospodar pointed. "It's our last chance." He rolled down the window and stuck his head out. "Next year," he yelled.

"They told Wayne to go down to New Haven for the play-offs and he told them to fuck off," Miller said.

"That guy is the tops," Hospodar marveled.

Herlihy's was dead. Except for the guys, there were one or two just post-pubescents hanging out by the tables, and a few non-Ranger-related revelers drinking at the bar. So it was almost a team party.

Or wake. Gresch was on his umpteenth beer, trying to drown the sorrow. Anders was brooding by the jukebox. "I can't believe we lost," Anders kept repeating. "I wish I was still playing. I really wish that."

Markham put a paternal hand on his shoulder. "Don't cry over spilt milk," the big, rawboned rookie lectured the vet. "We'll get 'em next year."

Over by the bar Walter Tkaczuk was holding forth, with Ciggy and Don Maloney doing the listening.

"I told you last year, goalscorers come and go, but checking players never die," Walter was telling them.

"I scored twenty-five goals this year," Donnie said. "That's scary. I think I can do it again."

"You'll score twenty-five for ten years," Wally poohpoohed. "Between twenty and thirty each year, then they'll reassign you as a checker. You won't have the scoring opportunities, but your job will be as important. Checking players never get the publicity, though." Tkaczuk smiled with self-satisfaction.

"Some do." EJ laughed. "Some make fifty thousand dollars, some make two hundred thousand dollars."

"I don't know many hockey players that make two hundred thousand dollars." Tkaczuk was wide-eyed.

"I do." EJ again. He was thinking of Tkaczuk's brand-new Mercedes.

"I'm talking about two hundred thousand dollars clear," Walter corrected. "Some make fifty thousand dollars clear, though."

They all slapped hands.

The rest of the guys kept drinking beer and talking, and then it was time for the Westchester guys to start their long drives back and, two and three at a time, they all filtered out, to start their summers.

• APRIL 25

We were standing at attention, waiting for the National Anthem. "And now to sing the Star-Spangled Banner is twelve-year-old Stephanie Vance," the announcer blared, "a good student who someday hopes to make a career out of singing." She was a skinny little black girl in a green dress, and they had her standing by the boards with a microphone. She was swallowing a lot of the words and her voice kept cracking. Welcome to New Haven.

The Nighthawks were playing the Hershey Bears, Washington's farm team, and I came down to see Boxcar and Soetaert and Conacher and Beater and LaRose and some of the other guys who were on the New York-New Haven Shero Shuttle all year. I was sitting in the first row, right next to the Bears' bench.

"Hey, Inness," the fans behind the bench screamed at Hershey's spare goaltender. "I had your mother last night." "Gary, you suck." Another leaned over. "Your mother wears combat boots, you potato picker you." The ledge behind the Bears' bench was festooned with little Hershey kisses.

On the ice it was mayhem. New Haven was pummeling Hershey all over the ice. Beaton creamed one guy against the boards so hard that everyone around me shivered. Chris Kotsopoulos, a big, rawboned defenseman, passed the puck and then gave the nearest Bear a gracious glove in the face. André Dore, another promising young defenseman, was slashing everyone in sight. These kids were not fooling around.

The Nighthawks were scoring, though—Mayer and Snopek and Nethery and LaRose—and by the middle of the third period, it was 8–2.

On the ice Beater threw a devastating check. "Why didn't Beater play like that when he was with us?" Murphy, the Rangers' trainer, shook his head. "He'd still be up."

Danny, who had driven up with him, had his mind on the Rangers, though. "Nykoluk's quitting," he whispered to me. "He told the guys at the final team meeting his hands were tied and he was leaving if he don't get his way."

"Didn't they have a farewell dinner again this year?" I asked.

"Not this year." Danny smiled. "It cost seventy thousand dollars last year. They didn't get fuckall this year. Six sticks and skates. I'll tell ya, it's not a team anymore. Everyone's got New Yorkitis. When Bubba first came here, he was nervous as hell when he came to the game. He was a wild animal, he had to take Bromo Seltzer. Now he jokes after the games. And did you see Bukka after the Philly series? He fucking went out on the ice and shook hands with the Flyers." Danny shook his head sadly. "What a team. Even the trainers hated each other."

It was 10–2 by now, and I made my way down to the Hawks' bench. In the waning seconds, Boxcar charged fifteen feet to run a Bear defenseman, and Tommy Laidlaw, another good-looking defenseman, began pummeling the shit out of another Bear. Laidlaw was banished to the penalty box. "Way to do," Seaweed, the Nighthawks' spare goalie, stuck his head through a hole at the end of the bench and gave the thumbs-up sign. "Kicked his ass."

The buzzer sounded and the teams filed off the ice. "We're gonna put ice on the bus and make you creeps practice all the way back to Hershey," someone shouted at the Bears. In the locker room the Nighthawks were whooping it up. There were a few reporters in the room and they were talking to Soapy and Beater. Beaton finished his interview and then gave a big toothless grin.

"Ratso." He grabbed my hand. "Some game, eh? The first two games we got away from their game plan and they got lucky. But today we destroyed them."

"You're a different person down here," I said. "Jesus, you were hitting the shit out of everyone."

Beaton scowled. His eyes narrowed, the way they do right before he drops his gloves. "Because they build up your self-confidence here," he fumed. "They give you a little bit of respect here. They don't treat you like a piece of shit. They give you a name here, not just a fucking number on a fucking team. You feel like somebody here."

He stalked off to shave and I wandered around the room, greeting the other ex-Rangers. The stereo was blasting and there were porno pictures in the back room on "Seaweed's Wall of Shame."

I said hello to Kotsopoulos. I had sat next to him back in Richmond when we made the iron-lung trip to Hershey during the exhibition season. He told me then he'd make New Haven, no sweat. He was right.

"So, Ratso," Chris barked. "You better put me in that fucking book. I'm having a hard time dealing with Keating. They won't give me a Ranger contract, just a minor league one. But I'm telling you, the next time I go up to that Garden, it'll be to sign a Ranger contract. I'll be with the Rangers next year, you'll see."

We chatted a while and then I said hello to Dore and then Wayne Thomas came over. "Did you see this yet?" He led me to the back room and pulled up one of the guys' storage bins. Someone had cut out *Hustler* magazine's "Asshole of the Month" feature. It was a picture of the Ayatollah gracing the rear of a donkey, only they had cut out the Ayatollah's face and in its place had affixed a publicity photo of Keating.

- MAY 9

Nykoluk resigned today.

Later that night I saw Sarge and his wife at a Felt Forum fund-raiser. It was a country-and-western benefit, and Kinky was featured.

Sarge had shaved his moustache off.

"Ask him why," Joanne prodded.

I complied.

" 'Cause it gave her a rash on the thigh," Sarge said, shrugging.

Joanne blushed. "No, that's not why, Ratso." She rolled her eyes. "He did it so he could kiss little Jimmy."

It was Sarge's turn to blush.

- MAY 24

It was like torture. I was sitting on the steps in an aisle of the Nassau Coliseum as the Islanders and the Flyers were about to begin overtime. Sudden death. If the Flyers could score, it would force a seventh game of the Stanley Cup finals. If the Islanders scored first, that was that. The Cup would belong to them.

What a horrible thought. I despised the Islanders.

I hated Long Island on principle. I had grown up in

Queens and had spent most of my formative years railing against the spoiled, split-level mentality of Islanders. I hated their sons' cars, and their long-nailed, whiny JAP daughters who never put out, and their endless rows of malls. I hated their clean parks and golf driving ranges, and I hated Nathan's in Oceanside. There was only one Nathan's and that was in Coney Island, and the frankfurters were frankfurters there, cooked on grills that were encrusted with the grease of decades. Tradition. Long Island was nouveau culture, nowhere culture.

And the Islanders were its team. I hated the Islanders because they had assimilated so well. Here were husky, rough-and-tumble Western Canadians who, in the space of a few years, were all dressed in three-piece suits, like their goddamn accountant and lawyer neighbors, worrying about their sewer systems and their lawns. They played like they were carrying goddamn briefcases. Most of them wore helmets before it was the style, the ultimate bureaucrats, each a tiny cog in the wheel of Islander efficiency. Torrey, their taskmaster GM, was fat and wore a bow tie.

And they choked. For years now, when the chips were down, they would bite the Big Apple and wind up getting eliminated earlier than expected. In 1978 the Toronto Maple Leafs, with much less talent, bullied the Islanders out of the quarter-final series. And last year, after they finished the season with the best record in hockey, they went down stiffly to the Rangers in six games in the semifinal round.

So losing became a tragedy of major proportions. And every time the team lost a game, even during the regular season, it became an occasion for tortured psychoanalysis. They would sit there in their pinstripes, talking to the press as if they were paying a hundred bucks an hour, exploring their weaknesses and their shortcomings, scraping the plaque out of the gums of their psyches. What a boring bunch of old farts.

But now they were one goal from their ultimate goal. I tensed as the puck was dropped and overtime began. It didn't take long. Seven minutes and eleven seconds, to be exact. Lorne Henning, a nice, balding guy who had been misused by Torrey and his coach Arbour, was finally seeing some ice and he made a nice play to break out of his own end. He gave the puck to Tonelli, one of the faceless cogs, who broke into the Flyer zone on a two on one with Nystrom. He slid the puck over to Nystrom, who got his backhand on it, deflecting it over Pete Peeters and into the net. For the Stanley Cup.

At least it was Nystrom, I was thinking, as the whole Coliseum exploded. Nystrom wasn't one of the helmet heads. He was a decent guy with some vestige of personality left, and a few months from this moment he would complain bitterly about the Islanders' utter inability to market his Cup-winning heroics. But right now, all he was worried about was getting out alive from under his jubilant teammates.

They milled around on the ice a bit, throwing their sticks and gloves and helmets in the air, hugging and kissing each other, and lining up for the traditional handshakes. Except for Islander goalie Billy Smith, one of the dirtiest stickmen in the league. Smith skated off to get first crack at the champagne.

Then they brought out the Cup. It looked like it was made of tin.

There was a mob waiting to get into the Islanders' dressing room after all the players had left the ice and gone in to celebrate. I was fighting off two juvenile delinquents from Merrick who were trying to snatch my press pass from my pocket. People were sardined in, pushing and cursing and sweating, trying to squeeze through the one door that gave access to the room. Larry Brooks was outside, desperately trying to get in with his heroes, moaning about what a disgrace the scene was and how John Ziegler was responsible. His nose was pressed up against the door.

We all finally got in and it was a scene. There was champagne and beer everywhere. Dennis Potvin was walking around in his long johns wearing a Pirates hat and chugging on a bottle of bubbly.

And then there was the Cup. It was being held by a beefy gas-station attendant named Muscle Mike who was strong-arming people out of the way, bringing it to each player to drink from. He had one hand around the bowl and the other was stuck all the way inside the base. The Cup was hollow.

He was waving it around like garbage men in New York do when they empty the trash into their compactor trucks, and all these Long Islanders were surrounding it, banging on its side. Every once in a while, to be perverse, Muscle Mike would tip it over, spewing the champagne contents onto the heads of those in the vicinity. It was in this manner that thick, syrupy, foamy wine penetrated the innards of my Sony, rendering it useless forever.

But that was a minor tragedy compared to what was happening to the Cup. Mike lugged it around for a while longer, and then everyone had had enough. I walked out to my car. In the parking lot, scores of cars were circling around, horns blaring, occupants sitting out of the windows. The ultimate suburban celebration, circling endlessly around a parking lot in Corvettes and jacked-up Fords.

They took the Cup out through those minicaravans to a private club where the Islanders partied into the wee hours. Then Bryan Trottier picked it up and posed for pictures, inching toward the door. With his wife as lookout, he skipped out with the hardware.

But, alas, he couldn't fit the Cup into his two-seat Mercedes, so he borrowed a bigger car from one of the Islander owners. They drove home and then Bryan took the

Cup to bed. It lay there between him and his wife, Nickey. "Like our little baby," Bryan later said. But Nickey refused to sleep in the same bed with the cold Cup, so it was cast out of their bed in their little bedroom of their nice condominium in Long Island. It wound up in the backyard the next day. They took pictures of it, posing the local policemen and the floor-waxer and some of the neighbors in the shots. Then they picked up Bryan, Jr., all two years old, and sat him in the Cup. He looked disoriented.

They were going to have him eat out of it except Clark Gillies had already beaten them to the punch. Earlier, he had used the Stanley Cup to feed his dogs.

• JUNE 14

Despite the protestations on the bathroom stall in Charlie O's, Captain Dave Maloney married his sweetheart, Vicki, today. It was a nice modern ceremony, complete with a handshaking fellowship greeting and Dave and Vicki reading from Paul's Letters to the Corinthians and the Book of Genesis.

It was not well attended, though. Gresch and brother Don, of course, were there. They were in the wedding party. A lot of the rookies showed up—Boxcar and Baker and Sully and Charlie Conacher and a few of the old vets, Vadnais, Tkaczuk, and Vickers. Of all the no-shows, the Swedes had the best excuse. They were in Sweden.

Surprisingly the complete Ranger troika management did show up. Although by now they weren't talking to each other. So by the time the reception started at a nearby country club, Freddie had staked out one corner of the bar, along with Keating, and Nykoluk was holding court at the other end.

Tkaczuk was talking to Nykoluk, and then he came over to

where a few of the players were standing. "Good scoops," Walter smiled. "Deep scoops. I really like to get the scoops."

"What did Nykoluk say?" I implored. Walter smiled enigmatically.

"C'mon." Sarge started off toward Nykoluk. "Let's try to provoke a brawl."

We walked over. "Ratso." Nykoluk seemed cheerful enough. "I finally figured out why Fred cut you off."

"What do you mean, cut me off?" I asked.

"Why he had me tell the players not to talk to you anymore." Nykoluk shrugged matter-of-factly. It had never crossed my mind that Shero had directed that on-ice talk. "He was pissed off about that *Playboy* article. You had those guys, Hickey and McEwen, implying he was drunk, staggering around early in the morning through parking lots, watching TV, and not caring what they say. He hated that article."

"So you're really bummed out, huh?" I changed the subject. Nykoluk nodded.

"I gave up a two-hundred-thousand-dollar-a-year-job with Toronto, it was my third offer, just to stay here, and then Fred lied to me," Nykoluk said.

I started defending Shero and went into my Zen-Fog routine, talking about delegating responsibility and remote authority figures and throwing people back on themselves. Then I mentioned the System. The fabled Shero System.

"System?" Nykoluk laughed. "He's bombed, Ratso. He's a drunk, he's bombed out of his mind. I know Fred better than anyone in the world. After that first play-off game in the finals when the Flyers played Boston, I had to cover his ass. He was drunk in a room, and we said he went back to Philly to study films. How about that time in Atlanta? He went out to a bar after practice during the play-offs and he got in a fight, and I had to coach my first NHL game, Ratso. They started winning in Philly when I came there. Fred's first year in Philly they didn't make the play-offs. After I came, we were first the next four years and we won two cups. Then they kick me upstairs to Maine to punish Fred because Snyder heard about Fred's drinking."

"What happened this year?" I asked.

"We lost too many guys in the draft because we didn't even send a representative to the WHA draft meetings. We didn't make any deals. I realized after the draft that we lost all these guys and nobody else lost anything. We just weren't prepared." Nykoluk shrugged.

"No way you'll be back, huh?" I wondered.

Nykoluk shook his head. "No way. He lied to me. And I'm going to get even."

Keating was watching our conversation from his side of the room, and as soon as I drifted away from Nykoluk, he struck.

"Ratso, how you doing?" He threw a paternal arm around my shoulders. I had never realized before that Mickey cared. "I told Fred that he should talk to you, eh? I told him you're a good guy. I figure you're gonna write about us anyway, eh? Might as well get our side of it, eh? Why don't you give me a call and I'll take you out to dinner, eh? Call me anytime."

Keating left and I drifted over to the other side of the bar. Freddie was standing by the champagne fountain, drinking Canadian Club, talking to Sulliman. He was telling him about the European system of play and how important it was to take a vacation from hockey in the summer and develop your mind and how the power of positive thinking works. And he was reminiscing about his playing days and how the owners had players over a barrel and about the time that his club offered him a contract without any sum specified after the warm-ups before the first game of the season. Sully was taking it all in, thrilled to hear Fred say more than two syllables.

I mentioned it was the most Shero had said all year.

"Coaches always used to say nothing." Freddie chuckled.

"The great ones, Toe Blake, Bunny Cook. The famous coaches didn't talk. Bunny Cook was my coach once, and all he'd say was 'Go Hump 'Em.' I didn't know if he meant before, during, or after the game."

We stood there and talked and drank and talked. Fred was reminiscing some more and he was talking about how he had delegated too much authority this year, but that the dilemma was if you don't give the assistants some power they can't gain any respect from the players. "You have to delegate authority," he stressed. "I always have. What is it to have a coach that just goes out and throws the pucks out in the practice?"

Just then we were interrupted by a large stranger. "Fred, I'm Dave Maloney's uncle." He offered a beefy hand. "Tell me, is Dave going somewhere?" There had been a rumor circulating that Maloney and another Ranger were going to Buffalo for Schoenfeld.

Shero just shrugged and resumed our conversation.

We were so engrossed in our talk that, before we knew it, everyone had moved out of this reception area and was sitting down at the tables. Keating came over and collected Fred.

But we met again a few minutes later, in the bathroom. I was already at the urinal when Fred walked in. He stood two urinals down.

"We stopped in a bar on the way here," he said suddenly, "and there was a sign over the urinals that said, 'Don't worry about the ice in the urinals. We only use it occasionally.' "

We finished and I led the way out. The band was playing a hot disco number, and our path back to the tables was obstructed by scores of writhing bodies. Freddie frowned.

"C'mon, Fred." I led him past the revelers. "You gotta take the body."

We made it past, and suddenly Shero stopped and pointed out a tall, attractive brunette. "I told Gresch to dance with her." Freddie chuckled. "He wants to meet her but he's too shy. Why don't you see what you can do?"

I went to talk to Gresch, but he wasn't interested. He was too busy putting the moves on Vicki's younger sister.

Back by our table, Walter was talking to Keating. The Rangers had just drafted and all the new prospects were centers, something of concern to Tkaczuk. "Hey, Mickey, just send those centers to my school this summer for a little seasoning. I'll turn them all into left wingers."

It was getting late now and it was time for the toast to the bride and groom, and Dave's other brother, the nomad, made it. "Dave used to sleep with a hockey stick," he said. "Used to. Now he's got Vicki, so he'll be happy to break that stick." Everyone cracked up.

Then they drank and danced some more and then it was time to go. There was a smaller get-together for the wedding party at Cliff's house, and Sarge decided to invite himself and the rest of the guys. But first we stopped at the bar and Gresch snuck behind it, searching for bottles for the trip.

We were almost out the door when I spied Shero again.

"Don't worry about Gresch." I pointed over to the defenseman, who was in final negotiations with Vicki's sister. "He just likes 'em young."

"I don't know," Freddie sighed. "I still think that tall one wasn't bad."

• FALL 1980

Maloney's wedding was the last time that the Ranger triumvirate would share the same roof. It didn't take Sonny long to see to that. On July 22, Halligan assembled the press, and Sonny took the floor at the Hall of Fame room at the Garden to announce the departure of Messrs. Nykoluk and Keating and the arrival of a new director of operations, Craig

Patrick. Patrick, a boyish blond who looked young enough to be Freddie's son, was a major cog in the triumphant U.S. Olympic Hockey Team, working under Herb Brooks. Suddenly, he was working over Fred Shero. Sonny assured everyone that Fred's job was not at all in jeopardy, that he was now free to do what he did best: coach. McPeek, for one, didn't go for it.

"Can you delay your book?" The reporter grinned at me. "This is Freddie's last stand. He's next."

He was right. And the press did all they could to hasten Shero's departure. Two months later, banner headlines blared from the *Post*: "SHERO: I DRANK TOO MUCH—Ranger Coach/GM claims he's beaten alcohol trouble." It seems that Delano had finally cajoled Shero into going public with a story that had been brewing for months and months. Freddie admitted drinking too much, but he maintained that it didn't affect his job. Sonny, for the record, backed his beleaguered coach.

"I think Fred is over his problem," Werblin told the papers. "Fred is like a new man. I mean that sincerely . . ."

A new man and a new season. But less than three weeks into the campaign, everyone wanted Fred's head. The Rangers had gotten off to their poorest start in years, 4–13–3, the result for the most part of some key injuries. But the bottle was in the back of most people's minds. So the press began floating their candidates for coach. Delano was trumpeting Cherry and Émile Francis, and Larry Brooks, in his infinite wisdom, was pumping up some ex-Islander for the Ranger position. But Sonny had other plans.

On November 22, Fred was dismissed and Patrick was named interim coach. But everyone knew who Sonny really lusted after. Herb Brooks, the Olympic hero. Only problem was he was in Switzerland, in the first year of a two-year contract. But contracts were never an obstacle in the rarefied air of the Garden top management. After all, Freddie still had about half of his five-year contract remaining when he was canned. Come to think of it, Nykoluk and Keating were probably still on the payroll too, wherever they were.

- JANUARY 11, 1981

It was a crisp Sunday afternoon, and I was sitting in the den of Fred Shero's sprawling ranch house in Hartsdale, N.Y. Fred looked relaxed and almost serene, and his wife, Mariette, was feeding us little melted-cheese finger sandwiches and bringing us beers as Freddie was being interviewed by me for *Inside Sports* magazine. Let's go to the tape:

ME: You once wrote on a blackboard: "A successful man appreciates the fact that failure is nothing more than a state of mind. He believes the way to react to it is not with fear but with curiosity. What can I learn from the mistake?" What have you learned from your experience with the Rangers?

SHERO: I've had more time with my family. I never realized how beautiful they are because with coaching your mind is on the game all the time. You even dream about hockey.

ME: What kind of dreams?

SHERO: Mostly of hockey. You're trying to get on the ice and you can't find your skates and your shift is ready, or you're coming off the ice and all of a sudden you've got no clothes on and you're trying to hide. (Laughs) They're always embarrassing.

ME: Do you analyze what these dreams mean?

SHERO: No.

ME: Mike Nykoluk, your longtime assistant coach, left the Rangers at the end of last season, saying that you lied to him and reneged on a promise that he'd be head coach for this season.

SHERO: All I can remember saying is that I would like him to be the coach of the Rangers *when* I felt like stepping down. I can't guarantee that I'm going to step down or that when I do someone is going to get a specific job.

ME: Didn't you encourage Nykoluk to take the Toronto job as coach when it was first offered to him?

SHERO: Yes. I said, you're crazy if you don't take it. I said he should go because I didn't know how I could get him more money. So he went to Mr. Werblin and told him his problems and said he'd like to stay, and they increased his salary. The setup he had was great. He didn't have to worry about accepting the responsibility, and last year I was letting him run things pretty much on the ice constantly, under my direction. I could have stopped him from going to Toronto when Harold Ballard asked for permission to talk to him. I could have said no, he's under contract. Or if I let him go that I wanted some money for him. But I wouldn't do that.

ME: Do you feel you delegated authority wisely?

SHERO: What I think I did wrong was delegate too much authority. You hate to hire somebody and give him nothing to do.

ME: When they brought in Craig Patrick over you last summer, one of the criticisms Werblin made was that there wasn't always communication with the top. Werblin once asked a player who André Beaulieu was, and the player told him that André was an assistant coach who had been with the team a few weeks.

SHERO: I'm sure whenever we'd do anything we always sent a memo. Imagine all the memos Mr. Werblin gets. How much can he remember?

ME: Do you feel he interfered too much in the day-to-day operation?

SHERO: You can't always do what you want with any team. This doesn't apply only to the Rangers, You have to live with that unless you own the damn team. Even in Philadelphia

I used to get mad because I was expected to go in the lounge with the executives and their wives and so-called friends for two hours and talk and drink and answer their stupid questions. After the game I want to be alone. When I had a basement a couple of years ago in Philadelphia, I'd go downstairs, even my wife wasn't allowed to talk to me. I don't want to be with thirty people and try to be nice to them. I'd sooner have a couple of hours by myself and think about the game.

ME: Didn't you try to trade Phil Esposito from the beginning?

SHERO: We thought we might get a younger man, a man that might have been better than Phil at the time, because Phil was getting old.

ME: Didn't you almost have a deal with Chicago?

SHERO: We found out that the other guy had some problems with his back and we weren't sure they could be corrected.

ME: Did you hear people saying that Esposito had a direct line to Werblin and undercut you?

SHERO: I don't believe that.

ME: How about losing Nicky Fotiu? On paper you might not think he was a big loss, but in terms of camaraderie, spirit off the ice.

SHERO: Yeah, but you can't keep people around because of camaraderie. He had a great heart but he didn't realize his role. He'd miss a shift sometimes and . . .

ME: Get depressed?

SHERO: It's okay to be depressed, but don't show it. You gotta be a hundred percent behind the team at all times on and off the ice, and you gotta accept your role.

ME: What do you think happened last year with Murdoch?

SHERO: I think he didn't have the personality to withstand the big city life. Maybe a couple of years from now he's gonna be okay. He may have been twenty-one years old, but he was more like a boy of fourteen or fifteen.

ME: Where does a team's responsibility end, though? I was close to him, it looked like he was falling apart, people outside of the team were trying to help him. Did it ever cross your mind that he might need outside help?

SHERO: We discussed it. We talked to him many times. I talked to him, Mike talked to him, André, the players tried to help him. When a man doesn't want help, he's not going to accept it from anyone. Sometimes it comes to a point where it takes maybe a couple of years where all of a sudden, the guy says, "Yeah, I'm gonna straighten out."

ME: So you had to give up on him?

SHERO: Well, because he gave up on himself, right? Nothing more you can do. You can bring in a psychiatrist, he's not going to listen. As good as the Flyers were, even Bobby Clark, we thought we'd hire a psychiatrist, and whatever the psychiatrist talked to them about, it was going to be free. We would not have the right to know anything that was said. But they wouldn't believe that. They were afraid.

ME: When you were removed, some Rangers said that you had lost control of the team. Had you?

SHERO: Definitely not.

ME: Did you have a drinking problem?

SHERO: I consider it something that's over with, and it's now under control. So why the big deal? I like beer as much as any player. Nobody said anything as long as we were winning. I think people got this impression because through the years when I first started coaching, I was a playing coach and I went with the players and had a beer or two with them or as much as they did. Maybe management didn't like that. Quite often when I'd walk into a bar and I was gonna have a drink, I'd see a couple of players and buy a bottle for them. Management maybe felt you're supposed to do it undercover. The problem was I didn't drink with the right people.

ME: This season you admitted that perhaps you drank too much last year.

SHERO: No. It could be any year. What's the difference? I drank the same everywhere and won.

ME: Some say that you said what you did about your drinking to take the pressure off the players.

SHERO: I had that motive in mind. I wanted to take the responsibility for them not playing well. The players have enough pressure.

ME: Do you think Ranger management used the drinking as an excuse to get rid of you?

SHERO: I have no idea and don't want to think about it.

ME: Do you think you have an unwarranted reputation?

SHERO: All I know is that I have no problem and I'm not worried about it. All I can do is ask people to trust me.

ME: Did you think about how the players would react to your statement that maybe you drank too much?

SHERO: I want them to realize that I'm human and I don't want their respect unless I earn it. That's what's wrong with a lot of people in government, big business. Suddenly they think that they're God and they're not God. People shouldn't be afraid to admit to something, a weakness of some kind, because there are no saints alive.

ME: Do you consider yourself shy? I remember a story in your first book in which you said that as a child you'd lock yourself in the bathroom for hours when relatives came.

SHERO: When I was young, yes. I still don't feel comfortable with relatives.

ME: You're not the kind of guy who chitchats?

SHERO: Not with relatives.

ME: Some of the players claim that you don't say two words to them all year.

SHERO: Through the years I've sometimes been accused

of talking too much to them. Sometimes you have to know where to draw the line. But I don't think it's true that I don't talk to them. They can't remember. (Laughs)

ME: How did that whole Fog image come about in Philadelphia?

SHERO: I think it started because sometimes you talk to the press and it's a difficult question and you look up for maybe ten, fifteen seconds. You've got to think. I find it very hard to think looking a guy right in the eye, right? (Laughs) We'd win a game 8–3 and I'd say we were lousy and they wouldn't believe me. The press would think I was nuts. I'm not nuts. I'd show you all the turning points in the game where we could have lost.

ME: It seemed that you used that Fog image effectively as a motivational tool. Players tell me that you'd call for someone to go on the ice when he already was in the penalty box, or call for the wrong line so the players had to correct you. Did the Fog thing serve to demystify you?

SHERO: That's just a coaching ploy you use. Pretend that you don't realize what you're doing and see if they're listening. Let them make fun of you because sometimes you make fun of them, right? Create a little atmosphere.

ME: Did you say much behind the bench?

SHERO: You talk to them about some little things that they're doing wrong or say, "Now see this coming up." You talk to them quietly. You do most of your coaching from behind the bench because you know they're listening. Everybody wants to win then. Sometimes their minds are somewhere else in practice.

ME: Don't you also use negative techniques, like getting guys angry to spur them on?

SHERO: I think the best example was a guy I used to coach. I named my son after him, that's how much I like him. He was the best man at my wedding. Jean-Paul Denis. He was a hell of a hockey player and a great fighter, one of the best, even though small. And as long as I coached him, every third game I'd come in the dressing room and really give him hell. Even though he was the star, I'd tell him he was no damned good, chicken, not backchecking, not working, thinking only of himself. This would frighten all the players. They'd say, "My God, if he says this to Jean-Paul Denis, who's the best player on the team, what does he think of us?" This went on about three years, and only one guy ever found out what was going on. Ted Hudson. He finally told me one summer. Well, I said, that's part of coaching.

ME: So Jean-Paul was in on it?

SHERO: Oh, yeah. Finally, he couldn't take it anymore. One night in St. Paul, he thought he was playing bad and he got upset and started to cry in front of everybody. He said, "I'm not takin' any more of this. Lay off, get off my back." So finally, after three years, it got too much. You have to use psychology.

ME: Ed Hospodar told me he was in the lobby of a hotel once late at night. He couldn't sleep before a game and was browsing at the card rack looking for one to send his girl friend. All of a sudden you were behind him and said, "Third row down, second card in. She'll like that." And you left. He was amazed. He told me he thought you have the ability to read minds.

SHERO: Everybody has it if they can develop it. I try a little bit. If a man studies it more, it would help him as a coach. He'd be able to read people better, understand them better. I read everything on the subject of parapsychology a few years ago to get a new insight on the game.

ME: You once said that at times you can almost direct the puck from behind the bench.

SHERO: I think if you pray hard enough, concentrate hard enough, sometimes you can change the flow or make things happen. A lot of people believe that. A lot of times I'll say, "Now, it's got to be now," and it goes in.

ME: It really works?

SHERO: Yes. And sometimes I feel touching a person is very important. I feel that when I'm touching someone I'm trying to reassure them that I'm with them and I understand the problems they're having. Sometimes if a guy comes off the ice and he's had a bad shift or an embarrassing moment and you just quietly touch him, maybe not even say anything, instead of giving him a dirty look, it helps. Because if you don't really believe in them or pray for them, how in hell are they going to play for you?

ME: How does mind over matter help?

SHERO: I read this one book and I was really praying. I had to do everything the book says. I was praying for Tommy Bladon because the fans were on his back. I figured if he could come up with three points, a goal, and two assists, maybe they'd get off him. So the night before the game, I was just laying there in bed starting to visualize flowers. Some things are harder than others, but your mind is opening now. Then you look at the television, pretend you're watching television. It's dark and you say, "I've got to see Tommy. Come up, Tommy, I've got to see your face." It just seemed impossible. All of a sudden his face came through. Then I started concentrating on the number three. I saw three clearly. It wasn't easy, you had to practice that— three, three. I could visualize a three perfectly all the time. The night of the game I saw Bladon's picture clearly on the scoreboard, but every time I tried to visualize the number three, it turned into an eight. I couldn't unlock the eight. So guess what happened that game? Eight points. I don't know if that had anything to do with it, but I was praying hard. One night I tried this same formula, going through the same routine for Rick MacLeish. The fans were on his back. "He's going to get three goals," I said, and I could see that three perfectly. Before the game I looked at the blackboard and I could see the three, beautiful in white, a perfect three. And I kept praying every time he went out there, "Rick, I'm with you. Three. Three." He got three goals. So there's nothing wrong with trying to transfer your thoughts. I believe that when there are fifteen thousand people cheering for you, the reason you win more at home is because somehow they are reaching you.

ME: When you say pray, you don't mean in a religious sense?

SHERO: I mean I'm pulling for you. I don't believe God's supposed to help you. A lot of times you pray before the game a little bit. You do the Hail Marys and whatnots.

ME: Are you religious?

SHERO: Just since I got married. I became a Catholic through marriage. I never have time to go to church. You're always practicing. So you have your beads and whatnots, maybe say a little prayer once in a while. I don't think that's supposed to help you win. I pray that my boys play up to their capabilities. I don't say, "Hey, how about helping us win?" One time in Philadelphia my first year, my goalie was badly hurt and my spare goalie was hurt and I had to put him in and he couldn't move. That's the only time I ever asked somebody to help. There were seconds to go and Gil Perreault of all guys walks in, no one to beat, and he pulled that goalie right over to the other side. He had the whole net, he could just slide it in, but he thought he was going to be fancy. And I hollered, "Hail Mary!" out loud, and everyone turned around. "Hail Mary!" and the puck went straight up and Perreault never could do that again in a million years. It must have gone a hundred feet straight up in the air and dropped over the glass. How can you miss a shot like that?

ME: Do you miss the game?

SHERO: A little rest is good for anybody. The trouble with life is that we don't get a chance every seven years to do something different for a year. People would come back

354 ∎

refreshed. I think some of the college professors do it, sabbaticals to get away from the students.

ME: You're under contract for another two years. You can get a lot of reading done.

SHERO: Yes, but I don't want to just read. I certainly don't want to sit out two years.

• FEBRUARY 24

It was Patrick's turn now. The Rangers were still struggling, seven games under .500, and the *Post*'s resident second-guessers, Delano and Brooks, were having a field day sticking it to the new coach.

Meanwhile, the old coach was going through his own private hell. We were back together again, me and Freddie, ensconced in someone's office up at *Inside Sports*. The editors there thought the interview was rich with philosophy, but they wanted more gritty stuff. They wanted to see Fred comment directly on the Nykoluk feud and his relationship with Werblin.

To this end, Mark Stewart was imported from Philadelphia. Stewart was a slick, shrewd attorney who, besides being up to his elbows in hot record business acts and notable sports figures, also managed to represent Fred. Stewart came down from Philly because he was concerned about Fred's reputation as of late, and he saw the *Inside Sports* piece as a vehicle for Fred to clear the air. But since when did a Fog ever clear the air?

I turned on the tape recorder and Stewart began what amounted to a cross-examination. Freddie looked pained, almost shell-shocked, as Stewart went to the offensive in an attempt to elicit some straight answers from him. I sat silently, for the most part, feeling like a sleazy voyeur as I watched Shero squirm.

STEWART: I said Freddie won't talk unless I'm with him, because I make him angry and he spills it all, see. Freddie, I think that it's high time that your story is told. I want you to listen to me carefully. Now, when Larry called up and said he wanted to do this story, I was surprised to find out that he had a pretty in-depth knowledge of what really went down, for instance with the Rangers. He probably has facts you're not fully aware of, and there's two sides to the story, you know. In my opinion you were set up and had, and were made to be the fall guy for certain other situations. I'm not putting words in anybody's mouth, but you can't sit here and defend that great Ranger organization, nor can you defend the great Flyer organization at the risk of your own integrity, reputation, and future. It can't happen that way, Freddie. You're a hockey legend, a hockey genius, and you know, I'll just ask you questions as your close friend and advisor. Okay? When you won two Stanley Cups in a row, did you drink any less than you did two years ago? Okay. You know the point I'm trying to make?

SHERO: Exactly. Didn't I say that?

STEWART: You know, you've been made out to appear in the eyes of the public as an alcoholic incompetent, and I don't fucking like it.

SHERO: Yeah, me neither.

STEWART: Let's put it the right way. You're not.

SHERO: No, I think every way that I would consider myself an average drinker in sports.

STEWART: You drink less than Sonny Werblin, for Chrissakes.

SHERO: I know that.

STEWART: Well, we both know, we've been out to dinner with him. I mean, come on. He drinks vodka. Freddie drank the same when he took the team to the finals, nobody said anything.

SHERO: I drank the same amount everywhere, and everywhere I won. I was the only coach in history to win in every championship in every professional league. So I've never had any more here than I had anywhere else. But I don't want to bring out anything bad or supposedly bad because I think my family's had enough of it.

STEWART: What do you mean?

SHERO: My wife and kids are concerned, right?

STEWART: I know that, Freddie, but how do you think your wife feels? and I know Mariette and I love Mariette, you know that, right? I've had conversations with Mariette, and she's cried on the phone to me. Okay? She feels so bad when you are the victim, and I'm just saying to you that you at this time have to declare exactly what the facts are as you view them. That's all I'm saying.

ME: Did you have a falling out with Sonny Werblin?

SHERO: I never had any problem with Werblin, he's probably one of the finest people I've ever worked with in my life. He's always nice to me.

STEWART: Well, do you think he was supportive of you?

SHERO: Well, I don't know really. There's so much going on at the Garden.

STEWART: No, no, Freddie, was he supportive of you?

SHERO: I have no idea.

STEWART: Did he respond to your requests? Did he give you what you asked for? Did he give you the latitude you wanted? Did he support your judgment? Did he do what you wanted to do as far as running the hockey club?

SHERO: I would say he was quite supportive. I mean, what else could you do, right?

STEWART: I'm asking you. When I came down here, remember the few meetings we had?

SHERO: Yes.

STEWART: The first time you went to his apartment with Keating and all that, and there seemed to be a problem there about who's running the hockey club, whether or not the players were responding, whether or not Mike Nykoluk was in fact causing dissension or a division among the players, remember that?

SHERO: Yeah.

STEWART: And Keating and André were extremely vocal as to their distrust and consternation with regard to the activities of Nykoluk, and you were defensive for Mike at that time. Fred, do you think it's right—you know, you and I have been through the Philadelphia era, right? Do you think it's right for the owner to have dinner with one or two of the players?

SHERO: Never.

STEWART: What? Never, right?

SHERO: I remember the old owner of Buffalo, he's a millionaire, he now owns Pepsi-Cola Company in Buffalo, and a beautiful person. And he used to be quite upset with me because I wouldn't go to his house for dinner. I said, I'm never going to go to your house for dinner. If I ever become a millionaire, I'll go to your house. I don't feel it's right. Even when I'm the coach.

ME: You said in all your books to socialize with management is a weakness for a coach.

SHERO: Yes, and it's worse for the players.

STEWART: Well, what about if management, the owner, solicits the presence of the players?

SHERO: I don't think that's right.

STEWART: Were you aware of these frequent meetings between the owner and your players? They were done without your knowledge, weren't they?

SHERO: They must have been because I didn't know about them.

STEWART: They were done without your knowledge. Don't you feel that those meetings inhibit your ability to coach those players?

SHERO: Well, you're not going to be able to coach them after that. 'Cause they know, they say, hey, just a minute, I've got the owner where I want him. Right? And I've got his ear.

STEWART: You know, Freddie, when we negotiated your contract with the Rangers, there was a clause in that contract which specifically states that you shall have complete control over hockey personnel as long as you stay within budgetary limitations. And it seems to me that those social meetings, etc., represent interference with the authority you're supposed to have and not really—none of us really know what went on with these meetings—if they were frequent enough—certain things could have been planted to try and prevent you from successfully coaching certain people. I'm going to ask you a question I've never asked you. Why do you think you're not still with the Rangers? And don't give me any cock-and-bull answer. I want to know why you think you're not with the Rangers.

SHERO: I don't know.

STEWART: Why do you think when you were retired from the Rangers your record was as poor as it was?

SHERO: I think it was mostly injuries.

STEWART: Okay. Why do you think there was such a big article . . . why am I asking all these questions? Why do you think there were so many articles and such a big acclaim referring to your drinking?

SHERO: I really don't know because I'd never—I drank the same amount anywhere I'd ever been.

STEWART: We know that. I want to know one thing. Do you think it's possible that the whole drinking bullshit was a plot against you to give the Rangers a reason to dismiss you?

SHERO: I hope not.

STEWART: So you think it's possible?

SHERO: Well, I think it's possible.

ME: Yeah. Why did you say that, why did you even admit you had a drinking problem?

SHERO: I don't know. Delano came one morning early, and he says it's gonna blow up in the paper. They're gonna say nasty things. Try to put it in a nice way.

STEWART: Why are you so worried about being Mr. Nice Guy when you're getting castrated, Freddie? Now you know, if you want to shut me up, you're gonna have to fire me because I'm gonna tell you exactly what I think. I think Larry's trying to give you an opportunity here in a national publication that can turn around your reputation in this country, and I want to see you seize upon that opportunity. Let me tell you right now, if we were to go out and get the kind of job you are deserving of, we've got to turn this around. And I want to see a declaration on your part that you're not an alcoholic.

SHERO: What else can I say?

STEWART: Are you an alcoholic?

SHERO: Definitely not. (Laughs) I'm not worried about that.

STEWART: And you never had a drinking problem?

SHERO: No.

STEWART: I'll tell you what. I've been with Fred in Toronto, I've never seen him drunk, and I've been with him in some more intimate times than with anybody. Right? Nobody has seen him drunk because he can handle his booze. He can drink you and I under the table. Fred, were you ever, as long as you were with New York, ever drunk behind the bench during a game?

SHERO: Definitely not. How can you be drunk behind the bench?

STEWART: I've heard those stories. I was told directly to my face by Werblin that you were.

ME: And Werblin got those stories from certain players.

SHERO: Definitely not.

STEWART: I'm not suggesting you were. I'm telling you what was told to me.

ME: Now, let me ask you something else. Mike Nykoluk at Dave Maloney's wedding told me that there were times in Philadelphia, like when you played Boston—you were in the finals, I think—that there was one time that he had to call up and make excuses to Flyers management for you because you took a bus back to Philly or something because you were dead drunk. You were comatose.

SHERO: Jeez, I don't believe that.

ME: You don't believe it?

SHERO: No.

ME: Or it's not true?

SHERO: Yeah.

ME: I mean, you know, I was talking to him at the wedding. I said, what about Fred's system? He goes, "System? There's no system, Ratso, he's a drunk." That's what Mike Nykoluk said to me. And you know, when I ask you about Nykoluk, you are so gracious to go out of your way not to say anything bad about Nykoluk.

SHERO: I don't believe it.

STEWART: You believe me? I told you about that . . .

ME: You don't believe it?

SHERO: No.

ME: You don't believe that he said that to me?

SHERO: Yeah, well, I don't want to believe it.

Epilogue

Well, Craig Patrick's Rangers didn't seem to do much better than Fred Shero's Rangers. They struggled through an up-and-down season, finishing thirteenth and making the play-offs by four points. With a fairly new cast of characters.

Espo was gone. The legs just gave out, and the reflexes too, sometime after Shero was exiled to Hartsdale. So they gave him a big retirement bash at the 21 Club (prompting Vadnais to note that when he retired the party would probably be at McDonalds). Phil tried assistant coaching for a while under Patrick, but that didn't work out, and by the end of the year, he was in limbo, reduced to watching the games on the tube, trying to figure out his future.

They lost Tkaczuk too, to a horrible, ill-fated puck-in-the-eye accident. He also became a coach, but he stayed. So did Wayne Thomas, who hung up his pads to assist the netminders.

Ulfie continued to prove brittle, and he missed almost thirty games, as did Duguay. So the load fell on the newcomers.

There was a new Captain, for one. Right from the start, Patrick and Maloney never saw eye to eye. A few games after Freddie was gone, out on the Island, rookie center Mike Allison was messing up, and after one horrendous shift he came back to the bench and ran right into a verbal barrage from Captain Dave. Allison almost started bawling.

Espo consoled the kid, and Patrick told Maloney to shut the fuck up. Soon afterward, Patrick announced his plan to rotate Captains.

It had been Fred's idea originally. By training camp Shero had felt that Maloney's leadership was questionable. He never publicly criticized his Captain, but he had called Greschner and Beck into his room after practice one day and told them that although Maloney wore the "C," they were the real leaders. So Patrick handed the "C" over to Tkaczuk for the second third of the season, and then announced he would bestow it on Beck for the final stretch. When Walter got hurt, Beck took over prematurely.

And he seemed to grow in stature, if that was possible. He called a team meeting and snapped the Rangers out of a horrible slump in Winnipeg. He led by example, regaining some of the ferocity that made him so attractive to Werblin during that Soviet Series. Of course, having Nicky back helped.

Fotiu returned in January and resumed his role as off-ice good-vibes man. He also was more than happy to be the policeman on the ice.

He had company. Shero had molded the team in his own image, and the bruisers that he had drafted were coming into their own. Hospodar was playing solid defense and refused to back down from anybody. Kotsopoulos made good on his prediction, and he was mean-spirited and tough around the net. Tommy Laidlaw, his teammate the previous season at New Haven, was playing well and, although for the most part mild-mannered, was as tough as nails when need be. And Allison was all heart, taking hit after hit to penetrate enemy ice, and he managed twenty-six goals his first year.

So they made the play-offs and drew LA in the first round and upset them. St. Louis was next and a by-now healthy Duguay was flying, and Greschner had been shifted to forward and teamed with the Swedes, and the combination was instant magic; and a skinny, gawky-looking skater named Lance Nethery was brilliant as a playmaker, and the next thing this suddenly Cinderella team knew, they were in the semis, playing the Islanders.

Without JD. The big guy was hobbling again, and Steve Baker was not your inspirational-type goalie. He had been heebie-jeebied by the Islanders picking him as a weak link in the preseries newspaper reports, and his jitters showed and oozed out to melt the confidence of the rest of the team. Of course, having Beck hurt didn't help. He was playing the series with a bum knee, unbeknownst to the fans and the press but not to the Islanders, who suddenly found their lost machismo as they took runs at the crippled defenseman. Nobody runs a healthy Bubba.

The Islanders won the first three games, and after the first period of the fourth game they were ahead 3–0, Baker letting in two soft goals. In the locker room, the goalie made a little speech, notifying his teammates not to blame him if they lost. When Werblin came in between the second and third periods to congratulate the guys on their season, everyone knew it was all over.

After the game, Krumpe came over to me in the locker room. "This is the last time you'll see this team." He made a sweeping gesture across the room with his beefy hand. "They'll be less individualism now. The team will be more boring, just like the Islanders. That's what you need to win. Less personality."

I nodded toward Duguay, who was playing out his option this year, to test the free-agent market.

"No, I don't mean him," Krumpe said.

But by fall it looked that way. Over the summer, to no one's surprise, Herb Brooks had rejoined his old crony, Patrick, as coach. And it took a week into the regular season for Duguay finally to sign another Ranger contract. And then a week later, Hitch was back. The Rangers had run into a lot of trouble of late. The Swedes had both been injured, Hedberg for the entire season, and an attempted comeback by their old left wing, Bobby Hull, had fizzled in the face of the injuries. So Hickey was brought back from Toronto for a draft pick. Full circle.

More changes. Vadnais was banished to the bench and Sarge was demoted to the minors. They didn't seem to fit into Brooks's "system." Dave Silk and Mark Pavelich, teammates from the Olympics, were freewheeling enough to make it, though.

Murdoch could have fit. Espo was pressuring Patrick to give the kid another shot, and he could have been had for a song last season when Edmonton had relegated him to Wichita in the Central League. But Patrick wanted no part of him, and now he was playing regular for Detroit, a new man, at last. Espo had his voice back too. Literally. He had taken over for Chadwick, doing the color on the telecasts.

Maloney had seemed to mature too. Maybe it was married life, maybe the pressure of the Captaincy removed, maybe the midsummer resolution he made to himself, whatever, Dave seemed to have a new attitude and it showed on the ice. Even Vadnais had mellowed in the absence of Nykoluk and he had become an elder statesman, of sorts, on the club.

Then there were the new faces of 1981–82. High-scoring Mike Rogers, who was obtained from Hartford for Sulliman and Kotsopoulos. Reijo Ruotsalainen, a Finnish defenseman who skated and stickhandled like a magician. Steve Weeks, who got a shot in the net when JD was injured again. Changes.

Even Charlie O's had changed. The girls had gone to greener pastures like NYU, and new lithe blondes had taken their seats. Head retired her Espo jersey and Marcus was seldom around; he was selling oil lot futures and trying to get into sportscasting.

So was the Chief. He was broadcasting too, his way. He would take the subway every week up to Thirty-second Street and Sixth Avenue, and pay fifteen dollars and get a tape and go to a booth, where he would do a fifteen-minute segment that would be broadcast over WBDJ in Brazil, Indiana. Public-access radio.

So the Chief would bring his Sammy Davis, Jr., records and Carpenters singles and spin a few discs and do some patter, and a month later they'd be digging this Bob Comas disc jockey fellow in the heartland.

He'd end each segment with the Tijuana Brass, and he'd snap his fingers and roll his head, holding the earphones with both hands, ecstatic in his little booth in the shadow of the Garden.

"Thanks for listening," he voiced-over in mellifluous tones. "Hey, remember to make the world a better place. Make up with a friend or a relative today. Because the life you save may be mine." Then he'd punch the music up and rock back in his chair and swing his arm as the studio clock ticked off the last few seconds of his show and he'd grab the mike for one last time and bellow, "Hang in there!"